asking would Miss Stein mind if her contribution appeared in the October number. She replied that nothing could be more suitable than the fifteenth of November on the fifteenth of October.

Once more a long silence and then this time came proof of the article. We were surprised but returned the proof promptly. Apparently a young man had sent it without authority because very shortly came an apologetic letter saying that there had been a mistake, the article was not to be printed just yet. This was also told to the passing english with the result that after all it was printed. Thereafter it was reprinted in the Georgian Stories. Gertrude Stein was delighted when later she was told that Eliot had said in Cambridge that the work of Gertrude Stein was very fine but not for us.

But to come back to Ezra. Ezra did come back and he came back with the editor of The Dial. This time it was worse than japanese prints, it was much more violent. In his surprise at the violence Ezra fell out of Gertrude Stein's favourite little armchair, the one I have since tapestried with Picasso designs, and Gertrude Stein was furious. Finally Ezra and the editor of The Dial left, nobody too well pleased. Gertrude Stein did not want to see Ezra again. Ezra did not quite see why. He met Gertrude Stein one day near the Luxembourg gardens and said, but I do want to come to see you. I am so sorry, answered Gertrude Stein, but Miss Toklas has a bad tooth and beside we are busy picking wild flowers. All of which was literally true, like all of Gertrude Stein's literature, but it upset Ezra, and we never saw him again.

During these months after the war we were one day going down a little street and saw a man looking in at a window and going backwards and forwards and right and left and otherwise behaving strangely. Lipschitz, said Gertrude Stein. Yes, said Lipschitz, I am buying an iron cock. Where is it, we asked. Why in there, he said, and in there it was. Gertrude Stein had known Lipschitz very slightly at one time but this incident made them friends and soon he asked

THE AUTOBIOGRAPHY OF

Alice B. Toklas

THE AUTOBIOGRAPHY OF

Alice B. Toklas

by Gertrude Stein

Illustrated by Maira Kalman

PENGUIN PRESS

NEW YORK

2020

PENGUIN PRESS
An imprint of Penguin Random House LLC
penguinrandomhouse.com

Originally published in 1933
by Harcourt, Brace and Company, New York.

Library of Congress Cataloging-in-Publication Data
Names: Stein, Gertrude, 1874–1946, author. | Kalman, Maira, illustrator.
Title: The autobiography of Alice B. Toklas / by Gertrude Stein; illustrated by Maira Kalman.
Description: New York: Penguin Press, 2020. | "Originally published in 1933
by Harcourt, Brace and Company, New York."
Identifiers: LCCN 2019004307 | ISBN 9781594204609 (hardcover)
Subjects: LCSH: Stein, Gertrude, 1874–1946—Friends and associates. | Toklas,
Alice B.—Friends and associates. | Paris (France)—Intellectual life—20th century. | Authors,
American—20th century—Biography. | Americans—France—Paris—Biography.
Classification: LCC PS3537.T323 Z46 2020 | DDC 818/.5209 [B]—dc23 LC record
available at https://lccn.loc.gov/2019004307

Printed in China
1 3 5 7 9 10 8 6 4 2

BOOK DESIGN BY CLAIRE VACCARO

Contents

I.

Before I Came to Paris

I WAS BORN IN San Francisco, California. I have in consequence always preferred living in a temperate climate
but it is difficult, on the continent of Europe or even in
America, to find a temperate climate and live in it. My mother's
father was a pioneer, he came to California in '49, he married my
grandmother who was very fond of music. She was a pupil of
Clara Schumann's father. My mother was a quiet charming woman named Emilie.

My father came of polish patriotic stock. His grand-uncle raised
a regiment for Napoleon and was its colonel. His father left his
mother just after their marriage, to fight at the barricades in Paris,
but his wife having cut off his supplies, he soon returned and led
the life of a conservative well to do land owner.

I myself have had no liking for violence and have always enjoyed the pleasures of needlework and gardening. I am fond of
paintings, furniture, tapestry, houses and flowers and even vege-
tables and fruit-trees. I like a view but I like to sit with my back
turned to it.

I led in my childhood and youth the gently bred existence of
my class and kind. I had some intellectual adventures at this period

I like a view but I like to sit with my back turned to it.

but very quiet ones. When I was about nineteen years of age I was a great admirer of Henry James. I felt that The Awkward Age would make a very remarkable play and I wrote to Henry James suggesting that I dramatise it. I had from him a delightful letter on the subject and then, when I felt my inadequacy, rather blushed for myself and did not keep the letter. Perhaps at that time I did not feel that I was justified in preserving it, at any rate it no longer exists.

Up to my twentieth year I was seriously interested in music. I studied and practised assiduously but shortly then it seemed futile, my mother had died and there was no unconquerable sadness, but there was no real interest that led me on. In the story Ada in Geography and Plays Gertrude Stein has given a very good description of me as I was at that time.

From then on for about six years I was well occupied. I led a pleasant life, I had many friends, much amusement many interests, my life was reasonably full and I enjoyed it but I was not very ardent in it. This brings me to the San Francisco fire which had as a consequence that the elder brother of Gertrude Stein and his wife came back from Paris to San Francisco and this led to a complete change in my life.

I was at this time living with my father and brother. My father was a quiet man who took things quietly, although he felt them deeply. The first terrible morning of the San Francisco fire I woke him and told him, the city has been rocked by an earthquake and is now on fire. That will give us a black eye in the East, he replied turning and going to sleep again. I remember that once when my brother and a comrade had gone horse-back riding, one of the horses returned riderless to the hotel, the mother of the other boy began to make a terrible scene. Be calm madam, said my father, perhaps it is my son who has been killed. One of his axioms I always remember, if you must do a thing do it graciously. He also told me that a hostess should never apologise for any failure in her household arrangements, if there is a hostess there is insofar as there is a hostess no failure.

As I was saying we were all living comfortably together and there had been in my mind no active desire or thought of change. The disturbance

but I was not very ardent in it

of the routine of our lives by the fire followed by the coming of Gertrude Stein's older brother and his wife made the difference.

Mrs. Stein brought with her three little Matisse paintings, the first modern things to cross the Atlantic. I made her acquaintance at this time of general upset and she showed them to me, she also told me many stories of her life in Paris. Gradually I told my father that perhaps I would leave San Francisco. He was not disturbed by this, after all there was at that time a great deal of going and coming and there were many friends of mine going. Within a year I also had gone and I had come to Paris. There I went to see Mrs. Stein who had in the meantime returned to Paris, and there at her house I met Gertrude Stein. I was impressed by the coral brooch she wore and by her voice. I may say that only three times in my life have I met a genius and each time a bell within me rang and I was not mistaken, and I may say in each case it was before there was any general recognition of the quality of genius in them. The three geniuses of whom I wish to speak are Gertrude Stein, Pablo Picasso and Alfred Whitehead. I have met many important people, I have met several great people but I have only known three first class geniuses and in each case on sight within me something rang. In no one of the three cases have I been mistaken. In this way my new full life began.

the coral brooch she wore and by her voice

II.

My Arrival in Paris

THIS WAS THE year 1907. Gertrude Stein was just seeing through the press Three Lives which she was having privately printed, and she was deep in The Making of Americans, her thousand page book. Picasso had just finished his portrait of her which nobody at that time liked except the painter and the painted and which is now so famous, and he had just begun his strange complicated picture of three women, Matisse had just finished his Bonheur de Vivre, his first big composition which gave him the name of fauve or a zoo. It was the moment Max Jacob has since called the heroic age of cubism. I remember not long ago hearing Picasso and Gertrude Stein talking about various things that had happened at that time, one of them said but all that could not have happened in that one year, oh said the other, my dear you forget we were young then and we did a great deal in a year.

There are a great many things to tell of what was happening then and what had happened before, which led up to then, but now I must describe what I saw when I came.

The home at 27 rue de Fleurus consisted then as it does now of a tiny pavillon of two stories with four small rooms, a kitchen and bath, and a very large atelier adjoining. Now the atelier is attached to the pavillon by a tiny hall passage added in 1914 but at that time the atelier had its own entrance, one rang the bell of the pavillon or knocked at the door of the atelier, and a great many people did both, but more knocked at the atelier. I was privileged to do both. I had been invited to dine on Saturday evening which was the evening when everybody came, and indeed everybody did come. I went to dinner. The dinner was cooked by Hélène. I must tell a little about Hélène.

Hélène had already been two years with Gertrude Stein and her brother. She was one of those admirable bonnes in other words excellent maids of all work, good cooks thoroughly occupied with the welfare of their employers and of themselves, firmly convinced that everything purchasable was far too dear. Oh but it is dear, was her answer to any question. She wasted nothing and carried on the household at the regular rate of eight francs a day. She even wanted to include guests at that price, it was her pride, but of course that was difficult since she for the honour of her house as well as to satisfy her employers always had to give every one enough to eat. She was a most excellent cook and she made a very good soufflé. In those days most of the guests were living more or less precariously, no one starved, some one always helped but still most of them did not live in abundance. It was Braque who said about four years later when they were all beginning to be known, with a sigh and a smile, how life has changed we all now have cooks who can make a soufflé.

Hélène had her opinions, she did not for instance like Matisse. She said a frenchman should not stay unexpectedly to a meal particularly if he asked the servant beforehand what there was for dinner. She said foreigners had a perfect right to do these things but not a frenchman and Matisse had once done it. So when Miss Stein said to her, Monsieur Matisse is staying for dinner this evening, she would say, in that case I will not make an omelette but fry the eggs. It takes the same number of eggs and the same amount of butter but it shows less respect, and he will understand.

Hélène stayed with the household until the end of 1913. Then her husband, by that time she had married and had a little boy, insisted that she work for others no longer. To her great regret she left and later she always said that life at home was never as amusing as it had been at the rue de Fleurus. Much later, only about three years ago, she came back for a year, she and her husband had fallen on bad times and her boy had died. She was as cheery as ever and enormously interested. She said isn't it extraordinary, all those people whom I knew when they were nobody are now always mentioned in the newspapers, and the other night over the radio they mentioned the name of Monsieur Picasso. Why they even speak in the newspapers of Monsieur Braque, who used to hold up the big pictures to hang because he was the strongest, while the janitor drove the nails, and they are putting into the Louvre, just imagine it, into the Louvre, a picture by that little poor Monsieur Rousseau, who was so timid he did not even have courage enough to knock at the door. She was terribly interested in seeing Monsieur Picasso and his wife and child and cooked her very best dinner for him, but how he has changed, she said, well, said she, I suppose that is natural but then he has a lovely son. We thought that really Hélène had come back to give the young generation the once over. She had in a way but she was not interested in them. She said they made no impression on her which made them all very sad because the legend of her was well known to all Paris. After a year things were going better again, her husband was earning more money, and she once more remains at home. But to come back to 1907.

Before I tell about the guests I must tell what I saw. As I said being invited to dinner I rang the bell of the little pavillon and was taken into the tiny hall and then into the small dining room lined with books. On the only free space, the doors, were tacked up a few drawings by Picasso and Matisse. As the other guests had not yet come Miss Stein took me into the atelier. It often rained in Paris and it was always difficult to go from the little pavillon to the atelier door in the rain in evening clothes, but you were not to mind such things as the hosts and most of the guests did not. We went into the atelier which opened with a yale key the only yale key in the quarter at that time, and this was not so much for safety, because in those days the pictures had no value, but because the key was small and could go into a purse instead of being enormous as french keys were. Against

She was a most excellent cook and she made a very good soufflé.

the walls were several pieces of large italian renaissance furniture and in the middle of the room was a big renaissance table, on it a lovely inkstand, and at one end of it note-books neatly arranged, the kind of note-books french children use, with pictures of earthquakes and explorations on the outside of them. And on all the walls right up to the ceiling were pictures. At one end of the room was a big cast iron stove that Hélène came in and filled with a rattle, and in one corner of the room was a large table on which were horseshoe nails and pebbles and little pipe cigarette holders which one looked at curiously but did not touch, but which turned out later to be accumulations from the pockets of Picasso and Gertrude Stein. But to return to the pictures. The pictures were so strange that one quite instinctively looked at anything rather than at them just at first. I have re freshed my memory by looking at some snap shots taken inside the atelier at that time. The chairs in the room were also all italian renaissance, not very comfortable for short-legged people and one got the habit of sitting on one's legs. Miss Stein sat near the stove in a lovely high-backed one and she peacefully let her legs hang, which was a matter of habit, and when any one of the many visitors came to ask her a question she lifted herself up out of this chair and usually replied in french, not just now. This usually referred to something they wished to see, drawings which were put away, some german had once spilled ink on one, or some other not to be fulfilled desire. But to return to the pictures. As I say they completely covered the whitewashed walls right up to the top of the very high ceiling. The room was lit at this time by high gas fixtures. This was the second stage. They had just been put in. Before that there had only been lamps, and a stalwart guest held up the lamp while the others looked. But gas had just been put in and an ingenious american painter named Sayen, to divert his mind from the birth of his first child, was arranging some mechanical contrivance that would light the high fixtures by themselves. The old landlady extremely conservative did not allow electricity in her houses and electricity was not put in until 1914, the old landlady by that time too old to know the difference, her house agent gave permission. But this time I am really going to tell about the pictures.

It is very difficult now that everybody is accustomed to everything to give some idea of the kind of uneasiness one felt when one first looked at all these pictures on these walls. In those days there were pictures of all kinds there, the time had not yet come when there were only Cézannes, Renoirs, Matisses and Picassos, nor as it was even later only Cézannes and Picassos. At that time there was a great deal of Matisse, Picasso, Renoir, Cézanne but there were also a great many other things. There were two Gauguins, there were Manguins, there was a big nude by Valloton that felt like only it was not like the Odalisque of Manet, there was a Toulouse-Lautrec. Once about this time Picasso looking at this and greatly daring said, but all the same I do paint better than he did. Toulouse-Lautrec had been the most important of his early influences. I later bought a little tiny picture by Picasso of that epoch. There was a portrait of Gertrude Stein by Valloton that might have been a David but was not, there was a Maurice Denis, a little Daumier, many Cézanne water colours, there was in short everything, there was even a little Delacroix and a moderate sized Greco. There were enormous Picassos of the Harlequin period, there were two rows of Matisses, there was a big portrait of a woman by Cézanne and some little Cézannes, all these pictures had a history and I will soon tell them. Now I was confused and I looked and I looked and I was confused. Gertrude Stein and her brother were so accustomed to this state of mind in a guest that they paid no attention to it. Then there was a sharp tap at the atelier door. Gertrude Stein opened it and a little dark dapper man came in with hair, eyes, face, hands and feet all very much alive. Hullo Alfy, she said, this is Miss Toklas. How do you do Miss Toklas, he said very solemnly. This was Alfy Maurer an old habitué of the house. He had been there before there were these pictures, when there were only japanese prints, and he was among those who used to light matches to light up a little piece of the Cézanne portrait. Of course you can tell it is a finished picture, he used to explain to the other american painters who came and looked dubiously, you can tell because it has a frame, now whoever heard of anybody framing a canvas if the picture isn't finished. He had followed, followed, followed always humbly always sincerely, it was he who selected

there was a Toulouse-Lautrec.

the first lot of pictures for the famous Barnes collection some years later faithfully and enthusiastically. It was he who when later Barnes came to the house and waved his cheque-book said, so help me God, I didn't bring him. Gertrude Stein who has an explosive temper, came in another evening and there were her brother, Alfy and a stranger. She did not like the stranger's looks. Who is that, said she to Alfy. I didn't bring him, said Alfy. He looks like a Jew, said Gertrude Stein, he is worse than that, says Alfy. But to return to that first evening. A few minutes after Alfy came in there was a violent knock at the door and, dinner is ready, from Hélène. It's funny the Picassos have not come, said they all, however we won't wait at least Hélène won't wait. So we went into the court and into the pavillon and dining room and began dinner. It's funny, said Miss Stein, Pablo is always promptness itself, he is never early and he is never late, it is his pride that punctuality is the politeness of kings, he even makes Fernande punctual. Of course he often says yes when he has no intention of doing what he says yes to, he can't say no, no is not in his vocabulary and you have to know whether his yes means yes or means no, but when he says a yes that means yes and he did about tonight he is always punctual. These were the days before automobiles and nobody worried about accidents. We had just finished the first course when there was a quick patter of footsteps in the court and Hélène opened the door before the bell rang. Pablo and Fernande as everybody called them at that time walked in. He, small, quick moving but not restless, his eyes having a strange faculty of opening wide and drinking in what he wished to see. He had the isolation and movement of the head of a bull-fighter at the head of their procession. Fernande was a tall beautiful woman with a won-derful big hat and a very evidently new dress, they were both very fussed. I am very upset, said Pablo, but you know very well Gertrude I am never late but Fernande had ordered a dress for the vernissage tomorrow and it didn't come. Well here you are anyway, said Miss Stein, since it's you Hélène won't mind. And we all sat down. I was next to Picasso who was silent and then gradually became peaceful. Alfy paid compliments to Fernande and she was soon calm and placid. After a little while I murmured to Picasso that I liked his portrait of Gertrude Stein. Yes, he said, everybody says that she does not look like it but that does not make any difference, she will, he said. The conversation soon became lively it was all about the opening day of the salon indépendant which was the great event of the year. Everybody was interested in all the scandals that would or would not break out. Picasso never exhibited but as his followers did and there were a great many stories connected with each follower the hopes and fears were vivacious.

While we were having coffee footsteps were heard in the court quite a number of footsteps and Miss Stein rose and said, don't hurry, I have to let them in. And she left.

When we went into the atelier there were already quite a number of people in the room, scattered groups, single and couples all looking and looking. Gertrude Stein sat by the stove talking and listening and getting up to open the door and go up to various people talking and listening. She usually opened the door to the knock and the usual formula was, de la part de qui venez-vous, who is your introducer. The idea was that anybody could come but for form's sake and in Paris you have to have a formula, everybody was supposed to be able to mention the name of somebody who had told them about it. It was a mere form, really everybody could come in and as at that time these pictures had no value and there was no social privilege attached to knowing any one there, only those came who really were interested. So as I say anybody could come in, however, there was the formula. Miss Stein once in opening the door said as she usually did by whose invitation do you come and we heard an aggrieved voice reply, but by yours, madame. He was a young man Gertrude Stein had met somewhere and with whom she had had a long conversation and to whom she had given a cordial invitation and then had as promptly forgotten.

The room was soon very very full and who were they all. Groups of hungarian painters and writers, it happened that some hungarian had once been brought and the word had spread from him throughout all Hungary, any village where there was a young man who had ambitions heard of 27 rue de Fleurus and then he lived but to get there and a great many did get there. They were always there, all sizes and shapes, all degrees of wealth and poverty, some very charming, some simply rough and every now and

she will, he said.

then a very beautiful young peasant. Then there were quantities of germans, not too popular because they tended always to want to see anything that was put away and they tended to break things and Gertrude Stein has a weakness for breakable objects, she has a horror of people who collect only the unbreakable. Then there was a fair sprinkling of americans, Mildred Aldrich would bring a group or Sayen, the electrician, or some painter and occasionally an architectural student would accidentally get there and then there were the habitués, among them Miss Mars and Miss Squires whom Gertrude Stein afterwards immortalised in her story of Miss Furr and Miss Skeene. On that first night Miss Mars and I talked of a subject then entirely new, how to make up your face. She was interested in types, she knew that there were femme décorative, femme d'intérieur and femme intrigante; there was no doubt that Fernande Picasso was a femme décorative, but what was Madame Matisse, femme d'intérieur, I said, and she was very pleased. From time to time one heard the high spanish whinnying laugh of Picasso and gay contralto outbreak of Gertrude Stein, people came and went, in and out. Miss Stein told me to sit with Fernande. Fernande was always beautiful but heavy in hand. I sat, it was my first sitting with a wife of a genius.

Before I decided to write this book my twenty-five years with Gertrude Stein, I had often said that I would write, The wives of geniuses I have sat with. I have sat with so many. I have sat with wives who were not wives, of geniuses who were real geniuses. I have sat with real wives of geniuses who were not real geniuses. I have sat with wives of geniuses, of near geniuses, of would be geniuses, in short I have sat very often and very long with many wives and wives of many geniuses.

As I was saying Fernande, who was then living with Picasso and had been with him a long time that is to say they were all twenty-four years old at that time but they had been together a long time, Fernande was the first wife of a genius I sat with and she was not the least amusing. We talked hats. Fernande had two subjects hats and perfumes. This first day we talked hats. She liked hats, she had the true french feeling about a hat, if a hat did not provoke some witticism from a man on the street the hat was not a success. Later on once in Montmartre she and I were walking together. She had on a large yellow hat and I had on a much smaller blue one. As we were walking along a workman stopped and called out, there go the sun and the moon shining together. Ah, said Fernande to me with a radiant smile, you see our hats are a success.

Miss Stein called me and said she wanted to have me meet Matisse. She was talking to a medium sized man with a reddish beard and glasses. He had a very alert although slightly heavy presence and Miss Stein and he seemed to be full of hidden meanings. As I came up I heard her say, Oh yes but it would be more difficult now. We were talking, she said, of a lunch party we had in here last year. We had just hung all the pictures and we asked all the painters. You know how painters are, I wanted to make them happy so I placed each one opposite his own picture, and they were happy so happy that we had to send out twice for more bread, when you know France you will know that that means that they were happy, because they cannot eat and drink without bread and we had to send out twice for bread so they were happy. Nobody noticed my little arrangement except Matisse and he did not until just as he left, and now he says it is a proof that I am very wicked, Matisse laughed and said, yes I know Mademoiselle Gertrude, the world is a theatre for you, but there are theatres and theatres, and when you listen so carefully to me and so attentively and do not hear a word I say then I do say that you are very wicked. Then they both began talking about the vernissage of the independent as every one else was doing and of course I did not know what it was all about. But gradually I knew and later on I will tell the story of the pictures, their painters and their followers and what this conversation meant.

Later I was near Picasso, he was standing meditatively. Do you think, he said, that I really do look like your president Lincoln. I had thought a good many things that evening but I had not thought that. You see, he went on, Gertrude, (I wish I could convey something of the simple affection and confidence with which he always pronounced her name and with which she always said, Pablo. In all their long friendship with all its sometimes troubled moments and its complications this has never changed.) Gertrude showed me a photograph of him and I have been trying to arrange my hair to look like his, I think my forehead does. I did not know whether he meant it or not but I was sympathetic. I did not realise then how completely and entirely american was Gertrude Stein. Later I often teased her, calling her a general, a civil war general of either or both sides. She had a series of photographs of the civil war, rather wonderful photographs and she and Picasso used to pore over them. Then he would suddenly remember the spanish war and he became very spanish and very bitter and Spain and America in their persons could say very bitter things about each other's country. But at this my first evening I knew nothing of all this and so I was polite and that was all.

And now the evening was drawing to a close. Everybody was leaving and everybody was still talking about the vernissage of the independent. I too left carrying with me a card of invitation for the vernissage. And so this, one of the most important evenings of my life, came to an end.

I went to the vernissage taking with me a friend, the invitation I had been given admitting two. We went very early. I had been told to go early otherwise we would not be able to see anything, and there would be no place to sit, and my friend liked to sit. We went to the building just put up for this salon. In France they always put things up just for the day or for a few days and then take them down again. Gertrude Stein's elder brother always says that the secret of the chronic employment or lack of unemployment in France is due to the number of men actively engaged in putting up and taking down temporary buildings. Human nature is so permanent in France that they can afford to be as temporary as they like with their buildings. We went to the long low certainly very very long temporary building that was put up every year for the independents. When after the war or just before, I forget, the independent was given permanent quarters in the big exposition building, the Grand Palais, it became much less interesting. After all it is the adventure that counts. The long building was beautifully alight with Paris light.

In earlier, still earlier days, in the days of Seurat, the independent had its exhibition in a building where the rain rained in. Indeed it was because of

Poor Monsieur Rousseau, who was so timid

poor Seurat caught his fatal cold

this, that in hanging pictures in the rain, poor Seurat caught his fatal cold. Now there was no rain coming in, it was a lovely day and we felt very festive. When we got in we were indeed early as nearly as possible the first to be there. We went from one room to another and quite frankly we had no idea which of the pictures the Saturday evening crowd would have thought art and which were just the attempts of what in France are known as the Sunday painters, workingmen, hair-dressers and veterinaries and visionaries who only paint once a week when they do not have to work. I say we did not know but yes perhaps we did know. But not about the Rousseau, and there was an enormous Rousseau there which was the scandal of the show, it was a picture of the officials of the republic, Picasso now owns it, no that picture we could not know as going to be one of the great pictures, and that as Hélène was to say, would come to be in the Louvre. There was also there if my memory is correct a strange picture by the same douanier Rousseau, a sort of apotheosis of Guillaume Apollinaire with an aged Marie Laurencin behind him as a muse. That also I would not have recognised as a serious work of art. At that time of course I knew nothing about Marie Laurencin and Guillaume Apollinaire but there is a lot to tell about them later. Then we went on and saw a Matisse. Ah there we were beginning to feel at home. We knew a Matisse when we saw it, knew at once and enjoyed it and knew that it was great art and beautiful. It was a big figure of a woman lying in among some cactuses. A picture which was after the show to be at the rue de Fleurus. There one day the five year old little boy of the janitor who often used to visit Gertrude Stein who was fond of him, jumped into her arms as she was standing at the open door of the atelier and looking over her shoulder and seeing the picture cried out in rapture, oh là là what a beautiful body of a woman. Miss Stein used always to tell this story when the casual stranger in the aggressive way of the casual stranger said, looking at this picture, and what is that supposed to represent.

In the same room as the Matisse, a little covered by a partition, was a hungarian version of the same picture by one Czobel whom I remembered to have seen at the rue de Fleurus, it was the happy independent way to put a violent follower opposite the violent but not quite as violent master.

We went on and on, there were a great many rooms and a great many pictures in the rooms and finally we came to a middle room and there was a garden bench and as there were people coming in quite a few people we sat down on the bench to rest.

We had been resting and looking at every body and it was indeed the vie de Bohème just as one had seen it in the opera and they were very wonderful to look at. Just then somebody behind us put a hand on our shoulders and burst out laughing. It was Gertrude Stein. You have seated yourselves admirably, she said. But why, we asked. Because right here in front of you is the whole story. We looked but we saw nothing except two big pictures that looked quite alike but not altogether alike. One is a Braque and one is a Derain, explained Gertrude Stein. They were strange pictures of strangely formed rather wooden blocked figures, one if I remember rightly a sort of man and women, the other three women. Well, she said still laughing. We were puzzled, we had seen so much strangeness we did not know why these two were any stranger. She was quickly lost in an excited and voluble crowd. We recognised Pablo Picasso and Fernande, we thought we recognised many more, to be sure everybody seemed to be interested in our corner and we stayed, but we did not know why they were so especially interested. After a considerable interval Gertrude Stein came back again, this time evidently even more excited and amused. She leaned over us and said solemnly, do you want to take french lessons. We hesitated, why yes we could take french lessons. Well Fernande will give you french lessons, go and find her and tell her how absolutely you are pining to take french lessons. But why should she give us french lessons, we asked. Because, well because she and Pablo have decided to separate forever. I suppose it has happened before but not since I have known them. You know Pablo says if you love a woman you give her money. Well now it is when you want to leave a woman you have to wait until you have enough money to give her. Vollard has just bought out his atelier and so he can afford to separate from her by giving her half. She wants to install herself in a room by herself and give french lessons, so that is how you come in. Well what has that to do with these two pictures, asked my ever curious friend. Nothing, said Gertrude Stein going off with a great shout of laughter.

I will tell the whole story as I afterward learnt it but now I must find Fernande and propose to her to take french lessons from her.

I wandered about and looked at the crowd, never had I imagined there could be so many kinds of men making and looking at pictures. In America, even in San Francisco, I had been accustomed to see women at picture shows and some men, but here there were men, men, men, sometimes women with them but more often three or four men with one woman, sometimes five or six men with two women. Later on I became accustomed to this proportion. In one of these groups of five or six men and two women I saw the Picassos, that is I saw Fernande with her characteristic gesture, one ringed forefinger straight in the air. As I afterwards found out she had the Napoleonic forefinger quite as long if not a shade longer than the middle finger, and this, whenever she was animated, which after all was not very often because Fernande was indolent, always went straight up into the air. I waited not wishing to break into this group of which she at one end and Picasso at the other end were the absorbed centres but finally I summoned up courage to go forward and draw her attention and tell her of my desire. Oh yes, she said sweetly, Gertrude has told me of your desire, it would give me great pleasure to give you lessons, you and your friend, I will be the next few days very busy installing myself in my new apartment. Gertrude is coming to see me the end of the week, if you and your friend would accompany her we could then make all arrangements. Fernande spoke a very elegant french, some lapses of course into montmartrois that I found difficult to follow, but she had been educated to be a schoolmistress, her voice was lovely and she was very very beautiful with a marvellous complexion. She was a big woman but not too big because she was indolent and she had the small round arms that give the characteristic beauty to all french women. It was rather a pity that short skirts ever came in because until then one never imagined the sturdy french legs of the average french woman, one thought only of the beauty of the small rounded arms. I agreed to Fernande's proposal and left her.

She was a big woman but not too big.

On my way back to where my friend was sitting I became more accustomed not so much to the pictures as to the people. I began to realise there was a certain uniformity of type. Many years after, that is just a few years ago, when Juan Gris whom we all loved very much died, (he was after Pablo Picasso Gertrude Stein's dearest friend) I heard her say to Braque, she and he were standing together at the funeral, who are all these people, there are so many and they are so familiar and I do not know who any of them are. Oh, Braque replied, they are all the people you used to see at the vernissage of the independent and the autumn salon and you saw their faces twice a year, year after year, and that is the reason they are all so familiar.

Gertrude Stein and I about ten days later went to Montmartre, I for the first time. I have never ceased to love it. We go there every now and then and I always have the same tender expectant feeling that I had then. It is a place where you were always standing and sometimes waiting, not for anything to happen, but just standing. The inhabitants of Montmartre did not sit much, they mostly stood which was just as well as the chairs, the dining room chairs of France, did not tempt one to sit. So I went to Montmartre and I began my apprenticeship of standing. We first went to see Picasso and then we went to see Fernande. Picasso now never likes to go to Montmartre, he does not like to think about it much less talk about it. Even to Gertrude Stein he is hesitant about talking of it, there were things that at that time cut deeply into his spanish pride and the end of his Montmartre life was bitterness and disillusion, and there is nothing more bitter than spanish disillusion.

But at this time he was in and of Montmartre and lived in the rue Ravignan.

We went to the Odéon and there got into an omnibus, that is we mounted on top of an omnibus, the nice old horse-pulled omnibuses that went pretty quickly and steadily across Paris and up the hill to the place Blanche. There we got out and climbed a steep street lined with shops with things to eat, the rue Lepic, and then turning we went around a corner and climbed even more steeply in fact almost straight up and came to the rue

Ravignan, now place Emile-Goudeau but otherwise unchanged, with its steps leading up to the little flat square with its few but tender little trees, a man carpentering in the corner of it, the last time I was there not very long ago there was still a man carpentering in a corner of it, and a little café just before you went up the steps where they all used to eat, it is still there, and to the left the low wooden building of studios that is still there.

We went up the couple of steps and through the open door passing on our left the studio in which later Juan Gris was to live out his martyrdom but where then lived a certain Vaillant, a nondescript painter who was to lend his studio as a ladies dressing room at the famous banquet for Rousscau, and then we passed a steep flight of steps leading down where Max Jacob had a studio a little later, and we passed another steep little stairway which led to the studio where not long before a young fellow had committed suicide, Picasso painted one of the most wonderful of his early pictures of the friends gathered round the coffin, we passed all this to a larger door where Gertrude Stein knocked and Picasso opened the door and we went in.

He was dressed in what the french call the singe or monkey costume, overalls made of blue jean or brown, I think his was blue and it is called a singe or monkey because being all of one piece with a belt, if the belt is not fastened, and it very often is not, it hangs down behind and so makes a monkey. His eyes were more wonderful than even I remembered, so full and so brown, and his hands so dark and delicate and alert. We went further in. There was a couch in one corner, a very small stove that did for cooking and heating in the other corner, some chairs, the large broken one Gertrude Stein sat in when she was painted and a general smell of dog and paint and there was a big dog there and Picasso moved her about from one place to another exactly as if the dog had been a large piece of furniture. He asked us to sit down but as all the chairs were full we all stood up and stood until we left. It was my first experience of standing but afterwards I found that they all stood that way for hours. Against the wall was an enormous picture, a strange picture of light and dark colours, that is all I can say, of a group, an enormous group and

But at this time he was in and of Montmartre

and lived in the Rue Ravignan.

next to it another in a sort of a red brown, of three women, square and posturing, all of it rather frightening. Picasso and Gertrude Stein stood together talking. I stood back and looked. I cannot say I realised anything but I felt that there was something painful and beautiful there and oppressive but imprisoned. I heard Gertrude Stein say, and mine. Picasso thereupon brought out a smaller picture, a rather unfinished thing that could not finish, very pale almost white, two figures, they were all there but very unfinished and not finishable. Picasso said, but he will never accept it. Yes, I know, answered Gertrude Stein. But just the same it is the only one in which it is all there. Yes, I know, he replied and they fell silent. After that they continued a low toned conversation and then Miss Stein said, well we have to go, we are going to have tea with Fernande. Yes, I know, replied Picasso. How often do you see her, she said, he got very red and looked sheepish. I have never been there, he said resentfully. She chuckled, well anyway we are going there, she said, and Miss Toklas is going to have lessons in french. Ah the Miss Toklas, he said, with small feet like a spanish woman and earrings like a gypsy and a father who is king of Poland like the Poniatowskis, of course she will take lessons. We all laughed and went to the door. There stood a very beautiful man, oh Agero, said Picasso, you know the ladies. He looks like a Greco, I said in english. Picasso caught the name, a false Greco, he said. Oh I forgot to give you these, said Gertrude Stein handing Picasso a package of newspapers, they will console you. He opened them up, they were the Sunday supplement of american papers, they were the Katzenjammer kids. Oh oui, Oh oui, he said, his face full of satisfaction, merci thanks Gertrude, and we left.

We left then and continued to climb higher up the hill. What did you think of what you saw, asked Miss Stein. Well I did see something. Sure you did, she said, but did you see what it had to do with those two pictures you sat in front of so long at the vernissage. Only that Picassos were rather awful and the others were not. Sure, she said, as Pablo once remarked, when you make a thing, it is so complicated making it that it is bound to be ugly, but those that do it after you they don't have to worry about making it and they can make it pretty, and so everybody can like it when the others make it.

We went on and turned down a little street and there was another little house and we asked for Mademoiselle Bellevallée and we were sent into a little corridor and we knocked and went into a moderate sized room in which was a very large bed and a piano and a little tea table and Fernande and two others.

One of them was Alice Princet. She was rather a madonna like creature, with large lovely eyes and charming hair. Fernande afterwards explained that she was the daughter of a workingman and had the brutal thumbs that of course were a characteristic of workingmen. She had been, so Fernande explained, for seven years with Princet who was in the government employ and she had been faithful to him in the fashion of Montmartre, that is to say she had stuck to him through sickness and health but she had amused herself by the way. Now they were to be married. Princet had become the head of his small department in the government service and it would be necessary for him to invite other heads of departments to his house and so of course he must regularise the relation. They were actually married a few months afterward and it was apropos of this marriage that Max Jacob made his famous remark, it is wonderful to long for a woman for seven years and to possess her at last. Picasso made the more practical one, why should they marry simply in order to divorce. This was a prophecy.

No sooner were they married than Alice Princet met Derain and Derain met her. It was what the french call un coup de foudre, or love at first sight. They went quite mad about each other. Princet tried to bear it but they were married now and it was different. Beside he was angry for the first time in his life and in his anger he tore up Alice's first fur coat which she had gotten for the wedding. That settled the matter, and within six months after the marriage Alice left Princet never to return. She and Derain went off together and they have never separated since. I always liked Alice Derain. She had a certain wild quality that perhaps had to do with her brutal thumbs and was curiously in accord with her madonna face.

The other woman was Germaine Pichot, entirely a different type. She

was quiet and serious and spanish, she had the square shoulders and the unseeing fixed eyes of a spanish woman. She was very gentle. She was married to a spanish painter Pichot, who was rather a wonderful creature, he was long and thin like one of those primitive Christs in spanish churches and when he did a spanish dance which he did later at the famous banquet to Rousseau, he was awe inspiringly religious.

Germaine, so Fernande said, was the heroine of many a strange story, she had once taken a young man to the hospital, he had been injured in a fracas at a music hall and all his crowd had deserted him. Germaine quite naturally stood by and saw him through. She had many sisters, she and all of them had been born and bred in Montmartre and they were all of different fathers and married to different nationalities, even to turks and armenians. Germaine, much later was very ill for years and she always had around her a devoted coterie. They used to carry her in her armchair to the nearest cinema and they, and she in the armchair, saw the performance through. They did this regularly once a week. I imagine they are still doing it.

The conversation around the tea table of Fernande was not lively, nobody had anything to say. It was a pleasure to meet, it was even an honour, but that was about all. Fernande complained a little that her charwoman had not adequately dusted and rinsed the tea things, and also that buying a bed and a piano on the instalment plan had elements of unpleasantness. Otherwise we really none of us had much to say.

Finally she and I arranged about the french lessons, I was to pay fifty cents an hour and she was to come to see me two days hence and we were to begin. Just at the end of the visit they were more natural. Fernande asked Miss Stein if she had any of the comic supplements of the american papers left. Gertrude Stein replied that she had just left them with Pablo.

They went quite mad about each other.

Fernande roused like a lioness defending her cubs. That is a brutality that I will never forgive him, she said. I met him on the street, he had a comic supplement in his hand, I asked him to give it to me to help me to distract myself and he brutally refused. It was a piece of cruelty that I will never forgive. I ask you, Gertrude, to give to me myself the next copies you have of the comic supplement. Gertrude Stein said, why certainly with pleasure.

As we went out she said to me, it is to be hoped that they will be together again before the next comic supplements of the Katzenjammer kids come out because if I do not give them to Pablo he will be all upset and if I do Fernande will make an awful fuss. Well I suppose I will have to lose them or have my brother give them to Pablo by mistake.

Fernande came quite promptly to the appointment and we proceeded to our lesson. Of course to have a lesson in french one has to converse and Fernande had three subjects, hats, we had not much more to say about hats, perfumes, we had something to say about perfumes. Perfumes were Fernande's really great extravagance, she was the scandal of Montmartre because she had once bought a bottle of perfume named Smoke and had paid eighty francs for it at that time sixteen dollars and it had no scent but such wonderful colour, like real bottled liquid smoke. Her third subject was the categories of furs. There were three categories of furs, there were first category, sables, second category ermine and chinchilla, third category martin fox and squirrel. It was the most surprising thing I had heard in Paris. I was surprised. Chinchilla second, squirrel called fur and no seal skin.

Our only other conversation was the description and names of the dogs that were then fashionable. This was my subject and after I had described she always hesitated, ah yes, she would say illuminated, you wish to describe a little belgian dog whose name is griffon.

There we were, she was very beautiful but it was a little heavy and monotonous, so I suggested we should meet out of doors, at a tea place or take walks in Montmartre. That was better. She began to tell me things. I met Max Jacob. Fernande and he were very funny together. They felt themselves to be a courtly couple of the first empire, he being le vieux

who made noises like an animal and annoyed Picasso

marquis kissing her hand and paying compliments and she the Empress Josephine receiving them. It was a caricature but a rather wonderful one. Then she told me about a mysterious horrible woman called Marie Laurencin who made noises like an animal and annoyed Picasso. I thought of her as a horrible old woman and was delighted when I met the young chic Marie who looked like a Clouet. Max Jacob read my horoscope. It was a great honour because he wrote it down. I did not realise it then but I have since and most of all very lately, as all the young gentlemen who nowadays so much admire Max are so astonished and impressed that he wrote mine down as he has always been supposed never to write them but just to say them off hand. Well anyway I have mine and it is written.

Then she also told me a great many stories about Van Dongen and his dutch wife and dutch little girl. Van Dongen broke into notoriety by a portrait he did of Fernande. It was in that way that he created the type of almond eyes that were later so much the vogue. But Fernande's almond eyes were natural, for good or for bad everything was natural in Fernande.

Of course Van Dongen did not admit that this picture was a portrait of Fernande, although she had sat for it and there was in consequence much bitterness. Van Dongen in these days was poor, he had a dutch wife who was a vegetarian and they lived on spinach. Van Dongen frequently escaped from the spinach to a joint in Montmartre where the girls paid for his dinner and his drinks.

The Van Dongen child was only four years old but terrific. Van Dongen used to do acrobatics with her and swing her around his head by a leg. When she hugged Picasso of whom she was very fond she used almost to destroy him, he had a great fear of her.

There were many other tales of Germaine Pichot and the circus where she found her lovers and there were tales of all the past and present life of Montmartre. Fernande herself had one ideal. It was Evelyn Thaw the heroine of the moment. And Fernande adored her in the way a later generation adored Mary Pickford, she was so blonde, so pale, so nothing and Fernande would give a heavy sigh of admiration.

The next time I saw Gertrude Stein she said to me suddenly, is Fernande wearing her earrings. I do not know, I said. Well notice, she said. The next time I saw Gertrude Stein I said, yes Fernande is wearing her earrings. Oh well, she said, there is nothing to be done yet, it's a nuisance because Pablo naturally having nobody in the studio cannot stay at home. In another week I was able to announce that Fernande was not wearing her earrings. Oh well it's alright then she has no more money left and it is all over, said Gertrude Stein. And it was. A week later I was dining with Fernande and Pablo at the rue de Fleurus.

I gave Fernande a chinese gown from San Francisco and Pablo gave me a lovely drawing.

And now I will tell you how two americans happened to be in the heart of an art movement of which the outside world at that time knew nothing.

III.

Gertrude Stein in Paris

1903–1907

D URING GERTRUDE STEIN'S last two years at
the Medical School, Johns Hopkins, Baltimore, 1900–
1903, her brother was living in Florence. There he heard
of a painter named Cézanne and saw paintings by him owned by
Charles Loeser. When he and his sister made their home in Paris
the following year they went to Vollard's the only picture dealer
who had Cézannes for sale, to look at them.

Vollard was a huge dark man who lisped a little. His shop was
on the rue Laffitte not far from the boulevard. Further along this
short street was Durand-Ruel and still further on almost at the
church of the Martyrs was Sagot the ex-clown. Higher up in Montmartre on the rue Victor-Massé was Mademoiselle Weill who sold
a mixture of pictures, books and bric-à-brac and in entirely another
part of Paris on the rue Faubourg-Saint-Honoré was the ex-café
keeper and photographer Druet. Also on the rue Laffitte was the
confectioner Fouquet where one could console oneself with delicious honey cakes and nut candies and once in a while instead of a
picture buy oneself strawberry jam in a glass bowl.

The first visit to Vollard has left an indelible impression on Gertrude Stein. It was an incredible place. It did not look like a picture

gallery. Inside there were a couple of canvases turned to the wall, in one corner was a small pile of big and little canvases thrown pell mell on top of one another, in the centre of the room stood a huge dark man glooming. This was Vollard cheerful. When he was really cheerless he put his huge frame against the glass door that led to the street, his arms above his head, his hands on each upper corner of the portal and gloomed darkly into the street. Nobody thought then of trying to come in.

They asked to see Cézannes. He looked less gloomy and became quite polite. As they found out afterward Cézanne was the great romance of Vollard's life. The name Cézanne was to him a magic word. He had first learned about Cézanne from Pissarro the painter. Pissarro indeed was the man from whom all the early Cézanne lovers heard about Cézanne. Cézanne at that time was living gloomy and embittered at Aix-en-Provence. Pissarro told Vollard about him, told Fabry, a Florentine, who told Loeser, told Picabia, in fact told everybody who knew about Cézanne at that time.

There were Cézannes to be seen at Vollard's. Later on Gertrude Stein wrote a poem called Vollard and Cézanne, and Henry McBride printed it in the New York Sun. This was the first fugitive piece of Gertrude Stein's to be so printed and it gave both her and Vollard a great deal of pleasure. Later on when Vollard wrote his book about Cézanne, Vollard at Gertrude Stein's suggestion sent a copy of the book to Henry McBride. She told Vollard that a whole page of one of New York's big daily papers would be devoted to his book. He did not believe it possible, nothing like that had ever happened to anybody in Paris. It did happen and he was deeply moved and unspeakably content. But to return to that first visit.

They told Monsieur Vollard they wanted to see some Cézanne landscapes, they had been sent to him by Mr. Loeser of Florence. Oh yes, said Vollard looking quite cheerful and he began moving about the room, finally he disappeared behind a partition in the back and was heard heavily mounting the steps. After a quite long wait he came down again and had in his hand a tiny picture of an apple with most of the canvas unpainted. They all looked at this thoroughly, then they said, yes but you see what we wanted to see was a landscape. Ah yes, sighed Vollard and he looked even more cheerful, after a moment he again disappeared and this time came back with a painting of a back, it was a beautiful painting there is no doubt about that but the brother and sister were not yet up to a full appreciation of Cézanne nudes and so they returned to the attack. They wanted to see a landscape. This time after even a longer wait he came back with a very large canvas and a very little fragment of a landscape painted on it. Yes that was it, they said, a landscape but what they wanted was a smaller canvas but one all covered. They said, they thought they would like to see one like that. By this time the early winter evening of Paris was closing in and just at this moment a very aged charwoman came down the same back stairs, mumbled, bon soir monsieur et madame, and quietly went out of the door, after a moment another old charwoman came down the same stairs, murmured, bon soir messieurs et mesdames and went quietly out of the door. Gertrude Stein began to laugh and said to her brother, it is all nonsense, there is no Cézanne. Vollard goes upstairs and tells these old women what to paint and he does not understand us and they do not understand him and they paint something and he brings it down and it is a Cézanne. They both began to laugh uncontrollably. Then they recovered and once more explained about the landscape. They said what they wanted was one of those marvellously yellow sunny Aix landscapes of which Loeser had several examples. Once more Vollard went off and this time he came back with a wonderful small green landscape. It was lovely, it covered all the canvas, it did not cost much and they bought it. Later on Vollard explained to every one that he had been visited by two crazy americans and they laughed and he had been much annoyed but gradually he found out that when they laughed most they usually bought something so of course he waited for them to laugh.

From that time on they went to Vollard's all the time. They had soon the privilege of upsetting his piles of canvases and finding what they liked in the heap. They bought a tiny little Daumier, head of an old woman. They began to take an interest in Cézanne nudes and they finally bought two tiny canvases of nude groups. They found a very very small Manet painted in black and white with Forain in the foreground and bought it, they found two tiny little Renoirs. They frequently bought in twos because one of them usually liked one more than the other one did, and so the year wore on. In the spring Vollard announced a show of Gauguin and they for the first time saw some Gauguins. They were rather awful but they finally liked them, and bought two Gauguins. Gertrude Stein liked his sun-flowers but not his figures and her brother preferred the figures. It sounds like a great deal now but in those days these things did not cost much. And so the winter went on.

There were not a great many people in and out of Vollard's but once Gertrude Stein heard a conversation there that pleased her immensely. Duret was a well known figure in Paris. He was now a very old and a very handsome man. He had been a friend of Whistler, Whistler had painted him in evening clothes with a white opera cloak over his arm. He was at Vollard's talking to a group of younger men and one of them Roussel, one of the Vuillard, Bonnard, the post impressionist group, said something complainingly about the lack of recognition of himself and his friends, that they were not even allowed to show in the salon. Duret looked at him kindly, my young friend, he said, there are two kinds of art, never forget this, there is art and there is official art. How can you, my poor young friend, hope to be official art. Just look at yourself. Supposing an important personage came to France, and wanted to meet the representative painters and have his portrait painted. My dear young friend, just look at yourself, the very sight of you would terrify him. You are a nice young man, gentle and intelligent, but to the important personage you would not seem so, you would be terrible. No they need as representative painter a medium sized, slightly stout man, not too well dressed but dressed in the fashion of his class, neither bald or well brushed hair and a respectful bow with it. You can see that you would not do. So never say another word about official recognition, or if you do look in the mirror and think of important personages. No, my dear young friend there is art and there is official art, there always has been and there always will be.

Before the winter was over, having gone so far Gertrude Stein and her brother decided to go further, they decided to buy a big Cézanne and then they would stop. After that they would be reasonable. They convinced their

44

elder brother that this last outlay was necessary, and it was necessary as will soon be evident. They told Vollard that they wanted to buy a Cézanne portrait. In those days practically no big Cézanne portraits had been sold. Vollard owned almost all of them. He was enormously pleased with this decision. They now were introduced into the room above the steps behind the partition where Gertrude Stein had been sure the old charwoman painted the Cézannes and there they spent days deciding which portrait they would have. There were about eight to choose from and the decision was difficult. They had often to go and refresh themselves with honey cakes at Fouquet's. Finally they narrowed the choice down to two, a portrait of a man and a portrait of a woman, but this time they could not afford to buy twos and finally they chose the portrait of the woman.

Vollard said of course ordinarily a portrait of a woman always is more expensive than a portrait of a man but, said he looking at the picture very carefully, I suppose with Cézanne it does not make any difference. They put it in a cab and they went home with it. It was this picture that Alfy Maurer used to explain was finished and that you could tell that it was finished because it had a frame.

It was an important purchase because in looking and looking at this picture Gertrude Stein wrote Three Lives.

She had begun not long before as an exercise in literature to translate Flaubert's Trois Contes and then she had this Cézanne and she looked at it and under its stimulus she wrote Three Lives.

The next thing that happened was in the autumn. It was the first year of the autumn salon, the first autumn salon that had ever existed in Paris and they, very eager and excited, went to see it. There they found Matisse's picture afterwards known as La Femme au Chapeau.

This first autumn salon was a step in official recognition of the outlaws of the independent salon. Their pictures were to be shown in the Petit Palais opposite the Grand Palais where the great spring salon was held. That is, those outlaws were to be shown there who had succeeded enough so that they began to be sold in important picture shops. These in collaboration with some rebels from the old salons had created the autumn salon.

The show had a great deal of freshness and was not alarming. There were a number of attractive pictures but there was one that was not attractive. It infuriated the public, they tried to scratch off the paint.

Gertrude Stein liked that picture, it was a portrait of a woman with a long face and a fan. It was very strange in its colour and in its anatomy. She said she wanted to buy it. Her brother had in the meantime found a white-clothed woman on a green lawn and he wanted to buy it. So as usual they decided to buy two and they went to the office of the secretary of the salon to find out about prices. They had never been in the little room of a secretary of a salon and it was very exciting. The secretary looked up the prices in his catalogue. Gertrude Stein has forgotten how much and even whose it was, the white dress and dog on the green grass, but the Matisse was five hundred francs. The secretary explained that of course one never paid what the artist asked, one suggested a price. They asked what price they should suggest. He asked them what they were willing to pay. They said they did not know. He suggested that they offer four hundred and he would let them know. They agreed and left.

The next day they received word from the secretary that Monsieur Matisse had refused to accept the offer and what did they want to do. They decided to go over to the salon and look at the picture again. They did. People were roaring with laughter at the picture and scratching at it. Gertrude Stein could not understand why, the picture seemed to her perfectly natural. The Cézanne portrait had not seemed natural, it had taken her some time to feel that it was natural but this picture by Matisse seemed perfectly natural and she could not understand why it infuriated everybody. Her brother was less attracted but all the same he agreed and they bought it. She then went back to look at it and it upset her to see them all mocking at it. It bothered her and angered her because she did not understand why because to her it was so alright, just as later she did not understand why since the writing was all so clear and natural they mocked at and were enraged by her work.

And so this was the story of the buying of La Femme au Chapeau by the buyers and now for the story from the seller's point of view as told some months after by Monsieur and Madame Matisse. Shortly after the purchase of the picture they all asked to meet each other. Whether Matisse wrote and asked or whether they wrote and asked Gertrude Stein does not remember. Anyway in no time they were knowing each other and knowing each other very well.

The Matisses lived on the quay just off the boulevard Saint-Michel. They were on the top floor in a small three-roomed apartment with a lovely view over Notre Dame and the river. Matisse painted it in winter. You went up and up the steps. In those days you were always going up stairs and down stairs. Mildred Aldrich had a distressing way of dropping her key down the middle of the stairs where an elevator might have been, in calling out goodbye to some one below, from her sixth story, and then you or she had to go all the way up or all the way down again. To be sure she would often call out, never mind, I am bursting open my door. Only americans did that. The keys were heavy and you either forgot them or dropped them. Sayen at the end of a Paris summer when he was congratulated on looking so well and sun-burned, said, yes it comes from going up and down stairs.

Madame Matisse was an admirable housekeeper. Her place was small but immaculate. She kept the house in order, she was an excellent cook and provider, she posed for all of Matisse's pictures. It was she who was La Femme au Chapeau, lady with a hat. She had kept a little millinery shop to keep them going in their poorest days. She was a very straight dark woman with a long face and a firm large loosely hung mouth like a horse. She had an abundance of dark hair. Gertrude Stein always liked the way she pinned her hat to her head and Matisse once made a drawing of his wife making this characteristic gesture and gave it to Miss Stein. She always wore black. She always placed a large black hat-pin well in the middle of the hat and the middle of the top of her head and then with a large firm gesture, down it came. They had with them a daughter of Matisse, a daughter he had had before his marriage and who had had diphtheria and had had to have an operation and for many years had to wear a black ribbon around her throat with a silver button. This Matisse put into many of his pictures. The girl was exactly like her father and Madame Matisse, as she once explained in her melodramatic simple way, did more than her duty by this child because having read in her youth a novel in which the heroine had done so and been consequently much loved all her life, had decided to do the same. She herself had had two boys but they were neither of them at that time living with them. The younger Pierre was in the south of France on the borders of Spain with Madame Matisse's father and mother, and the elder Jean with Monsieur Matisse's father and mother in the north of France on the borders of Belgium.

Matisse had an astonishing virility that always gave one an extraordinary pleasure when one had not seen him for some time. Less the first time of seeing him than later. And one did not lose the pleasure of this virility all the time he was with one. But there was not much feeling of life in this virility. Madame Matisse was very different, there was a very profound feeling of life in her for any one who knew her.

Matisse had at this time a small Cézanne and a small Gauguin and he said he needed them both. The Cézanne had been bought with his wife's marriage portion, the Gauguin with the ring which was the only jewel she had ever owned. And they were happy because he needed these two pictures. The Cézanne was a picture of bathers and a tent, the Gauguin the head of a boy. Later on in life when Matisse became a very rich man, he kept on buying pictures. He said he knew about pictures and had confidence in them and he did not know about other things. And so for his own pleasure and as the best legacy to leave his children he bought Cézannes. Picasso also later when he became rich bought pictures but they were his own. He too believed in pictures and wants to leave the best legacy he can to his son and so keeps and buys his own.

The Matisses had had a hard time. Matisse had come to Paris as a young man to study pharmacy. His people were small grain merchants in the north of France. He had become interested in painting, had begun copying the Poussins at the Louvre and become a painter fairly without the consent of his people who however continued to allow him the very small monthly sum he had had as a student. His daughter was born at this time and this further complicated his life. He had at first a certain amount of success. He married. Under the influence of the paintings of Poussin and Chardin he had painted still life pictures that had considerable success at the Champ-de-Mars salon, one of the two big spring salons. And then he fell under the influence of Cézanne, and then under the influence of negro sculpture. All this developed the Matisse of the period of La Femme au Chapeau. The year after his very considerable success at the salon he spent the winter painting a very large picture of a woman setting a table and on the table was a magnificent dish of fruit. It had strained the resources of the Matisse family to buy this fruit, fruit was horribly dear in Paris in those days, even ordinary fruit, imagine how much dearer was this very extraordinary fruit and it had to keep until the picture was completed and the picture was going to take a long time. In order to keep it as long as possible they kept the room as cold as possible, and that under the roof and in a Paris winter was not difficult, and Matisse painted in an overcoat and gloves and he painted at it all winter. It was finished at last and sent to the salon where the year before Matisse had had considerable success, and there it was refused. And now Matisse's serious troubles began, his daughter was very ill, he was in an agonising mental struggle concerning his work, and he had lost all possibility of showing his pictures. He no longer painted at home but in an atelier. It was cheaper so. Every morning he painted, every afternoon he worked at his sculpture, late every afternoon he drew in the sketch classes from the nude, and every evening he played his violin. These were very dark days and he was very despairful. His wife opened a small millinery shop and they managed to live. The two boys were sent away to the country to his and her people and they continued to live. The only encouragement came in the atelier where he worked and where a crowd of young men began to gather around him and be influenced by him. Among these the best known at that time was Manguin, the best known now Derain. Derain was a very young man at that time, he enormously admired Matisse, he went away to the country with them to Collioure near Perpignan, and he was a great comfort to them all. He began to paint landscapes outlining his trees with red and he had a sense of space that was quite his own and which first showed itself in a landscape of a cart going up a road bordered with trees

had had a hard time

lined in red. His paintings were coming to be known at the independent.

Matisse worked every day and every day and every day and he worked terribly hard. Once Vollard came to see him. Matisse used to love to tell the story. I have often heard him tell it. Vollard came and said he wanted to see the big picture which had been refused. Matisse showed it to him. He did not look at it. He talked to Madame Matisse and mostly about cooking, he liked cooking and eating as a frenchman should, and so did she. Matisse and Madame Matisse were both getting very nervous although she did not show it. And this door, said Vollard interestedly to Matisse, where does that lead to, does that lead into a court or does that lead on to a stairway. Into a court, said Matisse. Ah yes, said Vollard. And then he left.

The Matisses spent days discussing whether there was anything symbolic in Vollard's question or was it idle curiosity. Vollard never had any idle curiosity, he always wanted to know what everybody thought of everything because in that way he found out what he himself thought. This was very well known and therefore the Matisses asked each other and all their friends, why did he ask that question about that door. Well at any rate within the year he had bought the picture at a very low price but he bought it, and he put it away and nobody saw it, and that was the end of that.

From this time on things went neither better nor worse for Matisse and he was discouraged and aggressive. Then came the first autumn salon and he was asked to exhibit and he sent La Femme au Chapeau and it was hung. It was derided and attacked and it was sold.

Matisse was at this time about thirty-five years old, he was depressed. Having gone to the opening day of the salon and heard what was said of his picture and seen what they were trying to do to it he never went again. His wife went alone. He stayed at home and was unhappy. This is the way Madame Matisse used to tell the story.

Then a note came from the secretary of the salon saying that there had been an offer made for the picture, an offer of four hundred francs. Matisse was painting Madame Matisse as a gypsy holding a guitar. This guitar had already had a history. Madame Matisse was very fond of telling the story. She had a great deal to do and she posed beside and she was very healthy and sleepy. One day she was posing, he was painting, she began to nod and as she nodded the guitar made noises. Stop it, said Matisse, wake up. She woke up, he painted, she nodded and the guitar made noises. Stop it, said Matisse, wake up. She woke up and then in a little while she nodded again the guitar made even more noises. Matisse furious seized the guitar and broke it. And added Madame Matisse ruefully, we were very hard up then and we had to have it mended so he could go on with the picture. She was holding this same mended guitar and posing when the note from the secretary of the autumn salon came. Matisse was joyful, of course I will accept, said Matisse. Oh no, said Madame Matisse, if those people (ces gens) are interested enough to make an offer they are interested enough to pay the price you asked, and she added, the difference would make winter clothes for Margot. Matisse hesitated but was finally convinced and they sent a note saying he wanted his price. Nothing happened and Matisse was in a terrible state and very reproachful and then in a day or two when Madame Matisse was once more posing with the guitar and Matisse was painting, Margot brought them a little blue telegram. Matisse opened it and he made a grimace. Madame Matisse was terrified, she thought the worst had happened. The guitar fell. What is it, she said. They have bought it, he said. Why do you make such a face of agony and frighten me so and perhaps break the guitar, she said. I was winking at you, he said, to tell you, because I was so moved I could not speak.

And so, Madame Matisse used to end up the story triumphantly, you see it was I, and I was right to insist upon the original price, and Mademoiselle Gertrude, who insisted upon buying it, who arranged the whole matter.

The friendship with the Matisses grew apace. Matisse at that time was at work at his first big decoration, Le Bonheur de Vivre. He was making small and larger and very large studies for it. It was in this picture that Matisse first clearly realised his intention of deforming the drawing of the human body in order to harmonise and intensify the colour values of all the simple colours mixed only with white. He used his distorted drawing as a dissonance is used in music or as vinegar or lemons are used in cooking or egg shells in coffee to clarify. I do inevitably take my comparisons from

Cézanne had come to his unfinishedness

the kitchen because I like food and cooking and know something about it. However this was the idea. Cézanne had come to his unfinishedness and distortion of necessity, Matisse did it by intention.

Little by little people began to come to the rue de Fleurus to see the Matisses and the Cézannes, Matisse brought people, everybody brought somebody, and they came at any time and it began to be a nuisance, and it was in this way that Saturday evenings began. It was also at this time that Gertrude Stein got into the habit of writing at night. It was only after eleven o'clock that she could be sure that no one would knock at the studio door. She was at that time planning her long book, The Making of Americans, she was struggling with her sentences, those long sentences that had to be so exactly carried out. Sentences not only words but sentences and always sentences have been Gertrude Stein's life long passion. And so she had then and indeed it lasted pretty well to the war, which broke down so many habits, she had then the habit of beginning her work at eleven o'clock at night and working until the dawn. She said she always tried to stop before the dawn was too clear and the birds were too lively because it is a disagreeable sensation to go to bed then. There were birds in many trees behind high walls in those days, now there are fewer. But often the birds and the dawn caught her and she stood in the court waiting to get used to it before she went to bed. She had the habit then of sleeping until noon and the beating of the rugs into the court, because everybody did that in those days, even her household did, was one of her most poignant irritations.

So the Saturday evenings began.

Gertrude Stein and her brother were often at the Matisses and the Matisses were constantly with them. Madame Matisse occasionally gave them a lunch, this happened most often when some relation sent the Matisses a hare. Jugged hare prepared by Madame Matisse in the fashion of Perpignan was something quite apart. They also had extremely good wine, a little heavy, but excellent. They also had a sort of Madeira called Roncio which was very good indeed. Maillol the sculptor came from the same part of France as Madame Matisse and once when I met him at Jo Davidson's,

55

many years later, he told me about all these wines. He then told me how he had lived well in his student days in Paris for fifty francs a month. To be sure, he said, the family sent me homemade bread every week and when I came I brought enough wine with me to last a year and I sent my washing home every month.

Derain was present at one of these lunches in those early days. He and Gertrude Stein disagreed violently. They discussed philosophy, he basing his ideas on having read the second part of Faust in a french translation while he was doing his military service. They never became friends. Gertrude Stein was never interested in his work. He had a sense of space but for her his pictures had neither life nor depth nor solidity. They rarely saw each other after. Derain at that time was constantly with the Matisses and was of all Matisse's friends the one Madame Matisse liked the best.

It was about this time that Gertrude Stein's brother happened one day to find the picture gallery of Sagot, an ex-circus clown who had a picture shop further up the rue Laffitte. Here he, Gertrude Stein's brother, found the paintings of two young spaniards, one, whose name everybody has forgotten, the other one, Picasso. The work of both of them interested him and he bought a water colour by the forgotten one, a café scene. Sagot also sent him to a little furniture store where there were some paintings being shown by Picasso. Gertrude Stein's brother was interested and wanted to buy one and asked the price but the price asked was almost as expensive as Cézanne. He went back to Sagot and told him. Sagot laughed. He said, that is alright, come back in a few days and I will have a big one. In a few days he did have a big one and it was very cheap. When Gertrude Stein and Picasso tell about those days they are not always in agreement as to what happened but I think in this case they agree that the price asked was a hundred and fifty francs. The picture was the now well known painting of a nude girl with a basket of red flowers.

Gertrude Stein did not like the picture, she found something rather appalling in the drawing of the legs and feet, something that repelled and shocked her. She and her brother almost quarrelled about this picture. He wanted it and she did not want it in the house. Sagot gathering a little of

the Matisses were constantly with them

the discussion said, but that is alright if you do not like the legs and feet it is very easy to guillotine her and only take the head. No that would not do, everybody agreed, and nothing was decided.

Gertrude Stein and her brother continued to be very divided in this matter and they were very angry with each other. Finally it was agreed that since he, the brother, wanted it so badly they would buy it, and in this way the first Picasso was brought into the rue de Fleurus.

It was just about this time that Raymond Duncan, the brother of Isadora, rented an atelier in the rue de Fleurus. Raymond had just come back from his first trip to Greece and had brought back with him a greek girl and greek clothes. Raymond had known Gertrude Stein's elder brother and his wife in San Francisco. At that time Raymond was acting as advance agent for Emma Nevada who had also with her Pablo Casals the violincellist, at that time quite unknown.

The Duncan family had been then at the Omar Khayyám stage, they had not yet gone greek. They had after that gone italian renaissance, but now Raymond had gone completely greek and this included a greek girl. Isadora lost interest in him, she found the girl too modern a greek. At any rate Raymond was at this time without any money at all and his wife was enceinte. Gertrude Stein gave him coal and a chair for Penelope to sit in, the rest sat on packing cases. They had another friend who helped them, Kathleen Bruce, a very beautiful, very athletic English girl, a kind of sculptress, she later married and became the widow of the discoverer of the South Pole, Scott. She had at that time no money to speak of either and she used to bring a half portion of her dinner every evening for Penelope. Finally Penelope had her baby, it was named Raymond because when Gertrude Stein's brother and Raymond Duncan went to register it they had not thought of a name. Now he is against his will called Menalkas but he might be gratified if he knew that legally he is Raymond. However that is another matter.

Kathleen Bruce was a sculptress and she was learning to model figures of children and she asked to do a figure of Gertrude Stein's nephew. Gertrude Stein and her nephew went to Kathleen Bruce's studio. There they, one afternoon, met H. P. Roché. Roché was one of those characters that are always to be found in Paris. He was a very earnest, very noble, devoted, very faithful and very enthusiastic man who was a general introducer. He knew everybody, he really knew them and he could introduce anybody to anybody. He was going to be a writer. He was tall and red-headed and he never said anything but good good excellent and he lived with his mother and his grandmother. He had done a great many things, he had gone to the austrian mountains with the austrians, he had gone to Germany with the germans and he had gone to Hungary with hungarians and he had gone to England with the english. He had not gone to Russia although he had been in Paris with russians. As Picasso always said of him, Roché is very nice but he is only a translation.

Later he was often at 27 rue de Fleurus with various nationalities and Gertrude Stein rather liked him. She always said of him he is so faithful, perhaps one need never see him again but one knows that somewhere Roché is faithful. He did give her one delightful sensation in the very early days of their acquaintance. Three Lives, Gertrude Stein's first book was just then being written and Roché who could read english was very impressed by it. One day Gertrude Stein was saying something about herself and Roché said good good excellent that is very important for your biography. She was terribly touched, it was the first time that she really realised that some time she would have a biography. It is quite true that although she has not seen him for years somewhere Roché is probably perfectly faithful.

But to come back to Roché at Kathleen Bruce's studio. They all talked about one thing and another and Gertrude Stein happened to mention that they had just bought a picture from Sagot by a young spaniard named Picasso. Good good excellent, said Roché, he is a very interesting young fellow, I know him. Oh do you, said Gertrude Stein, well enough to take somebody to see him. Why certainly, said Roché. Very well, said Gertrude Stein, my brother I know is very anxious to make his acquaintance. And there and then the appointment was made and shortly after Roché and Gertrude Stein's brother went to see Picasso.

It was only a very short time after this that Picasso began the portrait of Gertrude Stein, now so widely known, but just how that came about is a little vague in everybody's mind. I have heard Picasso and Gertrude Stein talk about it often and they neither of them can remember. They can remember the first time that Picasso dined at the rue de Fleurus and they can remember the first time Gertrude Stein posed for her portrait at rue Ravignan but in between there is a blank. How it came about they do not know. Picasso had never had anybody pose for him since he was sixteen years old, he was then twenty-four and Gertrude Stein had never thought of having her portrait painted, and they do not either of them know how it came about. Anyway it did and she posed to him for this portrait ninety times and a great deal happened during that time. To go back to all the first times.

Picasso and Fernande came to dinner, Picasso in those days was, what a dear friend and schoolmate of mine, Nellie Jacot, called, a good-looking bootblack. He was thin dark, alive with big pools of eyes and a violent but not rough way. He was sitting next to Gertrude Stein at dinner and she took up a piece of bread. This, said Picasso, snatching it back with violence, this piece of bread is mine. She laughed and he looked sheepish. That was the beginning of their intimacy.

That evening Gertrude Stein's brother took out portfolio after portfolio of japanese prints to show Picasso, Gertrude Stein's brother was fond of japanese prints. Picasso solemnly and obediently looked at print after print and listened to the descriptions. He said under his breath to Gertrude Stein, he is very nice, your brother, but like all americans, like Haviland, he shows you japanese prints. Moi j'aime pas ça, no I don't care for it. As I say Gertrude Stein and Pablo Picasso immediately understood each other.

Then there was the first time of posing. The atelier of Picasso I have already described. In those days there was even more disorder, more coming and going, more red-hot fire in the stove, more cooking and more interruptions. There was a large broken armchair where Gertrude Stein posed. There was a couch where everybody sat and slept. There was a little kitchen chair upon which Picasso sat to paint, there was a large easel and there were many very large canvases. It was at the height of the end of the Harlequin period when the canvases were enormous, the figures also, and the groups.

There was a little fox terrier there that had something the matter with it and had been and was again about to be taken to the veterinary. No frenchman or frenchwoman is so poor or so careless or so avaricious but that they can and do constantly take their pet to the vet.

Fernande was as always, very large, very beautiful and very gracious. She offered to read La Fontaine's stories aloud to amuse Gertrude Stein while Gertrude Stein posed. She took her pose, Picasso sat very tight on his chair and very close to his canvas and on a very small palette which was of a uniform brown grey colour, mixed some more brown grey and the painting began. This was the first of some eighty or ninety sittings.

Toward the end of the afternoon Gertrude Stein's two brothers and her sister-in-law and Andrew Green came to see. They were all excited at the beauty of the sketch and Andrew Green begged and begged that it should be left as it was. But Picasso shook his head and said, non.

It is too bad but in those days no one thought of taking a photograph of the picture as it was then and of course no one of the group that saw it then remembers at all what it looked like any more than do Picasso or Gertrude Stein.

Andrew Green, none of them knew how they had met Andrew Green, he was the great-nephew of Andrew Green known as the father of Greater New York. He had been born and reared in Chicago but he was a typical tall gaunt new englander, blond and gentle. He had a prodigious memory and could recite all of Milton's Paradise Lost by heart and also all the translations of chinese poems of which Gertrude Stein was very fond. He had been in China and he was later to live permanently in the South Sea islands after he finally inherited quite a fortune from his great-uncle who was fond of Milton's Paradise Lost. He had a passion for oriental stuffs. He adored as he said a simple centre and a continuous design. He loved pictures in museums and he hated everything modern. Once when during the family's absence he had stayed at the rue de Fleurus for a month, he had outraged Hélène's feelings by having his bed-sheets changed every day and covering all the pictures with cashmere shawls. He said the pictures were very restful, he could not deny that, but he could not bear it. He said that after the month was over that he had of course never come to like the new pictures but the worst of it was that not liking them he had lost his taste for the old and he never again in his life could go to any museum or look at any picture. He was tremendously impressed by Fernande's beauty. He was indeed quite overcome. I would, he said to Gertrude Stein, if I could talk french, I would make love to her and take her away from that little Picasso. Do you make love with words, laughed Gertrude Stein. He went away before I came to Paris and he came back eighteen years later and he was very dull.

This year was comparatively a quiet one. The Matisses were in the South of France all winter, at Collioure on the Mediterranean coast not far from Perpignan, where Madame Matisse's people lived. The Raymond Duncans had disappeared after having been joined first by a sister of Penelope who was a little actress and was very far from being dressed greek, she was as nearly as she possibly could be a little Parisian. She had accompanying her a very large dark greek cousin. He came in to see Gertrude Stein and he looked around and he announced, I am greek, that is the same as saying that I have perfect taste and I do not care for any of these pictures. Very shortly Raymond, his wife and baby, the sister-in-law and the greek cousin disappeared out of the court at 27 rue de Fleurus and were succeeded by a german lady.

This german lady was the niece and god-daughter of german field-marshals and her brother was a captain in the german navy. Her mother was english and she herself had played the harp at the bavarian court. She was very amusing and had some strange friends, both english and french. She was a sculptress and she made a typical german sculpture of little Roger, the concierge's boy. She made three heads of him, one laughing, one crying and one sticking out his tongue, all three together on one pedestal. She sold this piece to the royal museum at Potsdam. The concierge during the war often wept at the thought of her Roger being there, sculptured, in the museum at Potsdam. She invented clothes that could be worn inside out and taken to pieces and be made long or short and she showed these to everybody with great pride. She had as an instructor in painting a weird looking frenchman one who looked exactly like the pictures of Huckleberry Finn's father. She explained that she employed him out of charity, he had won a gold medal at the salon in his youth and after that had had no success. She also said that she never employed a servant of the servant class. She said that decayed gentlewomen were more appetising and more efficient and she always had some widow of some army officer or functionary sewing or posing for her. She had an austrian maid for a while who cooked perfectly delicious austrian pastry but she did not keep her long. She was in short very amusing and she and Gertrude Stein used to talk to each other in the court. She always wanted to know what Gertrude Stein thought of everybody who came in and out. She wanted to know if she came to her conclusions by deduction, observation, imagination or analysis. She was amusing and then she disappeared and nobody thought anything about her until the war came and then everybody wondered if after all there had not been something sinister about this german woman's life in Paris.

Practically every afternoon Gertrude Stein went to Montmartre, posed and then later wandered down the hill usually walking across Paris to the rue de Fleurus. She then formed the habit which has never left her of walking around Paris, now accompanied by the dog, in those days alone. And Saturday evenings the Picassos walked home with her and dined and then there was Saturday evening.

During these long poses and these long walks Gertrude Stein meditated and made sentences. She was then in the middle of her negro story Melanctha Herbert, the second story of Three Lives and the poignant incidents that she wove into the life of Melanctha were often these she noticed in walking down the hill from the rue Ravignan.

It was at that time that the hungarians began their pilgrimages to the rue de Fleurus. There were strange groups of americans then, Picasso unaccustomed to the virginal quality of these young men and women used to say of them, ils sont pas des hommes, ils sont pas des femmes, ils sont des américains. They are not men, they are not women, they are americans. Once there was a Bryn Mawr woman there, wife of a well known portrait painter, who was very tall and beautiful and having once fallen on her head had a strange vacant expression. Her, he approved of, and used to call the Empress. There was a type of american art student, male, that used very much to afflict him, he used to say no it is not he who will make the future glory of America. He had a characteristic reaction when he saw the first photograph of a skyscraper. Good God, he said, imagine the pangs of jealousy a lover would have while his beloved came up all those flights of stairs to his top story studio.

It was at this time that a Maurice Denis, a Toulouse-Lautrec and many enormous Picassos were added to the collection. It was at this time also that the acquaintance and friendship with the Vallotons began.

Vollard once said when he was asked about a certain painter's picture, oh ça c'est un Cézanne pour les pauvres, that is a Cézanne for the poor collector. Well Valloton was a Manet for the impecunious. His big nude had all the hardness, the stillness and none of the quality of the Olympe of Manet and his portraits had the aridity but none of the elegance of David. And further he had the misfortune of having married the sister of an important picture-dealer. He was very happy with his wife and she was a very charming woman but then there were the weekly family reunions, and there was also the wealth of his wife and the violence of his step-sons. He was a gentle soul, Valloton, with a keen wit and a great deal of ambition but a feeling of impotence, the result of being the brother-in-law of picture dealers. However for a time his pictures were very interesting. He asked Gertrude Stein to pose for him. She did the following year. She had come to like posing, the long still hours followed by a long dark walk intensified the concentration with which she was creating her sentences. The sentences of which Marcel Brion, the french critic has written, by exactitude, austerity, absence of variety in light and shade, by refusal of the use of the subconscious Gertrude Stein achieves a symmetry which has a close analogy to the symmetry of the musical fugue of Bach.

She often described the strange sensation she had as a result of the way in which Valloton painted. He was not at that time a young man as painters go, he had already had considerable recognition as a painter in the Paris exposition of 1900. When he painted a portrait he made a crayon sketch and then began painting at the top of the canvas straight across. Gertrude Stein said it was like pulling down a curtain as slowly moving as one of his swiss glaciers. Slowly he pulled the curtain down and by the time he was at the bottom of the canvas, there you were. The whole operation took about two weeks and then he gave the canvas to you. First however he exhibited it in the autumn salon and it had considerable notice and everybody was pleased.

Everybody went to the Cirque Médrano once a week, at least, and usually everybody went on the same evening. There the clowns had commenced dressing up in misfit clothes instead of the old classic costume and these clothes later so well known on Charlie Chaplin were the delight of Picasso and all his friends in Montmartre. There also were the english jockeys and their costumes made the mode that all Montmartre followed. Not very long ago somebody was talking about how well the young painters of to-day dressed and what a pity it was that they spent money in that way. Picasso laughed. I am quite certain, he said, they pay less for the fashionable complet, their suits of clothes, than we did for our rough and common ones. You have no idea how hard it was and expensive it was in those days to find english tweed or a french imitation that would look rough and dirty enough. And it was quite true one way and another the painters in those days did spend a lot of money and they spent all they got hold of because in those happy days you could owe money for years for your paints and canvases and rent and restaurant and practically everything except coal and luxuries.

The winter went on. Three Lives was written. Gertrude Stein asked her sister-in-law to come and read it. She did and was deeply moved. This pleased Gertrude Stein immensely, she did not believe that any one could read anything she wrote and be interested. In those days she never asked any one what they thought of her work, but were they interested enough to read it. Now she says if they can bring themselves to read it they will be interested.

Her elder brother's wife has always meant a great deal in her life but never more than on that afternoon. And then it had to be typewritten.

Gertrude Stein had at that time a wretched little portable typewriter which she never used. She always then and for many years later wrote on scraps of paper in pencil, copied it into french school note-books in ink and then often copied it over again in ink. It was in connection with these various series of scraps of paper that her elder brother once remarked, I do not know whether Gertrude has more genius than the rest of you all, that I know nothing about, but one thing I have always noticed, the rest of you paint and write and are not satisfied and throw it away or tear it up, she does not say whether she is satisfied or not, she copies it very often but she never throws away any piece of paper upon which she has written.

Gertrude Stein tried to copy Three Lives on the typewriter but it was no use, it made her nervous, so Etta Cone came to the rescue. The Miss Etta Cones as Pablo Picasso used to call her and her sister. Etta Cone was a Baltimore connection of Gertrude Stein's and she was spending a winter in Paris. She was rather lonesome and she was rather interested.

Etta Cone found the Picassos appalling but romantic. She was taken there by Gertrude Stein whenever the Picasso finances got beyond everybody and was made to buy a hundred francs' worth of drawings. After all a hundred francs in those days was twenty dollars. She was quite willing to indulge in this romantic charity. Needless to say these drawings became in very much later years the nucleus of her collection.

Etta Cone offered to typewrite Three Lives and she began. Baltimore is famous for the delicate sensibilities and conscientiousness of its inhabitants. It suddenly occurred to Gertrude Stein that she had not told Etta Cone to read the manuscript before beginning to typewrite it. She went to see her and there indeed was Etta Cone faithfully copying the manuscript letter by letter so that she might not by any indiscretion become conscious of the meaning. Permission to read the text having been given the typewriting went on.

Spring was coming and the sittings were coming to an end. All of a sudden one day Picasso painted out the whole head. I can't see you any longer when I look, he said irritably. And so the picture was left like that.

Nobody remembers being particularly disappointed or particularly annoyed at this ending to the long series of posings. There was the spring independent and then Gertrude Stein and her brother were going to Italy as was at that time their habit. Pablo and Fernande were going to Spain, she for the first time, and she had to buy a dress and a hat and perfumes and a cooking stove. All french women in those days when they went from one country to another took along a french oil stove to cook on. Perhaps they still do. No matter where they were going this had to be taken with them. They always paid a great deal of excess baggage, all french women who went travelling. And the Matisses were back and they had to meet the Picassos and to be enthusiastic about each other, but not to like each other very well. And in their wake, Derain met Picasso and with him came Braque.

It may seem very strange to every one nowadays that before this time Matisse had never heard of Picasso and Picasso had never met Matisse. But at that time every little crowd lived its own life and knew practically nothing of any other crowd. Matisse on the Quai Saint-Michel and in the indépendant did not know anything of Picasso and Montmartre and Sagot. They all, it is true, had been in the very early stages bought one after the other by Mademoiselle Weill, the bric-à-brac shop in Montmartre, but as she bought everybody's pictures, pictures brought by any one, not necessarily by the painter, it was not very likely that any painter would, except by some rare chance, see there the paintings of any other painter. They were however all very grateful to her in later years because after all practically everybody who later became famous had sold their first little picture to her.

As I was saying the sittings were over, the vernissage of the independent was over and everybody went away.

It had been a fruitful winter. In the long struggle with the portrait of Gertrude Stein, Picasso passed from the Harlequin, the charming early italian period to the intensive struggle which was to end in cubism. Gertrude Stein had written the story of Melanctha the negress, the second story of Three Lives which was the first definite step away from the nineteenth century and into the twentieth century in literature. Matisse had painted the Bonheur de Vivre and had created the new school of colour which was

soon to leave its mark on everything. And everybody went away. That summer the Matisses came to Italy. Matisse did not care about it very much, he preferred France and Morocco but Madame Matisse was deeply touched. It was a girlish dream fulfilled. She said, I say to myself all the time, I am in Italy. And I say it to Henri all the time and he is very sweet about it, but he says, what of it.

The Picassos were in Spain and Fernande wrote long letters describing Spain and the spaniards and earthquakes.

In Florence except for the short visit of the Matisses and a short visit from Alfy Maurer the summer life was in no way related to the Paris life.

Gertrude Stein and her brother rented for the summer a villa on top of the hill at Fiesole near Florence, and there they spent their summers for several years. The year I came to Paris a friend and myself took this villa, Gertrude Stein and her brother having taken a larger one on the other side of Fiesole, having been joined that year by their elder brother, his wife and child. The small one, the Casa Ricci, was very delightful. It had been made livable by a Scotch woman who born Presbyterian became an ardent Catholic and took her old Presbyterian mother from one convent to another. Finally they came to rest in Casa Ricci and there she made for herself a chapel and there her mother died. She then abandoned this for a larger villa which she turned into a retreat for retired priests and Gertrude Stein and her brother rented the Casa Ricci from her. Gertrude Stein delighted in her landlady who looked exactly like a lady-in-waiting to Mary Stuart and with all her trailing black robes genuflected before every Catholic symbol and would then climb up a precipitous ladder and open a little window in the roof to look at the stars. A strange mingling of Catholic and Protestant exaltation.

Hélène the french servant never came down to Fiesole. She had by that time married. She cooked for her husband during the summer and mended the stockings of Gertrude Stein and her brother by putting new feet into them. She also made jam. In Italy there was Maddalena quite as important

They all, it is true, had been in the very early stages bought one after the other by Mademoiselle Weill.

in Italy as Hélène in Paris, but I doubt if with as much appreciation for notabilities. Italy is too accustomed to the famous and the children of the famous. It was Edwin Dodge who apropos of these said, the lives of great men oft remind us we should leave no sons behind us.

Gertrude Stein adored heat and sunshine although she always says that Paris winter is an ideal climate. In those days it was always at noon that she preferred to walk. I, who have and had no fondness for a summer sun, often accompanied her. Sometimes later in Spain I sat under a tree and wept but she in the sun was indefatigable. She could even lie in the sun and look straight up into a summer noon sun, she said it rested her eyes and head.

There were amusing people in Florence. There were the Berensons and at that time with them Gladys Deacon, a well known international beauty, but after a winter of Montmartre Gertrude Stein found her too easily shocked to be interesting. Then there were the first russians, von Heiroth and his wife, she who afterwards had four husbands and once pleasantly remarked that she had always been good friends with all her husbands. He was foolish but attractive and told the usual russian stories. Then there were the Thorolds and a great many others. And most important there was a most excellent english lending library with all sorts of strange biographies which were to Gertrude Stein a source of endless pleasure. She once told me that when she was young she had read so much, read from the Elizabethans to the moderns, that she was terribly uneasy lest some day she would be without anything to read. For years this fear haunted her but in one way and another although she always reads and reads she seems always to find more to read. Her eldest brother used to complain that although he brought up from Florence every day as many books as he could carry, there always were just as many to take back.

It was during this summer that Gertrude Stein began her great book, The Making of Americans.

It began with an old daily theme that she had written when at Radcliffe,

"Once an angry man dragged his father along the ground through his own orchard. 'Stop!' cried the groaning old man at last. 'Stop! I did not drag my father beyond this tree.'

"It is hard living down the tempers we are born with. We all begin well. For in our youth there is nothing we are more intolerant of than our own sins writ large in others and we fight them fiercely in ourselves; but we grow old and we see that these our sins are of all sins the really harmless ones to own, nay that they give a charm to any character, and so our struggle with them dies away." And it was to be the history of a family. It was a history of a family but by the time I came to Paris it was getting to be a history of all human beings, all who ever were or are or could be living.

Gertrude Stein in all her life has never been as pleased with anything as she is with the translation that Bernard Faÿ and Madame Seillière are making of this book now. She has just been going over it with Bernard Faÿ and as she says, it is wonderful in english and it is even as wonderful in french. Elliot Paul, when editor of transition once said that he was certain that Gertrude Stein could be a best-seller in France. It seems very likely that his prediction is to be fulfilled.

But to return to those old days in the Casa Ricci and the first beginnings of those long sentences which were to change the literary ideas of a great many people.

Gertrude Stein was working tremendously over the beginning of The Making of Americans and came back to Paris under the spell of the thing she was doing. It was at this time that working every night she often was caught by the dawn coming while she was working. She came back to a Paris fairly full of excitement. In the first place she came back to her finished portrait. The day he returned from Spain Picasso sat down and out of his head painted the head in without having seen Gertrude Stein again. And when she saw it he and she were content. It is very strange but neither can remember at all what the head looked like when he painted it out. There is another charming story of the portrait.

Only a few years ago when Gertrude Stein had had her hair cut short, she had always up to that time worn it as a crown on top of her head as Picasso has painted it, when she had had her hair cut, a day or so later she happened to come into a room and Picasso was several rooms away. She had a hat on but he caught sight of her through two doorways and approaching her quickly called out, Gertrude, what is it, what is it. What is what, Pablo, she said. Let me see, he said. She let him see. And my portrait, said he sternly. Then his face softening he added, mais, quand même tout y est, all the same it is all there.

Matisse was back and there was excitement in the air. Derain, and Braque with him, had gone Montmartre. Braque was a young painter who had known Marie Laurencin when they were both art students, and they had then painted each other's portraits. After that Braque had done rather geographical pictures, rounded hills and very much under the colour influence of Matisse's independent painting. He had come to know Derain, I am not sure but that they had known each other while doing their military service, and now they knew Picasso. It was an exciting moment.

They began to spend their days up there and they all always ate together at a little restaurant opposite, and Picasso was more than ever as Gertrude Stein said the little bullfighter followed by his squadron of four, or as later in her portrait of him, she called him, Napoleon followed by his four enormous grenadiers. Derain and Braque were great big men, so was Guillaume a heavy set man and Salmon was not small. Picasso was every inch a chief.

This brings the story to Salmon and Guillaume Apollinaire, although Gertrude Stein had known these two and Marie Laurencin a considerable time before all this was happening.

Salmon and Guillaume Apollinaire both lived in Montmarte in these days. Salmon was very lithe and alive but Gertrude Stein never found him particularly interesting. She liked him. Guillaume Apollinaire on the contrary was very wonderful. There was just about that time, that is about the time when Gertrude Stein first knew Apollinaire, the excitement of a duel that he was to fight with another writer. Fernande and Pablo told about it with so much excitement and so much laughter and so much Montmartre slang, this was in the early days of their acquaintance, that she was always a little vague about just what did happen. But the gist of the matter was that Guillaume challenged the other man and Max Jacob was to be the second and witness for Guillaume. Guillaume and his antagonist each sat in their

Sometimes later in Spain
I sat under a tree and wept.

favourite café all day and waited while their seconds went to and fro. How it all ended Gertrude Stein does not know except that nobody fought, but the great excitement was the bill each second and witness brought to his principal. In these was itemised each time they had a cup of coffee and of course they had to have a cup of coffee every time they sat down at one or other café with one or other principal, and again when the two seconds sat with each other. There was also the question under what circumstances were they under the absolute necessity of having a glass of brandy with the cup of coffee. And how often would they have had coffee if they had not been seconds. All this led to endless meetings and endless discussion and endless additional items. It lasted for days, perhaps weeks and months and whether anybody finally was paid, even the café keeper, nobody knows. It was notorious that Apollinaire was parted with the very greatest difficulty from even the smallest piece of money. It was all very absorbing.

Apollinaire was very attractive and very interesting. He had a head like one of the late roman emperors. He had a brother whom one heard about but never saw. He worked in a bank and therefore he was reasonably well dressed. When anybody in Montmartre had to go anywhere where they had to be conventionally clothed, either to see a relation or attend to a business matter, they always wore a piece of a suit that belonged to the brother of Guillaume.

Guillaume was extraordinarily brilliant and no matter what subject was started, if he knew anything about it or not, he quickly saw the whole meaning of the thing and elaborated it by his wit and fancy carrying it further than anybody knowing anything about it could have done, and oddly enough generally correctly.

Once, several years later, we were dining with the Picassos, and in a conversation I got the best of Guillaume. I was very proud, but, said Eve (Picasso was no longer with Fernande), Guillaume was frightfully drunk or it would not have happened. It was only under such circumstances that anybody could successfully turn a phrase against Guillaume. Poor Guillaume. The last time we saw him was after he had come back to Paris from the war. He had been badly wounded in the head and had had a piece of his skull removed. He looked very wonderful with his bleu horizon and his bandaged head. He lunched with us and we all talked a long time together. He was tired and his heavy head nodded. He was very serious almost solemn. We went away shortly after, we were working with the American Fund for French Wounded, and never saw him again. Later Olga Picasso, the wife of Picasso, told us that the night of the armistice Guillaume Apollinaire died, that they were with him that whole evening and it was warm and the windows were open and the crowd passing were shouting, à bas Guillaume, down with William and as every one always called Guillaume Apollinaire Guillaume, even in his death agony it troubled him.

He had really been heroic. As a foreigner, his mother was a pole, his father possibly an italian, it was not at all necessary that he should volunteer to fight. He was a man of full habit, accustomed to a literary life and the delights of the table, and in spite of everything he volunteered. He went into the artillery first. Every one advised this as it was less dangerous and easier than the infantry, but after a while he could not bear this half protection and he changed into the infantry and was wounded in a charge. He was a long time in hospital, recovered a little, it was at this time that we saw him, and finally died on the day of the armistice.

The death of Guillaume Apollinaire at this time made a very serious difference to all his friends apart from their sorrow at his death. It was the moment just after the war when many things had changed and people naturally fell apart. Guillaume would have been a bond of union, he always had a quality of keeping people together, and now that he was gone everybody ceased to be friends. But all that was very much later and now to go back again to the beginning when Gertrude Stein first met Guillaume and Marie Laurencin.

Everybody called Gertrude Stein Gertrude, or at most Mademoiselle Gertrude, everybody called Picasso Pablo and Fernande Fernande and everybody called Guillaume Apollinaire Guillaume and Max Jacob Max but everybody called Marie Laurencin Marie Laurencin.

The first time Gertrude Stein ever saw Marie Laurencin, Guillaume Apollinaire brought her to the rue de Fleurus, not on a Saturday evening,

guillaume was extraordinarily brilliant.

but another evening. She was very interesting. They were an extraordinary pair. Marie Laurencin was terribly near-sighted and of course she never wore eye-glasses, no french woman and few frenchmen did in those days. She used a lorgnette.

She looked at each picture carefully that is, every picture on the line, bringing her eye close and moving over the whole of it with her lorgnette, an inch at a time. The pictures out of reach she ignored. Finally she remarked, as for myself, I prefer portraits and that is of course quite natural, as I myself am a Clouet. And it was perfectly true, she was a Clouet. She had the square thin build of the mediaeval french women in the french primitives. She spoke in a high pitched beautifully modulated voice. She sat down beside Gertrude Stein on the couch and she recounted the story of her life, told that her mother who had always had it in her nature to dislike men had been for many years the mistress of an important personage, had borne her, Marie Laurencin. I have never, she added, dared let her know Guillaume although of course he is so sweet that she could not refuse to like him but better not. Some day you will see her.

And later on Gertrude Stein saw the mother and by that time I was in Paris and I was taken along.

Marie Laurencin, leading her strange life and making her strange art, lived with her mother, who was a very quiet, very pleasant, very dignified woman, as if the two were living in a convent. The small apartment was filled with needlework which the mother had executed after the designs of Marie Laurencin. Marie and her mother acted toward each other exactly as a young nun with an older one. It was all very strange. Later just before the war the mother fell ill and died. Then the mother did see Guillaume Apollinaire and liked him.

After her mother's death Marie Laurencin lost all sense of stability. She and Guillaume no longer saw each other. A relation that had existed as long as the mother lived without the mother's knowledge now that the mother was dead and had seen and liked Guillaume could no longer endure. Marie against the advice of all her friends married a german. When her friends remonstrated with her she said, but he is the only one who can give me a feeling of my mother.

Six weeks after the marriage the war came and Marie had to leave the country, having been married to a german. As she told me later when once during the war we met in Spain, naturally the officials could make no trouble for her, her passport made it clear that no one knew who her father was and they naturally were afraid because perhaps her father might be the president of the french republic.

During these war years Marie was very unhappy. She was intensely french and she was technically german. When you met her she would say, let me present to you my husband a boche, I do not remember his name. The official french world in Spain with whom she and her husband occasionally came in contact made things very unpleasant for her, constantly referring to Germany as her country. In the meanwhile Guillaume with whom she was in correspondence wrote her passionately patriotic letters. It was a miserable time for Marie Laurencin.

Finally Madame Groult, the sister of Poiret, coming to Spain, managed to help Marie out of her troubles. She finally divorced her husband and after the armistice returned to Paris, at home once more in the world. It was then that she came to the rue de Fleurus again, this time with Erik Satie. They were both Normans and so proud and happy about it.

In the early days Marie Laurencin painted a strange picture, portraits of Guillaume, Picasso, Fernande and herself. Fernande told Gertrude Stein about it. Gertrude Stein bought it and Marie Laurencin was so pleased. It was the first picture of hers any one had ever bought.

It was before Gertrude Stein knew the rue Ravignan that Guillaume Apollinaire had his first paid job, he edited a little pamphlet about physical culture. And it was for this that Picasso made his wonderful caricatures, including one of Guillaume as an exemplar of what physical culture could do.

And now once more to return to the return from all their travels and to Picasso becoming the head of a movement that was later to be known as the cubists. Who called it cubist first I do not know but very likely it was Apollinaire. At any rate he wrote the first little pamphlet about them all and illustrated it with their paintings.

I can so well remember the first time Gertrude Stein took me to see Guillaume Apollinaire. It was a tiny bachelor's apartment on the rue des Martyrs. The room was crowded with a great many small young gentlemen. Who, I asked Fernande, are all these little men. They are poets, answered Fernande. I was overcome. I had never seen poets before, one poet yes but not poets. It was on that night too that Picasso, just a little drunk and to Fernande's great indignation persisted in sitting beside me and finding for me in a spanish album of photographs the exact spot where he was born. I came away with rather a vague idea of its situation

Derain and Braque became followers of Picasso about six months after Picasso had, through Gertrude Stein and her brother, met Matisse. Matisse had in the meantime introduced Picasso to negro sculpture.

At that time negro sculpture had been well known to curio hunters but not to artists. Who first recognised its potential value for the modern artist I am sure I do not know. Perhaps it was Maillol who came from the Perpignan region and knew Matisse in the south and called his attention to it. There is a tradition that it was Derain. It is also very possible that it was Matisse himself because for many years there was a curio-dealer in the rue de Rennes who always had a great many things of this kind in his window and Matisse often went up the rue de Rennes to go to one of the sketch classes.

In any case it was Matisse who first was influenced, not so much in his painting but in his sculpture, by the african statues and it was Matisse who drew Picasso's attention to it just after Picasso had finished painting Gertrude Stein's portrait.

The effect of this african art upon Matisse and Picasso was entirely different. Matisse through it was affected more in his imagination than in his vision. Picasso more in his vision than in his imagination. Strangely enough it is only very much later in his life that this influence has affected his imagination and that may be through its having been re-enforced by the Orientalism of the russians when he came in contact with that through Diaghilev and the russian ballet.

In these early days when he created cubism the effect of the african art was purely upon his vision and his forms, his imagination remained purely spanish. The spanish quality of ritual and abstraction had been indeed stimulated by his painting the portrait of Gertrude Stein. She had a definite impulse then and always toward elemental abstraction. She was not at any time interested in african sculpture. She always says that she liked it well enough but that it has nothing to do with europeans, that it lacks naïveté, that it is very ancient, very narrow, very sophisticated but lacks the elegance of the egyptian sculpture from which it is derived. She says that as an american she likes primitive things to be more savage.

Matisse and Picasso then being introduced to each other by Gertrude Stein and her brother became friends but they were enemies. Now they are neither friends nor enemies. At that time they were both.

They exchanged pictures as was the habit in those days. Each painter chose the one of the other one that presumably interested him the most. Matisse and Picasso chose each one of the other one the picture that was undoubtedly the least interesting either of them had done. Later each one used it as an example, the picture he had chosen, of the weaknesses of the other one. Very evidently in the two pictures chosen the strong qualities of each painter were not much in evidence.

The feeling between the Picassoites and the Matisseites became bitter. And this, you see, brings me to the independent where my friend and I sat without being aware of it under the two pictures which first publicly showed that Derain and Braque had become Picassoites and were definitely not Matisseites.

In the meantime naturally a great many things had happened.

Matisse showed in every autumn salon and every independent. He was beginning to have a considerable following. Picasso, on the contrary, never

who, I asked Fernande, are all these little men.

in all his life has shown in any salon. His pictures at that time could really only be seen at 27 rue de Fleurus. The first time as one might say that he had ever shown at a public show was when Derain and Braque, completely influenced by his recent work, showed theirs. After that he too had many followers.

Matisse was irritated by the growing friendship between Picasso and Gertrude Stein. Mademoiselle Gertrude, he explained, likes local colour and theatrical values. It would be impossible for any one of her quality to have a serious friendship with any one like Picasso. Matisse still came frequently to the rue de Fleurus but there was no longer any frankness of intercourse between them all. It was about this time that Gertrude Stein and her brother gave a lunch for all the painters whose pictures were on the wall. Of course it did not include the dead or the old. It was at this lunch that as I have already said Gertrude Stein made them all happy and made the lunch a success by seating each painter facing his own picture. No one of them noticed it, they were just naturally pleased, until just as they were all leaving Matisse, standing up with his back to the door and looking into the room suddenly realised what had been done.

Matisse intimated that Gertrude Stein had lost interest in his work. She answered him, there is nothing within you that fights itself and hitherto you have had the instinct to produce antagonism in others which stimulated you to attack. But now they follow.

That was the end of the conversation but a beginning of an important part of The Making of Americans. Upon this idea Gertrude Stein based some of her most permanent distinctions in types of people.

It was about this time that Matisse began his teaching. He now moved from the Quai Saint-Michel, where he had lived ever since his marriage, to the boulevard des Invalides. In consequence of the separation of church and state which had just taken place in France the french government had become possessed of a great many convent schools and other church property. As many of these convents ceased to exist, there were at that time a great many of their buildings empty. Among others a very splendid one on the boulevard des Invalides.

These buildings were being rented at very low prices because no lease was given, as the government when it decided how to use them permanently would put the tenants out without warning. It was therefore an ideal place for artists as there were gardens and big rooms and they could put up with the inconveniences of housekeeping under the circumstances. So the Matisses moved in and Matisse instead of a small room to work in had an immense one and the two boys came home and they were all very happy. Then a number of those who had become his followers asked him if he would teach them if they organised a class for him in the same building in which he was then living. He consented and the Matisse atelier began.

The applicants were of all nationalities and Matisse was at first appalled at the number and variety of them. He told with much amusement as well as surprise that when he asked a very little woman in the front row, what in particular she had in mind in her painting, what she was seeking, she replied, Monsieur je cherche le neuf. He used to wonder how they all managed to learn french when he knew none of their languages. Some one got hold of some of these facts and made fun of the school in one of the french weeklies. This hurt Matisse's feelings frightfully. The article said, and where did these people come from, and it was answered, from Massachusetts. Matisse was very unhappy.

But in spite of all this and also in spite of many dissensions the school flourished. There were difficulties. One of the hungarians wanted to earn his living posing for the class and in the intervals when some one else posed go on with his painting. There were a number of young women who protested, a nude model on a model stand was one thing but to have it turn into a fellow student was another. A hungarian was found eating the bread for rubbing out crayon drawings that the various students left on their painting boards and this evidence of extreme poverty and lack of hygiene had an awful effect upon the sensibilities of the americans. There were quite a number of americans. One of these americans under the plea of poverty was receiving his tuition for nothing and then was found to have purchased for himself a tiny Matisse and a tiny Picasso and a tiny Seurat. This was not only unfair, because many of the others wanted and could not afford to own a picture by the master and they were paying their tuition, but, since he also bought a Picasso, it was treason. And then every once in a while some one said something to Matisse in such bad french that it sounded like something very different from what it was and Matisse grew very angry and the unfortunate had to be taught how to apologise properly. All the students were working under such a state of tension that explosions were frequent. One would accuse another of undue influence with the master and then there were long and complicated scenes in which usually some one had to apologise. It was all very difficult since they themselves organised themselves.

Gertrude Stein enjoyed all these complications immensely. Matisse was a good gossip and so was she and at this time they delighted in telling tales to each other.

She began at that time always calling Matisse the C.M. or cher maître. She told him the favourite Western story, pray gentlemen, let there be no bloodshed. Matisse came not unfrequently to the rue de Fleurus. It was indeed at this time that Hélène prepared him the fried eggs instead of an omelet.

Three Lives had been typewritten and now the next thing was to show it to a publisher. Some one gave Gertrude Stein the name of an agent in New York and she tried that. Nothing came of it. Then she tried publishers directly. The only one at all interested was Bobbs-Merrill and they said they could not undertake it. This attempt to find a publisher lasted some time and then without being really discouraged she decided to have it printed. It was not an unnatural thought as people in Paris often did this. Some one told her about the Grafton Press in New York, a respectable firm that printed special historical things that people wanted to have printed. The arrangements were concluded, Three Lives was to be printed and the proofs to be sent.

One day some one knocked at the door and a very nice very american young man asked if he might speak to Miss Stein. She said, yes come in. He said, I have come at the request of the Grafton Press. Yes, she said. You see, he said slightly hesitant, the director of the Grafton Press is under the impression that perhaps your knowledge of english. But I am an american, said Gertrude Stein indignantly. Yes yes I understand that perfectly now, he said, but perhaps you have not had much experience in writing. I suppose, said she laughing, you were under the impression that I was imperfectly educated. He blushed, why no, he said, but you might not have had much experience in writing. Oh yes, she said, oh yes. Well it's alright. I will write to the director and you might as well tell him also that everything that is written in the manuscript is written with the intention of its being so written and all he has to do is to print it and I will take the responsibility. The young man bowed himself out.

Later when the book was noticed by interested writers and newspaper men the director of the Grafton Press wrote Gertrude Stein a very simple letter in which he admitted he had been surprised at the notice the book had received but wished to add that now that he had seen the result he wished to say that he was very pleased that his firm had printed the book. But this last was after I came to Paris.

IV.

Gertrude Stein
Before She Came to Paris

ONCE MORE I have come to Paris and now I am one of the habitués of the rue de Fleurus. Gertrude Stein was writing The Making of Americans and she had just commenced correcting the proofs of Three Lives. I helped her correct them.

Gertrude Stein was born in Allegheny, Pennsylvania. As I am an ardent californian and as she spent her youth there I have often begged her to be born in California but she has always remained firmly born in Allegheny, Pennsylvania. She left it when she was six months old and has never seen it again and now it no longer exists being all of it Pittsburgh. She used however to delight in being born in Allegheny, Pennsylvania when during the war, in connection with war work, we used to have papers made out and they always immediately wanted to know one's birth-place. She used to say if she had been really born in California as I wanted her to have been she would never have had the pleasure of seeing the various french officials try to write, Allegheny, Pennsylvania.

When I first knew Gertrude Stein in Paris I was surprised never to see a french book on her table, although there were always plenty of english ones, there were even no french newspapers. But do you never read french, I as well as many other people asked her. No, she replied, you see I feel with my eyes and it does not make any difference to me what language I hear, I don't hear a language, I hear tones of voice and rhythms, but with my eyes I see words and sentences and there is for me only one language and that is english. One of the things that I have liked all these years is to be surrounded by people who know no english. It has left me more intensely alone with my eyes and my english. I do not know if it would have been possible to have english be so all in all to me otherwise. And they none of them could read a word I wrote, most of them did not even know that I did write. No, I like living with so very many people and being all alone with english and myself.

One of her chapters in The Making of Americans begins: I write for myself and strangers.

She was born in Allegheny, Pennsylvania, of a very respectable middle class family. She always says that she is very grateful not to have been born of an intellectual family, she has a horror of what she calls intellectual people. It has always been rather ridiculous that she who is good friends with all the world and can know them and they can know her, has always been the admired of the precious. But she always says some day they, anybody, will find out that she is of interest to them, she and her writing. And she always consoles herself that the newspapers are always interested. They always say, she says, that my writing is appalling but they always quote it and what is more, they quote it correctly, and those they say they admire they do not quote. This at some of her most bitter moments has been a consolation. My sentences do get under their skin, only they do not know that they do, she has often said.

She was born in Allegheny, Pennsylvania, in a house, a twin house. Her family lived in one and her father's brother's family lived in the other one. These two families are the families described in The Making of Americans. They had lived in these houses for about eight years when Gertrude Stein was born. A year before her birth, the two sisters-in-law who had never gotten along any too well were no longer on speaking terms.

Gertrude Stein's mother as she describes her in The Making of Americans, a gentle pleasant little woman with a quick temper, flatly refused to see her sister-in-law again. I don't know quite what had happened but something. At any rate the two brothers who had been very successful business partners broke up their partnership, the one brother went to New York where he and all his family after him became very rich and the other brother, Gertrude Stein's family, went to Europe. They first went to Vienna and stayed there until Gertrude Stein was about three years old. All she remembers of this is that her brother's tutor once, when she was allowed to sit with her brothers at their lessons, described a tiger's snarl and that that pleased and terrified her. Also that in a picture-book that one of her brothers used to show her there was a story of the wanderings of Ulysses who when sitting sat on bent-wood dining room chairs. Also she remembers that they used to play in the public gardens and that often the old Kaiser Francis Joseph used to stroll through the gardens and sometimes a band played the austrian national hymn which she liked. She believed for many years that Kaiser was the real name of Francis Joseph and she never could come to accept the name as belonging to anybody else.

They lived in Vienna for three years, the father having in the meanwhile gone back to America on business and then they moved to Paris. Here Gertrude Stein has more lively memories. She remembers a little school where she and her elder sister stayed and where there was a little girl in the corner of the school yard and the other little girls told her not to go near her, she scratched. She also remembers the bowl of soup with french bread for breakfast and she also remembers that they had mutton and spinach for lunch and as she was very fond of spinach and not fond of mutton she used to trade mutton for spinach with the little girl opposite. She also remembers all of her three older brothers coming to see them at the school and coming on horse-back. She also remembers a black cat jumping from the ceiling of their house at Passy and scaring her mother and some unknown person rescuing her.

The family remained in Paris a year and then they came back to America. Gertrude Stein's elder brother charmingly describes the last days when he and his mother went shopping and bought everything that pleased their fancy, seal skin coats and caps and muffs for the whole family from the mother to the small sister Gertrude Stein, gloves dozens of gloves, wonderful hats, riding costumes, and finally ending up with a microscope and a whole set of the famous french history of zoology. Then they sailed for America.

This visit to Paris made a very great impression upon Gertrude Stein. When in the beginning of the war, she and I having been in England and there having been caught by the outbreak of the war and so not returning until October, were back in Paris, the first day we went out Gertrude Stein said, it is strange, Paris is so different but so familiar. And then reflectively, I see what it is, there is nobody here but the french (there were no soldiers or allies there yet), you can see the little children in their black aprons, you can see the streets because there is nobody on them, it is just like my memory of Paris when I was three years old. The pavements smell like they used (horses had come back into use), the smell of french streets and french public gardens that I remember so well.

They went back to America and in New York, the New York family tried to reconcile Gertrude Stein's mother to her sister-in-law but she was obdurate.

This story reminds me of Miss Etta Cone, a distant connection of Gertrude Stein, who typed Three Lives. When I first met her in Florence she confided to me that she could forgive but never forget. I added that as for myself I could forget but not forgive. Gertrude Stein's mother in this case was evidently unable to do either.

The family went west to California after a short stay in Baltimore at the home of her grandfather, the religious old man she describes in The Making of Americans, who lived in an old house in Baltimore with a large number of those cheerful pleasant little people, her uncles and her aunts.

Gertrude Stein has never ceased to be thankful to her mother for neither forgetting or forgiving. Imagine, she has said to me, if my mother had forgiven her sister-in-law and my father had gone into business with my

I have often begged her to be born in California.

uncle and we had lived and been brought up in New York, imagine, she says, how horrible. We would have been rich instead of being reasonably poor but imagine how horrible to have been brought up in New York.

I as a californian can very thoroughly sympathise.

And so they took the train to California. The only thing Gertrude Stein remembers of this trip was that she and her sister had beautiful big austrian red felt hats trimmed each with a beautiful ostrich feather and at some stage of the trip her sister leaning out of the window had her hat blown off. Her father rang the emergency bell, stopped the train, got the hat to the awe and astonishment of the passengers and the conductor. The only other thing she remembers is that they had a wonderful hamper of food given them by the aunts in Baltimore and that in it was a marvellous turkey. And that later as the food in it diminished it was renewed all along the road whenever they stopped and that that was always exciting. And also that somewhere in the desert they saw some red indians and that somewhere else in the desert they were given some very funny tasting peaches to eat.

When they arrived in California they went to an orange grove but she does not remember any oranges but remembers filling up her father's cigar boxes with little limes which were very wonderful.

They came by slow stages to San Francisco and settled down in Oakland. She remembers there the eucalyptus trees seeming to her so tall and thin and savage and the animal life very wild. But all this and much more, all the physical life of these days, she has described in the life of the Hersland family in her Making of Americans. The important thing to tell about now is her education.

Her father having taken his children to Europe so that they might have the benefit of a european education now insisted that they should forget their french and german so that their american english would be pure. Gertrude Stein had prattled in german and then in french but she had never read until she read english. As she says eyes to her were more important than ears and it happened then as always that english was her only language.

Her bookish life commenced at this time. She read anything that was printed that came her way and a great deal came her way. In the house

her hat blown off

were a few stray novels, a few travel books, her mother's well bound gift books Wordsworth Scott and other poets, Bunyan's Pilgrim's Progress a set of Shakespeare with notes, Burns, Congressional Records encyclopedias etcetera. She read them all and many times. She and her brothers began to acquire other books. There was also the local free library and later in San Francisco there were the mercantile and mechanics libraries with their excellent sets of eighteenth century and nineteenth century authors. From her eighth year when she absorbed Shakespeare to her fifteenth year when she read Clarissa Harlowe, Fielding, Smollett etcetera and used to worry lest in a few years more she would have read everything and there would be nothing unread to read, she lived continuously with the english language. She read a tremendous amount of history, she often laughs and says she is one of the few people of her generation that has read every line of Carlyle's Frederick the Great and Lecky's Constitutional History of England besides Charles Grandison and Wordsworth's longer poems. In fact she was as she still is always reading. She reads anything and everything and even now hates to be disturbed and above all however often she has read a book and however foolish the book may be no one must make fun of it or tell her how it goes on. It is still as it always was real to her.

The theatre she has always cared for less. She says it goes too fast, the mixture of eye and ear bothers her and her emotion never keeps pace. Music she only cared for during her adolescence. She finds it difficult to listen to it, it does not hold her attention. All of which of course may seem strange because it has been so often said that the appeal of her work is to the ear and to the subconscious. Actually it is her eyes and mind that are active and important and concerned in choosing.

Life in California came to its end when Gertrude Stein was about seventeen years old. The last few years had been lonesome ones and had been passed in an agony of adolescence. After the death of first her mother and then her father she and her sister and one brother left California for the East. They came to Baltimore and stayed with her mother's people. There she began to lose her lonesomeness. She has often described to me how strange it was to her coming from the rather desperate inner life that she had been living for the last few years to the cheerful life of all her aunts and uncles. When later she went to Radcliffe she described this experience in the first thing she ever wrote. Not quite the first thing she ever wrote. She remembers having written twice before. Once when she was about eight and she tried to write a Shakespearean drama in which she got as far as a stage direction, the courtiers making witty remarks. And then as she could not think of any witty remarks gave it up.

The only other effort she can remember must have been at about the same age. They asked the children in the public schools to write a description. Her recollection is that she described a sunset with the sun going into a cave of clouds. Anyway it was one of the half dozen in the school chosen to be copied out on beautiful parchment paper. After she had tried to copy it twice and the writing became worse and worse she was reduced to letting some one else copy it for her. This, her teacher considered a disgrace. She does not remember that she herself did.

As a matter of fact her handwriting has always been illegible and I am very often able to read it when she is not.

She has never been able or had any desire to indulge in any of the arts. She never knows how a thing is going to look until it is done, in arranging a room, a garden, clothes or anything else. She cannot draw anything. She feels no relation between the object and the piece of paper. When at the medical school, she was supposed to draw anatomical things she never found out in sketching how a thing was made concave or convex. She remembers when she was very small she was to learn to draw and was sent to a class. The children were told to take a cup and saucer at home and draw them and the best drawing would have as its reward a stamped leather medal and the next week the same medal would again be given for the best drawing. Gertrude Stein went home, told her brothers and they put a pretty cup and saucer before her and each one explained to her how to draw it. Nothing happened. Finally one of them drew it for her. She took it to the class and won the leather medal. And on the way home in playing some game she lost the leather medal. That was the end of the drawing class.

She says it is a good thing to have no sense of how it is done in the things that amuse you. You should have one absorbing occupation and as for the other things in life for full enjoyment you should only contemplate results. In this way you are bound to feel more about it than those who know a little of how it is done.

She is passionately addicted to what the french call métier and she contends that one can only have one métier as one can only have one language. Her métier is writing and her language is english.

Observation and construction make imagination, that is granting the possession of imagination, is what she has taught many young writers. Once when Hemingway wrote in one of his stories that Gertrude Stein always knew what was good in a Cézanne, she looked at him and said, Hemingway, remarks are not literature.

The young often when they have learnt all they can learn accuse her of an inordinate pride. She says yes of course. She realises that in english literature in her time she is the only one. She has always known it and now she says it.

She understands very well the basis of creation and therefore her advice and criticism is invaluable to all her friends. How often have I heard Picasso say to her when she has said something about a picture of his and then illustrated by something she was trying to do, racontez-moi cela. In other words tell me about it. These two even to-day have long solitary conversations. They sit in two little low chairs up in his apartment studio, knee to knee and Picasso says, expliquez-moi cela. And they explain to each other. They talk about everything, about pictures, about dogs, about death, about unhappiness. Because Picasso is a spaniard and life is tragic and bitter and unhappy. Gertrude Stein often comes down to me and says, Pablo has been persuading me that I am as unhappy as he is. He insists that I am and with as much cause. But are you, I ask. Well I don't think I look it, do I, and she laughs. He says, she says, that I don't look it because I have more courage, but I don't think I am, she says, no I don't think I am.

And so Gertrude Stein having been in Baltimore for a winter and having become more humanised and less adolescent and less lonesome went to Radcliffe. There she had a very good time.

She was one of a group of Harvard men and Radcliffe women and they all lived very closely and very interestingly together. One of them, a young philosopher and mathematician who was doing research work in psychology left a definite mark on her life. She and he together worked out a series of experiments in automatic writing under the direction of Münsterberg. The result of her own experiments, which Gertrude Stein wrote down and which was printed in the Harvard Psychological Review was the first writing of hers ever to be printed. It is very interesting to read because the method of writing to be afterwards developed in Three Lives and Making of Americans already shows itself.

The important person in Gertrude Stein's Radcliffe life was William James. She enjoyed her life and herself. She was the secretary of the philosophical club and amused herself with all sorts of people. She liked making sport of question asking and she liked equally answering them. She liked it all. But the really lasting impression of her Radcliffe life came through William James.

It is rather strange that she was not then at all interested in the work of Henry James for whom she now has a very great admiration and whom she considers quite definitely as her forerunner, he being the only nineteenth century writer who being an american felt the method of the twentieth century. Gertrude Stein always speaks of America as being now the oldest country in the world because by the methods of the civil war and the commercial conceptions that followed it America created the twentieth century, and since all the other countries are now either living or commencing to be living a twentieth century of life, America having begun the creation of the twentieth century in the sixties of the nineteenth century is now the oldest country in the world.

In the same way she contends that Henry James was the first person in literature to find the way to the literary methods of the twentieth century. But oddly enough in all of her formative period she did not read him and was not interested in him. But as she often says one is always naturally antagonistic to one's parents and sympathetic to one's grandparents. The parents are too close, they hamper you, one must be alone. So perhaps that is the reason why only very lately Gertrude Stein reads Henry James.

William James delighted her. His personality and his teaching and his way of amusing himself with himself and his students all pleased her. Keep your mind open, he used to say, and when some one objected, but Professor James, this that I say, is true. Yes, said James, it is abjectly true.

Gertrude Stein never had subconscious reactions, nor was she a successful subject for automatic writing. One of the students in the psychological seminar of which Gertrude Stein, although an undergraduate was at William James' particular request a member, was carrying on a series of experiments on suggestions to the subconscious. When he read his paper upon the result of his experiments, he began by explaining that one of the subjects gave absolutely no results and as this much lowered the average and made the conclusion of his experiments false he wished to be allowed to cut this record out. Whose record is it, said James. Miss Stein's, said the student. Ah, said James, if Miss Stein gave no response I should say that it was as normal not to give a response as to give one and decidedly the result must not be cut out.

It was a very lovely spring day, Gertrude Stein had been going to the opera every night and going also to the opera in the afternoon and had been otherwise engrossed and it was the period of the final examinations, and there was the examination in William James' course. She sat down with the examination paper before her and she just could not. Dear Professor James, she wrote at the top of her paper. I am so sorry but really I do not feel a bit like an examination paper in philosophy to-day, and left.

The next day she had a postal card from William James saying, Dear Miss Stein, I understand perfectly how you feel I often feel like that myself. And underneath it he gave her work the highest mark in his course.

When Gertrude Stein was finishing her last year at Radcliffe, William James one day asked her what she was going to do. She said she had no idea. Well, he said, it should be either philosophy or psychology. Now for philosophy you have to have higher mathematics and I don't gather that that has ever interested you. Now for psychology you must have a medical

James delighted her

education, a medical education opens all doors, as Oliver Wendell Holmes told me and as I tell you. Gertrude Stein had been interested in both biology and chemistry and so medical school presented no difficulties.

There were no difficulties except that Gertrude Stein had never passed more than half of her entrance examinations for Radcliffe, having never intended to take a degree. However with considerable struggle and enough tutoring that was accomplished and Gertrude Stein entered Johns Hopkins Medical School.

Some years after when Gertrude Stein and her brother were just beginning knowing Matisse and Picasso, William James came to Paris and they met. She went to see him at his hotel. He was enormously interested in what she was doing, interested in her writing and in the pictures she told him about. He went with her to her house to see them. He looked and gasped, I told you, he said, I always told you that you should keep your mind open.

Only about two years ago a very strange thing happened. Gertrude Stein received a letter from a man in Boston. It was evident from the letter head that he was one of a firm of lawyers. He said in his letter that he had not long ago in reading in the Harvard library found that the library of William James had been given as a gift to the Harvard library. Among these books was the copy of Three Lives that Gertrude Stein had dedicated and sent to James. Also on the margins of the book were notes that William James had evidently made when reading the book. The man then went on to say that very likely Gertrude Stein would be very interested in these notes and he proposed, if she wished, to copy them out for her as he had appropriated the book, in other words taken it and considered it as his. We were very puzzled what to do about it. Finally a note was written saying that Gertrude Stein would like to have a copy of William James' notes. In answer came a manuscript the man himself had written and of which he wished Gertrude Stein to give him an opinion. Not knowing what to do about it all, Gertrude Stein did nothing.

After having passed her entrance examinations she settled down in Baltimore and went to the medical school. She had a servant named Lena and it is her story that Gertrude Stein afterwards wrote as the first story of the Three Lives.

The first two years of the medical school were alright. They were purely laboratory work and Gertrude Stein under Llewelys Barker immediately betook herself to research work. She began a study of all the brain tracts, the beginning of a comparative study. All this was later embodied in Llewelys Barker's book. She delighted in Doctor Mall, professor of anatomy, who directed her work. She always quotes his answer to any student excusing him or herself for anything. He would look reflective and say, yes that is just like our cook. There is always a reason. She never brings the food to the table hot. In summer of course she can't because it is too hot, in winter of course she can't because it is too cold, yes there is always a reason. Doctor Mall believed in everybody developing their own technique. He also remarked, nobody teaches anybody anything, at first every student's scalpel is dull and then later every student's scalpel is sharp, and nobody has taught anybody anything.

These first two years at the medical school Gertrude Stein liked well enough. She always liked knowing a lot of people and being mixed up in a lot of stories and she was not awfully interested but she was not too bored with what she was doing and besides she had quantities of pleasant relatives in Baltimore and she liked it. The last two years at the medical school she was bored, frankly openly bored. There was a good deal of intrigue and struggle among the students, that she liked, but the practice and theory of medicine did not interest her at all. It was fairly well known among all her teachers that she was bored, but as her first two years of scientific work had given her a reputation, everybody gave her the necessary credits and the end of her last year was approaching. It was then that she had to take her turn in the delivering of babies and it was at that time that she noticed the negroes and the places that she afterwards used in the second of the Three Lives stories, Melanctha Herbert, the story that was the beginning of her revolutionary work.

As she always says of herself, she has a great deal of inertia and once started keeps going until she starts somewhere else.

As the graduation examinations drew near some of her professors were getting angry. The big men like Halstead, Osler etcetera knowing her reputation for original scientific work made the medical examinations merely a matter of form and passed her. But there were others who were not so amiable. Gertrude Stein always laughed, and this was difficult. They would ask her questions although as she said to her friends, it was foolish of them to ask her, when there were so many eager and anxious to answer. However they did question her from time to time and as she said, what could she do, she did not know the answers and they did not believe that she did not know them, they thought that she did not answer because she did not consider the professors worth answering. It was a difficult situation, as she said, it was impossible to apologise and explain to them that she was so bored she could not remember the things that of course the dullest medical student could not forget. One of the professors said that although all the big men were ready to pass her he intended that she should be given a lesson and he refused to give her a pass mark and so she was not able to take her degree. There was great excitement in the medical school. Her very close friend Marion Walker pleaded with her, she said, but Gertrude Gertrude remember the cause of women, and Gertrude Stein said, you don't know what it is to be bored.

The professor who had flunked her asked her to come to see him. She did. He said, of course Miss Stein all you have to do is to take a summer course here and in the fall naturally you will take your degree. But not at all, said Gertrude Stein, you have no idea how grateful I am to you. I have so much inertia and so little initiative that very possibly if you had not kept me from taking my degree I would have, well, not taken to the practice of medicine, but at any rate to pathological psychology and you don't know how little I like pathological psychology, and how all medicine bores me. The professor was completely taken aback and that was the end of the medical education of Gertrude Stein.

She always says she dislikes the abnormal, it is so obvious. She says the normal is so much more simply complicated and interesting.

It was only a few years ago that Marion Walker, Gertrude Stein's old friend, came to see her at Bilignin where we spend the summer. She and Gertrude Stein had not met since those old days nor had they corresponded but they were as fond of each other and disagreed as violently about the cause of women as they did then. Not, as Gertrude Stein explained to Marion Walker, that she at all minds the cause of women or any other cause but it does not happen to be her business.

During these years at Radcliffe and Johns Hopkins she often spent the summers in Europe. The last couple of years her brother had been settled in Florence and now that everything medical was over she joined him there and later they settled down in London for the winter.

They settled in lodgings in London and were not uncomfortable. They knew a number of people through the Berensons, Bertrand Russell, the Zangwills, then there was Willard (Josiah Flynt) who wrote Tramping With Tramps, and who knew all about London pubs, but Gertrude Stein was not very much amused. She began spending all her days in the British Museum reading the Elizabethans. She returned to her early love of Shakespeare and the Elizabethans, and became absorbed in Elizabethan prose and particularly in the prose of Greene. She had little note-books full of phrases that pleased her as they had pleased her when she was a child. The rest of the time she wandered about the London streets and found them infinitely depressing and dismal. She never really got over this memory of London and never wanted to go back there, but in nineteen hundred and twelve she went over to see John Lane, the publisher and then living a very pleasant life and visiting very gay and pleasant people she forgot the old memory and became very fond of London.

She always said that that first visit had made London just like Dickens and Dickens had always frightened her. As she says anything can frighten her and London when it was like Dickens certainly did.

There were some compensations, there was the prose of Greene and it was at this time that she discovered the novels of Anthony Trollope, for her the greatest of the Victorians. She then got together the complete collection of his work some of it difficult to get and only obtainable in Tauchnitz and it is of this collection that Robert Coates speaks when he tells about Gertrude Stein lending books to young writers. She also bought a quantity of eighteenth century memoirs among them the Creevy papers and Walpole and it is these that she loaned to Bravig Imbs when he wrote what she believes to be an admirable life of Chatterton. She reads books but she is not fussy about them, she cares about neither editions nor make-up as long as the print is not too bad and she is not even very much bothered about that. It was at this time too that, as she says, she ceased to be worried about there being in the future nothing to read, she said she felt that she would always somehow be able to find something.

But the dismalness of London and the drunken women and children and the gloom and the lonesomeness brought back all the melancholy of her adolescence and one day she said she was leaving for America and she left. She stayed in America the rest of the winter. In the meantime her brother also had left London and gone to Paris and there later she joined him. She immediately began to write. She wrote a short novel.

The funny thing about this short novel is that she completely forgot about it for many years. She remembered herself beginning a little later writing the Three Lives but this first piece of writing was completely forgotten, she had never mentioned it to me, even when I first knew her. She must have forgotten about it almost immediately. This spring just two days before our leaving for the country she was looking for some manuscript of The Making of Americans that she wanted to show Bernard Faÿ and she came across these two carefully written volumes of this completely forgotten first novel. She was very bashful and hesitant about it, did not really want to read it. Louis Bromfield was at the house that evening and she handed him the manuscript and said to him, you read it.

V.

1907-1914

AND SO LIFE in Paris began and as all roads lead to Paris, all of us are now there, and I can begin to tell what happened when I was of it.

When I first came to Paris a friend and myself stayed in a little hotel in the boulevard Saint-Michel, then we took a small apartment in the rue Notre-Dame-des-Champs and then my friend went back to California and I joined Gertrude Stein in the rue de Fleurus.

I had been at the rue de Fleurus every Saturday evening and I was there a great deal beside. I helped Gertrude Stein with the proofs of Three Lives and then I began to typewrite The Making of Americans. The little badly made french portable was not strong enough to type this big book and so we bought a large and imposing Smith Premier which at first looked very much out of place in the atelier but soon we were all used to it and it remained until I had an american portable, in short until after the war.

As I said Fernande was the first wife of a genius I was to sit with. The geniuses came and talked to Gertrude Stein and the wives sat with me. How they unroll, an endless vista through the years. I began with Fernande and then there were Madame Matisse and Marcelle Braque and Josette Gris and Eve Picasso and Bridget Gibb and Marjory Gibb and Hadley and Pauline Hemingway and Mrs. Sherwood Anderson and Mrs. Bravig Imbs and the Mrs. Ford Madox Ford and endless others, geniuses, near geniuses and might be geniuses, all having wives, and I have sat and talked with them all all the wives and later on, well later on too, I have sat and talked with all. But I began with Fernande.

I went too to the Casa Ricci in Fiesole with Gertrude Stein and her brother. How well I remember the first summer I stayed with them. We did charming things. Gertrude Stein and I took a Fiesole cab, I think it was the only one and drove in this old cab all the way to Siena. Gertrude Stein had once walked it with a friend but in those hot italian days I preferred a cab. It was a charming trip. Then another time we went to Rome and we brought back a beautiful black renaissance plate. Maddalena, the old italian cook, came up to Gertrude Stein's bedroom one morning to bring the water for her bath. Gertrude Stein had the hiccoughs. But cannot the signora stop it, said Maddalena anxiously. No, said Gertrude Stein between hiccoughs. Maddalena shaking her head sadly went away. In a minute there was an awful crash. Up flew Maddalena, oh signora, signora, she said, I was so upset because the signora had the hiccoughs that I broke the black plate that the signora so carefully brought from Rome. Gertrude Stein began to swear, she has a reprehensible habit of swearing whenever anything unexpected happens and she always tells me she learned it in her youth in California, and as I am a loyal californian I can then say nothing. She swore and the hiccoughs ceased. Maddalena's face was wreathed in smiles. Ah the signorina, she said, she has stopped hiccoughing. Oh no I did not break the beautiful plate, I just made the noise of it and then said I did it to make the signorina stop hiccoughing.

Gertrude Stein is awfully patient over the breaking of even her most cherished objects, it is I, I am sorry to say who usually break them. Neither she nor the servant nor the dog do, but then the servant never touches them, it is I who dust them and alas sometimes accidentally break them. I always beg her to promise to let me have them mended by an expert before I tell her which it is that is broken, she always replies she gets no pleasure out of them if they are mended but alright have it mended and it is mended and it gets put away. She loves objects that are breakable, cheap objects and valuable objects, a chicken out of a grocery shop or a pigeon out of a fair, one just broke this morning, this time it was not I who did it, she loves them all and she remembers them all but she knows that sooner or later they will break and she says that like books there are always more to find. However to me this is no consolation. She says she likes what she has and she likes the adventure of a new one. That is what she always says about young painters, about anything, once everybody knows they are good the adventure is over. And adds Picasso with a sigh, even after everybody knows they are good not any more people really like them than they did when only the few knew they were good.

I did have to take one hot walk that summer. Gertrude Stein insisted that no one could go to Assisi except on foot. She has three favourite saints, Saint Ignatius Loyola, Saint Theresa of Avila and Saint Francis. I alas have only one favourite saint, Saint Anthony of Padua because it is he who finds lost objects and as Gertrude Stein's elder brother once said of me, if I were a general I would never lose a battle, I would only mislay it. Saint Anthony helps me find it. I always put a considerable sum in his box in every church I visit. At first Gertrude Stein objected to this extravagance but now she realises its necessity and if I am not with her she remembers Saint Anthony for me.

It was a very hot italian day and we started as usual about noon, that being Gertrude Stein's favourite walking hour, because it was hottest and beside presumably Saint Francis had walked it then the oftenest as he had walked it at all hours. We started from Perugia across the hot valley. I gradually undressed, in those days one wore many more clothes than one does now, I even, which was most unconventional in those days, took off my stockings, but even so I dropped a few tears before we arrived and we did arrive. Gertrude Stein was very fond of Assisi for two reasons, because of Saint Francis and the beauty of his city and because the old women used to lead instead of a goat a little pig up and down the hills of Assisi. The little black pig was always decorated with a red ribbon. Gertrude Stein had always liked little pigs and she always said that in her old age she expected to wander up and down the hills of Assisi with a little black pig. She now wanders about the hills of the Ain with a large white dog and a small black one, so I suppose that does as well.

She was always fond of pigs, and because of this Picasso made and gave her some charming drawings of the prodigal son among the pigs. And one delightful study of pigs all by themselves. It was about this time too that he made for her the tiniest of ceiling decorations on a tiny wooden panel and it was an hommage à Gertrude with women and angels bringing fruits and trumpeting. For years she had this tacked to the ceiling over her bed. It was only after the war that it was put upon the wall.

But to return to the beginning of my life in Paris. It was based upon the rue de Fleurus and the Saturday evenings and it was like a kaleidoscope slowly turning.

What happened in those early years. A great deal happened.

As I said when I became an habitual visitor at the rue de Fleurus the Picassos were once more together, Pablo and Fernande. That summer they went again to Spain and he came back with some spanish landscapes and one may say that these landscapes, two of them still at the rue de Fleurus and the other one in Moscow in the collection that Stchoukine founded and that is now national property, were the beginning of cubism. In these there was no african sculpture influence. There was very evidently a strong Cézanne influence, particularly the influence of the late Cézanne water colours, the cutting up the sky not in cubes but in spaces.

But the essential thing, the treatment of the houses was essentially spanish and therefore essentially Picasso. In these pictures he first emphasised the way of building in spanish villages, the line of the houses not following the landscape but cutting across and into the landscape, becoming undistinguishable in the landscape by cutting across the landscape. It was the principle of the camouflage of the guns and the ships in the war. The first year of the war, Picasso and Eve, with whom he was living then, Gertrude Stein and myself, were walking down the boulevard Raspail a cold winter evening. There is nothing in the world colder than the Raspail on a cold

I dropped a few tears

winter evening, we used to call it the retreat from Moscow. All of a sudden down the street came some big cannon, the first any of us had seen painted, that is camouflaged. Pablo stopped, he was spell-bound. C'est nous qui avons fait ça, he said, it is we that have created that, he said. And he was right, he had. From Cézanne through him they had come to that. His foresight was justified.

But to go back to the three landscapes. When they were first put up on the wall naturally everybody objected. As it happened he and Fernande had taken some photographs of the villages which he had painted and he had given copies of these photographs to Gertrude Stein. When people said that the few cubes in the landscapes looked like nothing but cubes, Gertrude Stein would laugh and say, if you had objected to these landscapes as being too realistic there would be some point in your objection. And she would show them the photographs and really the pictures as she rightly said might be declared to be too photographic a copy of nature. Years after Elliot Paul at Gertrude Stein's suggestion had a photograph of the painting by Picasso and the photographs of the village reproduced on the same page in transition and it was extraordinarily interesting. This then was really the beginning of cubism. The colour too was characteristically spanish, the pale silver yellow with the faintest suggestion of green, the colour afterwards so well known in Picasso's cubist pictures, as well as in those of his followers.

Gertrude Stein always says that cubism is a purely spanish conception and only spaniards can be cubists and that the only real cubism is that of Picasso and Juan Gris. Picasso created it and Juan Gris permeated it with his clarity and his exaltation. To understand this one has only to read the life and death of Juan Gris by Gertrude Stein, written upon the death of one of her two dearest friends, Picasso and Juan Gris, both spaniards.

She always says that americans can understand spaniards. That they are the only two western nations that can realise abstraction. That in americans it expresses itself by disembodiedness, in literature and machinery, in Spain by ritual so abstract that it does not connect itself with anything but ritual.

I always remember Picasso saying disgustedly apropos of some germans who said they liked bull-fights, they would, he said angrily, they like bloodshed. To a spaniard it is not bloodshed, it is ritual.

Americans, so Gertrude Stein says, are like spaniards, they are abstract and cruel. They are not brutal they are cruel. They have no close contact with the earth such as most europeans have. Their materialism is not the materialism of existence, of possession, it is the materialism of action and abstraction. And so cubism is spanish.

We were very much struck, the first time Gertrude Stein and I went to Spain, which was a year or so after the beginning of cubism, to see how naturally cubism was made in Spain. In the shops in Barcelona instead of post cards they had square little frames and inside it was placed a cigar, a real one, a pipe, a bit of handkerchief etcetera, all absolutely the arrangement of many a cubist picture and helped out by cut paper representing other objects. That is the modern note that in Spain had been done for centuries.

Picasso in his early cubist pictures used printed letters as did Juan Gris to force the painted surface to measure up to something rigid, and the rigid thing was the printed letter. Gradually instead of using the printed thing they painted the letters and all was lost, it was only Juan Gris who could paint with such intensity a printed letter that it still made the rigid contrast. And so cubism came little by little but it came.

It was in these days that the intimacy between Braque and Picasso grew. It was in these days that Juan Gris, a raw rather effusive youth came from Madrid to Paris and began to call Picasso cher maître to Picasso's great annoyance. It was apropos of this that Picasso used to address Braque as cher maître, passing on the joke, and I am sorry to say that some foolish people have taken this joke to mean that Picasso looked up to Braque as a master.

But I am once more running far ahead of those early Paris days when I first knew Fernande and Pablo.

In those days then only the three landscapes had been painted and he was beginning to paint some heads that seemed cut out in planes, also long loaves of bread.

At this time Matisse, the school still going on, was really beginning to be

Bonnard and Poucette

fairly well known, so much so that to everybody's great excitement Bernheim jeune, a very middle class firm indeed, was offering him a contract to take all his work at a very good price. It was an exciting moment.

This was happening because of the influence of a man named Fénéon. Il est très fin, said Matisse, much impressed by Fénéon. Fénéon was a journalist, a french journalist who had invented the thing called a feuilleton en deux lignes, that is to say he was the first one to hit off the news of the day in two lines. He looked like a caricature of Uncle Sam made french and he had been painted standing in front of a curtain in a circus picture by Toulouse-Lautrec.

And now the Bernheims, how or wherefor I do not know, taking Fénéon into their employ, were going to connect themselves with the new generation of painters.

Something happened, at any rate this contract did not last long, but for all that it changed the fortunes of Matisse. He now had an established position. He bought a house and some land in Clamart and he started to move out there. Let me describe the house as I saw it.

This home in Clamart was very comfortable, to be sure the bath-room, which the family much appreciated from long contact with americans, although it must be said that the Matisses had always been and always were scrupulously neat and clean, was on the ground floor adjoining the dining room. But that was alright, and is and was a french custom, in french houses. It gave more privacy to a bath-room to have it on the ground floor. Not so long ago in going over the new house Braque was building the bath-room was again below, this time underneath the dining room. When we said, but why, they said because being nearer the furnace it would be warmer.

The grounds at Clamart were large and the garden was what Matisse between pride and chagrin called un petit Luxembourg. There was also a glass forcing house for flowers. Later they had begonias in them that grew smaller and smaller. Beyond were lilacs and still beyond a big demountable studio. They liked it enormously. Madame Matisse with simple recklessness went out every day to look at it and pick flowers, keeping a cab waiting for

Fénéon was a journalist.

her. In those days only millionaires kept cabs waiting and then only very occasionally.

They moved out and were very comfortable and soon the enormous studio was filled with enormous statues and enormous pictures. It was that period of Matisse. Equally soon he found Clamart so beautiful that he could not go home to it, that is when he came into Paris to his hour of sketching from the nude, a thing he had done every afternoon of his life ever since the beginning of things, and he came in every afternoon. His school no longer existed, the government had taken over the old convent to make a Lycée of it and the school had come to an end.

These were the beginning of very prosperous days for the Matisses. They went to Algeria and they went to Tangiers and their devoted german pupils gave them Rhine wines and a very fine black police dog, the first of the breed that any of us had seen.

And then Matisse had a great show of his pictures in Berlin. I remember so well one spring day, it was a lovely day and we were to lunch at Clamart with the Matisses. When we got there they were all standing around an enormous packing case with its top off. We went up and joined them and there in the packing case was the largest laurel wreath that had ever been made, tied with a beautiful red ribbon. Matisse showed Gertrude Stein a card that had been in it. It said on it, To Henri Matisse, Triumphant on the Battlefield of Berlin, and was signed Thomas Whittemore. Thomas Whittemore was a bostonian archeologist and professor at Tufts College, a great admirer of Matisse and this was his tribute. Said Matisse, still more rueful, but I am not dead yet. Madame Matisse, the shock once over said, but Henri look, and leaning down she plucked a leaf and tasted it, it is real laurel, think how good it will be in soup. And, said she still further brightening, the ribbon will do wonderfully for a long time as hair ribbon for Margot.

The Matisses stayed in Clamart more or less until the war. During this period they and Gertrude Stein were seeing less and less of each other. Then after the war broke out they came to the house a good deal. They were lonesome and troubled, Matisse's family in Saint-Quentin, in the north, were within the german lines and his brother was a hostage. It was

Madame Matisse who taught me how to knit woollen gloves. She made them wonderfully neatly and rapidly and I learned to do so too. Then Matisse went to live in Nice and in one way and another, although remaining perfectly good friends, Gertrude Stein and the Matisses never see each other.

The Saturday evenings in those early days were frequented by many hungarians, quite a number of germans, quite a few mixed nationalities, a very thin sprinkling of americans and practically no english. These were to commence later, and with them came aristocracy of all countries and even some royalty.

Among the germans who used to come in those early days was Pascin. He was at that time a thin brilliant-looking creature, he already had a considerable reputation as maker of neat little caricatures in Simplicissimus, the most lively of the german comic papers. The other germans told strange stories of him. That he had been brought up in a house of prostitution of unknown and probably royal birth, etcetera.

He and Gertrude Stein had not met since those early days but a few years ago they saw each other at the vernissage of a young dutch painter Kristians Tonny who had been a pupil of Pascin and in whose work Gertrude Stein was then interested. They liked meeting each other and had a long talk.

Pascin was far away the most amusing of the germans although I cannot quite say that because there was Uhde.

Uhde was undoubtedly well born, he was not a blond german, he was a tallish thin dark man with a high forehead and an excellent quick wit. When he first came to Paris he went to every antiquity shop and bric-à-brac shop in the town in order to see what he could find. He did not find much, he found what purported to be an Ingres, he found a few very early Picassos, but perhaps he found other things. At any rate when the war broke out he was supposed to have been one of the super spies and to have belonged to the german staff.

He was said to have been seen near the french war office after the declaration of war, undoubtedly he and a friend had a summer home very near what was afterward the Hindenburg line. Well at any rate he was very pleasant and very amusing. He it was who was the first to commercialise the douanier Rousseau's pictures. He kept a kind of private art shop. It was here that Braque and Picasso went to see him in their newest and roughest clothes and in their best Cirque Médrano fashion kept up a constant fire of introducing each other to him and asking each other to introduce each other.

Uhde used often to come Saturday evening accompanied by very tall blond good-looking young men who clicked their heels and bowed and then all evening stood solemnly at attention. They made a very effective background to the rest of the crowd. I remember one evening when the son of the great scholar Bréal and his very amusing clever wife brought a spanish guitarist who wanted to come and play. Uhde and his bodyguard were the background and it came on to be a lively evening, the guitarist played and Manolo was there. It was the only time I ever saw Manolo the sculptor, by that time a legendary figure in Paris. Picasso very lively undertook to dance a southern spanish dance not too respectable, Gertrude Stein's brother did the dying dance of Isadora, it was very lively, Fernande and Pablo got into a discussion about Frédéric of the Lapin Agile and apaches. Fernande contended that the apaches were better than the artists and her forefinger went up in the air. Picasso said, yes apaches of course have their universities, artists do not. Fernande got angry and shook him and said, you think you are witty, but you are only stupid. He ruefully showed that she had shaken off a button and she very angry said, and you, your only claim to distinction is that you are a precocious child. Things were not in those days going any too well between them, it was just about the time that they were quitting the rue Ravignan to live in an apartment in the boulevard Clichy, where they were to have a servant and to be prosperous.

But to return to Uhde and first to Manolo. Manolo was perhaps Picasso's oldest friend. He was a strange spaniard. He, so the legend said, was the brother of one of the greatest pickpockets in Madrid. Manolo himself was gentle and admirable. He was the only person in Paris with whom Picasso spoke spanish. All the other spaniards had french wives or french mistresses and having so much the habit of speaking french they always talked french to each other. This always seemed very strange to me. However Picasso and Manolo always talked spanish to each other.

There were many stories about Manolo, he had always loved and he had always lived under the protection of the saints. They told the story of how when he first came to Paris he entered the first church he saw and there he saw a woman bring a chair to some one and receive money. So Manolo did the same, he went into many churches and always gave everybody a chair and always got money, until one day he was caught by the woman whose business it was and whose chairs they were and there was trouble.

He once was hard up and he proposed to his friends to take lottery tickets for one of his statues, everybody agreed, and then when everybody met they found they all had the same number. When they reproached him he explained that he did this because he knew his friends would be unhappy if they did not all have the same number. He was supposed to have left Spain while he was doing his military service, that is to say he was in the cavalry and he went across the border, and sold his horse and his accoutrement, and so had enough money to come to Paris and be a sculptor. He once was left for a few days in the house of a friend of Gauguin. When the owner of the house came back all his Gauguin souvenirs and all his Gauguin sketches were gone. Manolo had sold them to Vollard and Vollard had to give them back. Nobody minded. Manolo was like a sweet crazy religiously uplifted spanish beggar and everybody was fond of him. Moréas, the greek poet, who in those days was a very well known figure in Paris was very fond of him and used to take him with him for company whenever he had anything to do. Manolo always went in hopes of getting a meal but he used to be left to wait while Moréas ate. Manolo was always patient and always hopeful although Moréas was as well known then as Guillaume Apollinaire was later, to pay rarely or rather not at all.

Manolo used to make statues for joints in Montmartre in return for meals etcetera, until Alfred Stieglitz heard of him and showed his things in New York and sold some of them and then Manolo returned to the french frontier, Céret and there he has lived ever since, turning night into day, he and his catalan wife.

But Uhde. Uhde one Saturday evening presented his fiancée to Gertrude Stein. Uhde's morals were not all that they should be and as his fiancée seemed a very well to do and very conventional young woman we were all surprised. But it turned out that it was an arranged marriage. Uhde wished to respectabilise himself and she wanted to come into possession of her inheritance, which she could only do upon marriage. Shortly after she married Uhde and shortly after they were divorced. She then married Delaunay the painter who was just then coming into the foreground. He was the founder of the first of the many vulgarisations of the cubist idea, the painting of houses out of plumb, what was called the catastrophic school.

Delaunay was a big blond frenchman. He had a lively little mother. She used to come to the rue de Fleurus with old vicomtes who looked exactly like one's youthful idea of what an old french marquis should look like. These always left their cards and then wrote a solemn note of thanks and never showed in any way how entirely out of place they must have felt. Delaunay himself was amusing. He was fairly able and inordinately ambitious. He was always asking how old Picasso had been when he had painted a certain picture. When he was told he always said, oh I am not as old as that yet. I will do as much when I am that age.

As a matter of fact he did progress very rapidly. He used to come a great deal to the rue de Fleurus. Gertrude Stein used to delight in him. He was funny and he painted one rather fine picture, the three graces standing in front of Paris, an enormous picture in which he combined everybody's ideas and added a certain french clarity and freshness of his own. It had a rather remarkable atmosphere and it had a great success. After that his pictures lost all quality, they grew big and empty or small and empty. I remember his bringing one of these small ones to the house, saying, look I am bringing you a small picture, a jewel. It is small, said Gertrude Stein, but is it a jewel.

It was Delaunay who married the ex-wife of Uhde and they kept up quite an establishment. They took up Guillaume Apollinaire and it was he

He was at that time a
thin, brilliant looking creature.

They were rather awful but they finally
liked them, and bought two Gauguins.

who taught them how to cook and how to live. Guillaume was extraordinary. Nobody but Guillaume, it was the italian in Guillaume, Stella the New York painter could do the same thing in his early youth in Paris, could make fun of his hosts, make fun of their guests, make fun of their food and spur them to always greater and greater effort.

It was Guillaume's first opportunity to travel, he went to Germany with Delaunay and thoroughly enjoyed himself.

Uhde used to delight in telling how his former wife came to his house one day and dilating upon Delaunay's future career, explained to him that he should abandon Picasso and Braque, the past, and devote himself to the cause of Delaunay, the future. Picasso and Braque at this time it must be remembered were not yet thirty years old. Uhde told everybody this story with a great many witty additions and always adding, I tell you all this sans discrétion, that is tell it to everybody.

The other german who came to the house in those days was a dull one. He is, I understand a very important man now in his own country and he was a most faithful friend to Matisse, at all times, even during the war. He was the bulwark of the Matisse school. Matisse was not always or indeed often very kind to him. All women loved him, so it was supposed. He was a stocky Don Juan. I remember one big scandinavian who loved him and who would never come in on Saturday evening but stood in the court and whenever the door opened for some one to come in or go out you could see her smile in the dark of the court like the smile of the Cheshire cat. He was always bothered by Gertrude Stein. She did and bought such strange things. He never dared to criticise anything to her but to me he would say, and you, Mademoiselle, do you, pointing to the despised object, do you find that beautiful.

Once when we were in Spain, in fact the first time we went to Spain, Gertrude Stein had insisted upon buying in Cuenca a brand new enormous turtle made of Rhine stones. She had very lovely old jewellery, but with great satisfaction to herself she was wearing this turtle as a clasp. Purrmann this time was dumbfounded. He got me into a corner. That jewel, he said, that Miss Stein is wearing, are those stones real.

She then married Delaunay.

Speaking of Spain also reminds me that once we were in a crowded restaurant. Suddenly in the end of the room a tall form stood up and a man bowed solemnly at Gertrude Stein who as solemnly replied. It was a stray hungarian from Saturday evening, surely.

There was another german whom I must admit we both liked. This was much later, about nineteen twelve. He too was a dark tall german. He talked english, he was a friend of Marsden Hartley whom we liked very much, and we liked his german friend, I cannot say that we did not.

He used to describe himself as the rich son of a not so rich father. In other words he had a large allowance from a moderately poor father who was a university professor. Rönnebeck was charming and he was always invited to dinner. He was at dinner one evening when Berenson the famous critic of Italian art was there. Rönnebeck had brought with him some photographs of pictures by Rousseau. He had left them in the atelier and we were all in the dining room. Everybody began to talk about Rousseau. Berenson was puzzled, but Rousseau, Rousseau, he said, Rousseau was an honourable painter but why all this excitement. Ah, he said with a sigh, fashions change, that I know, but really I never thought that Rousseau would come to be the fashion for the young. Berenson had a tendency to be supercilious and so everybody let him go on and on. Finally Rönnebeck said gently, but perhaps Mr. Berenson, you have never heard of the great Rousseau, the douanier Rousseau. No, admitted Berenson, he hadn't, and later when he saw the photographs he understood less than ever and was fairly fussed. Mabel Dodge who was present, said, but Berenson, you must remember that art is inevitable. That, said Berenson recovering himself, you understand, you being yourself a femme fatale.

We were fond of Rönnebeck and beside the first time he came to the house he quoted some of Gertrude Stein's recent work to her. She had loaned some manuscript to Marsden Hartley. It was the first time that anybody had quoted her work to her and she naturally liked it. He also made a translation into german of some of the portraits she was writing at that time and thus brought her her first international reputation. That however is not quite true, Roché the faithful Roché had introduced some young germans to Three Lives and they were already under its spell. However Rönnebeck was charming and we were very fond of him.

Rönnebeck was a sculptor, he did small full figure portraits and was doing them very well, he was in love with an american girl who was studying music. He liked France and all french things and he was very fond of us. We all separated as usual for the summer. He said he had a very amusing summer before him. He had a commission to do a portrait figure of a countess and her two sons, the little counts and he was to spend the summer doing this in the home of the countess who had a magnificent place on the shores of the Baltic.

When we all came back that winter Rönnebeck was different. In the first place he came back with lots of photographs of ships of the german navy and insisted upon showing them to us. We were not interested. Gertrude Stein said, of course, Rönnebeck, you have a navy, of course, we americans have a navy, everybody has a navy, but to anybody but the navy, one big ironclad looks very much like any other, don't be silly. He was different though. He had had a good time. He had photos of himself with all the counts and there was also one with the crown prince of Germany who was a great friend of the countess. The winter, it was the winter of 1913-1914, wore on. All the usual things happened and we gave as usual some dinner parties. I have forgotten what the occasion of one was but we thought Rönnebeck would do excellently for it. We invited him. He sent word that he had to go to Munich for two days but he would travel at night and get back for the dinner party. This he did and was delightful as he always was.

Pretty soon he went off on a trip to the north, to visit the cathedral towns. When he came back he brought us a series of photographs of all these northern towns seen from above. What are these, Gertrude Stein asked. Oh, he said, I thought you would be interested, they are views I have taken of all the cathedral towns. I took them from the tip top of the steeples and I thought you would be interested because see, he said, they look exactly like the pictures of the followers of Delaunay, what you call the earthquake school, he said turning to me. We thanked him and thought no more about it. Later when during the war I found them, I tore them up in a rage.

Then we all began to talk about our summer plans. Gertrude Stein was to go to London in July to see John Lane to sign the contract for Three Lives. Rönnebeck said, why don't you come to Germany instead or rather before or immediately after, he said. Because, said Gertrude Stein, as you know I don't like germans. Yes I know, said Rönnebeck, I know, but you like me and you would have such a wonderful time. They would be so interested and it would mean so much to them, do come, he said. No, said Gertrude Stein, I like you alright but I don't like germans.

We went to England in July and when we got there Gertrude Stein had a letter from Rönnebeck saying that he still awfully wanted us to come to Germany but since we wouldn't had we not better spend the summer in England or perhaps in Spain but not as we had planned come back to Paris. That was naturally the end. I tell the story for what it is worth.

When I first came to Paris there was a very small sprinkling of americans Saturday evenings, this sprinkling grew gradually more abundant but before I tell about americans I must tell all about the banquet to Rousseau.

In the beginning of my stay in Paris a friend and I were living as I have already said in a little apartment on the rue Notre-Dame-des-Champs. I was no longer taking french lessons from Fernande because she and Picasso were together again but she was not an infrequent visitor. Autumn had come and I can remember it very well because I had bought my first winter Paris hat. It was a very fine hat of black velvet, a big hat with a brilliant yellow fantaisie. Even Fernande gave it her approval.

Fernande was lunching with us one day and she said that there was going to be a banquet given for Rousseau and that she was giving it. She counted up the number of the invited. We were included. Who was Rousseau. I did not know but that really did not matter since it was to be a banquet and everybody was to go, and we were invited.

Next Saturday evening at the rue de Fleurus everybody was talking about the banquet to Rousseau and then I found out that Rousseau was the painter whose picture I had seen in that first independent. It appeared that Picasso had recently found in Montmartre a large portrait of a woman by Rousseau, that he had bought it and that this festivity was in honour of the purchase and the painter. It was going to be very wonderful.

Fernande told me a great deal about the menu. There was to be riz à la Valenciennes, Fernande had learnt how to cook this on her last trip to Spain, and then she had ordered, I forget now what it was that she had ordered, but she had ordered a great deal at Félix Potin, the chain store of groceries where they made prepared dishes. Everybody was excited. It was Guillaume Apollinaire, as I remember, who knowing Rousseau very well had induced him to promise to come and was to bring him and everybody was to write poetry and songs and it was to be very rigolo, a favourite Montmartre word meaning a jokeful amusement. We were all to meet at the café at the foot of the rue Ravignan and to have an apéritif and then go up to Picasso's atelier and have dinner. I put on my new hat and we all went to Montmartre and all met at the café.

As Gertrude Stein and I came into the café there seemed to be a great many people present and in the midst was a tall thin girl who with her long thin arms extended was swaying forward and back. I did not know what she was doing, it was evidently not gymnastics, it was bewildering but she looked very enticing. What is that, I whispered to Gertrude Stein. Oh that is Marie Laurencin, I am afraid she has been taking too many preliminary apéritifs. Is she the old lady that Fernande told me about who makes noises like animals and annoys Pablo. She annoys Pablo alright but she is a very young lady and she has had too much, said Gertrude Stein going in. Just then there was a violent noise at the door of the café and Fernande appeared very large, very excited and very angry. Félix Potin, said she, has not sent the dinner. Everybody seemed overcome at these awful tidings but I, in my american way said to Fernande, come quickly, let us telephone. In those days in Paris one did not telephone and never to a provision store. But Fernande consented and off we went. Everywhere we went there was either no telephone or it was not working, finally we got one that worked but Félix Potin was closed or closing and it was deaf to our appeals. Fernande was completely upset but finally I persuaded her to tell me just what we were to have had from Félix Potin and then in one little shop and another little shop in Montmartre we found substitutes, Fernande finally announcing that she had made so much riz à la Valenciennes that it would take the place of everything and it did.

When we were back at the café almost everybody who had been there had gone and some new ones had come, Fernande told them all to come along. As we toiled up the hill we saw in front of us the whole crowd. In the middle was Marie Laurencin supported on the one side by Gertrude Stein and on the other by Gertrude Stein's brother and she was falling first into one pair of arms and then into another, her voice always high and sweet and her arms always thin graceful and long. Guillaume of course was not there, he was to bring Rousseau himself after every one was seated.

Fernande passed this slow moving procession, I following her and we arrived at the atelier. It was rather impressive. They had gotten trestles, carpenter's trestles, and on them had placed boards and all around these boards were benches. At the head of the table was the new acquisition, the Rousseau, draped in flags and wreaths and flanked on either side by big statues, I do not remember what statues. It was very magnificent and very festive. The riz à la Valenciennes was presumably cooking below in Max Jacob's studio. Max not being on good terms with Picasso was not present but they used his studio for the rice and for the men's overcoats. The ladies were to put theirs in the front studio which had been Van Dongen's in his spinach days and now belonged to a frenchman by the name of Vaillant. This was the studio which was later to be Juan Gris'.

I had just time to deposit my hat and admire the arrangements, Fernande violently abusing Marie Laurencin all the time, when the crowd arrived. Fernande large and imposing, barred the way, she was not going to have her party spoiled by Marie Laurencin. This was a serious party, a serious banquet for Rousseau and neither she nor Pablo would tolerate such conduct. Of course Pablo, all this time, was well out of sight in the rear. Gertrude Stein remonstrated, she said half in english half in french, that she would be hanged if after the struggle of getting Marie Laurencin up that terrific hill it was going to be for nothing. No indeed and beside she reminded Fernande that Guillaume and Rousseau would be along any minute and it was necessary that every one should be decorously seated before that event. By this time Pablo had made his way to the front and he joined in and said, yes yes, and Fernande yielded. She was always a little afraid of Guillaume Apollinaire, of his solemnity and of his wit, and they all came in. Everybody sat down.

Everybody sat down and everybody began to eat rice and other things, that is as soon as Guillaume Apollinaire and Rousseau came in which they did very presently and were wildly acclaimed. How well I remember their coming. Rousseau a little small colourless frenchman with a little beard, like any number of frenchmen one saw everywhere. Guillaume Apollinaire with finely cut florid features, dark hair and a beautiful complexion. Everybody was presented and everybody sat down again. Guillaume slipped into a seat beside Marie Laurencin. At the sight of Guillaume, Marie who had become comparatively calm seated next to Gertrude Stein, broke out again in wild movements and outcries. Guillaume got her out of the door and downstairs and after a decent interval they came back Marie a little bruised but sober. By this time everybody had eaten everything and poetry began. Oh yes, before this Frédéric of the Lapin Agile and the University of Apaches had wandered in with his usual companion a donkey, was given a drink and wandered out again. Then a little later some italian street singers hearing of the party came in. Fernande rose at the end of the table and flushed and her forefinger straight into the air said it was not that kind of a party, and they were promptly thrown out.

Who was there. We were there and Salmon, André Salmon, then a rising young poet and journalist, Pichot and Germaine Pichot, Braque and perhaps Marcelle Braque but this I do not remember, I know that there was talk of her at that time, the Raynals, the Ageros the false Greco and his wife, and several other pairs who I did not know and do not remember and Vaillant, a very amiable ordinary young frenchman who had the front studio.

The ceremonies began. Guillaume Apollinaire got up and made a solemn eulogy, I do not remember at all what he said but it ended up with a poem he had written and which he half chanted and in which everybody joined in the refrain, La peinture de ce Rousseau. Somebody else then, possibly Raynal, I don't remember, got up and there were toasts, and then all of a sudden André Salmon who was sitting next to my friend and solemnly discoursing of literature and travels, leaped upon the by no means solid table and poured out an extemporaneous eulogy and poem. At the end he seized a big glass and drank what was in it, then promptly went off his head, being completely drunk, and began to fight. The men all got hold of him, the statues tottered, Braque, a great big chap, got hold of a statue in either arm and stood there holding them while Gertrude Stein's brother another big chap, protected little Rousseau and his violin from harm. The others with Picasso leading because Picasso though small is very strong, dragged Salmon into the front atelier and locked him in. Everybody came back and sat down.

Thereafter the evening was peaceful. Marie Laurencin sang in a thin voice some charming old norman songs. The wife of Agero sang some charming old limousin songs, Pichot danced a wonderful religious spanish dance ending in making of himself a crucified Christ upon the floor. Guillaume Apollinaire solemnly approached myself and my friend and asked us to sing some of the native songs of the red indians. We did not either of us feel up to that to the great regret of Guillaume and all the company. Rousseau blissful and gentle played the violin and told us about the plays he had written and his memories of Mexico. It was all very peaceful and about three o'clock in the morning we all went into the atelier where Salmon had been deposited and where we had left our hats and coats to get them to go home. There on the couch lay Salmon peacefully sleeping and surrounding him, half chewed, were a box of matches, a petit bleu and my yellow fantaisie. Imagine my feelings even at three o'clock in the morning. However, Salmon woke up very charming and very polite and we all went out into the street together. All of a sudden with a wild yell Salmon rushed down the hill.

Gertrude Stein and her brother, my friend and I, all in one cab, took Rousseau home.

It was about a month later that one dark Paris winter afternoon I was hurrying home and felt myself being followed. I hurried and hurried and the footsteps drew nearer and I heard, mademoiselle, mademoiselle. I turned. It was Rousseau. Oh mademoiselle, he said, you should not be out alone after dark, may I see you home. Which he did.

It was not long after this that Kahnweiler came to Paris. Kahnweiler was a german married to a frenchwoman and they had lived for many years in England. Kahnweiler had been in England in business, saving money to carry out a dream of some day having a picture shop in Paris. The time had come and he started a neat small gallery in the rue Vignon. He felt his way a little and then completely threw in his lot with the cubist group. There were difficulties at first, Picasso always suspicious did not want to go too far with him. Fernande did the bargaining with Kahnweiler but finally they all realised the genuineness of his interest and his faith, and that he could and would market their work. They all made contracts with him and until the war he did everything for them all. The afternoons with the group coming in and out of his shop were for Kahnweiler really afternoons with Vasari. He believed in them and their future greatness. It was only the year before the war that he added Juan Gris. It was just two months before the outbreak of the war that Gertrude Stein saw the first Juan Gris paintings at Kahnweiler's and bought three of them.

Picasso always says that he used in those days to tell Kahnweiler that he should become a french citizen, that war would come and there would be the devil to pay. Kahnweiler always said he would when he had passed the military age but that he naturally did not want to do military service a second time. The war came, Kahnweiler was in Switzerland with his family on his vacation and he could not come back. All his possessions were sequestrated.

The auction sale by the government of Kahnweiler's pictures, practically all the cubist pictures of the three years before the war, was the first occasion after the war where everybody of the old crowd met. There had been quite a conscious effort on the part of all the older merchants, now that the war was over, to kill cubism. The expert for the sale, who was a well known picture dealer, had avowed this as his intention. He would keep the prices down as low as possible and discourage the public as much as possible. How could the artists defend themselves.

We happened to be with the Braques a day or two before the public show of pictures for the sale and Marcelle Braque, Braque's wife, told us that they had come to a decision. Picasso and Juan Gris could do nothing they were spaniards, and this was a french government sale. Marie Laurencin was technically a german, Lipschitz was a russian at that time not a popular thing to be. Braque a frenchman, who had won the croix de guerre in a charge, who had been made an officer and had won the légion d'honneur and had had a bad head wound could do what he pleased. He had a technical reason too for picking a quarrel with the expert. He had sent in a list of people likely to buy his pictures, a privilege always accorded to an artist whose pictures are to be publicly sold, and catalogues had not been sent to these people. When we arrived Braque had already done his duty. We came in just at the end of the fray. There was a great excitement.

Braque had approached the expert and told him that he had neglected his obvious duties. The expert had replied that he had done and would do as he pleased and called Braque a norman pig. Braque had hit him. Braque is a big man and the expert is not and Braque tried not to hit hard but nevertheless the expert fell. The police came in and they were taken off to the police station. There they told their story. Braque of course as a hero of the war was treated with all due respect, and when he spoke to the expert using the familiar thou the expert completely lost his temper and his head and was publicly rebuked by the magistrate. Just after it was over Matisse came in and wanted to know what had happened and was happening, Gertrude Stein told him. Matisse said, and it was a Matisse way to say it, Braque a raison, celui-là a volé la France, et on sait bien ce que c'est que voler la France.

As a matter of fact the buyers were frightened off and all the pictures except those of Derain went for little. Poor Juan Gris whose pictures went for very little tried to be brave. They after all did bring an honourable price, he said to Gertrude Stein, but he was sad.

Fortunately Kahnweiler, who had not fought against France, was allowed to come back the next year. The others no longer needed him but Juan needed him desperately and Kahnweiler's loyalty and generosity to Juan Gris all those hard years can only be matched by Juan's loyalty and generosity when at last just before his death and he had become famous tempting offers from other dealers were made to him.

Kahnweiler coming to Paris and taking on commercially the cause of the cubists made a great difference to all of them. Their present and future were secure.

The Picassos moved from the old studio in the rue Ravignan to an apartment in the boulevard Clichy. Fernande began to buy furniture and have a servant and the servant of course made a soufflé. It was a nice apartment with lots of sunshine. On the whole however Fernande was not quite as happy as she had been. There were a great many people there and even afternoon tea. Braque was there a great deal, it was the height of the intimacy between Braque and Picasso, it was at that time they first began to put musical instruments into their pictures. It was also the beginning of Picasso's making constructions. He made still lifes of objects and photographed them. He made paper constructions later, he gave one of these to Gertrude Stein. It is perhaps the only one left in existence.

This was also the time when I first heard of Poiret. He had a houseboat on the Seine and he had given a party on it and he had invited Pablo and Fernande. He gave Fernande a handsome rose-coloured scarf with gold fringe and he also gave her a spun glass fantaisie to put on a hat, an entirely new idea in those days. This she gave to me and I wore it on a little straw pointed cap for years after. I may even have it now.

Then there was the youngest of the cubists. I never knew his name. He was doing his military service and was destined for diplomacy. How he drifted in and whether he painted I do not know. All I know is that he was known as the youngest of the cubists.

Fernande had at this time a new friend of whom she often spoke to me. This was Eve who was living with Marcoussis. And one evening all four of them came to the rue de Fleurus, Pablo, Fernande, Marcoussis and Eve.

It was the only time we ever saw Marcoussis until many many years later.

I could perfectly understand Fernande's liking for Eve. As I said Fernande's great heroine was Evelyn Thaw, small and negative. Here was a little french Evelyn Thaw, small and perfect.

Not long after this Picasso came one day and told Gertrude Stein that he had decided to take an atelier in the rue Ravignan. He could work better there. He could not get back his old one but he took one on the lower floor. One day we went to see him there. He was not in and Gertrude Stein as a joke left her visiting card. In a few days we went again and Picasso was at work on a picture on which was written ma jolie and at the lower corner painted in was Gertrude Stein's visiting card. As we went away Gertrude Stein said, Fernande is certainly not ma jolie, I wonder who it is. In a few days we knew. Pablo had gone off with Eve.

This was in the spring. They all had the habit of going to Céret near Perpignan for the summer probably on account of Manolo, and they all in spite of everything went there again. Fernande was there with the Pichots and Eve was there with Pablo. There were some redoubtable battles and then everybody came back to Paris.

One evening, we too had come back, Picasso came in. He and Gertrude Stein had a long talk alone. It was Pablo, she said when she came in from having bade him goodbye, and he said a marvellous thing about Fernande, he said her beauty always held him but he could not stand any of her little ways. She further added that Pablo and Eve were now settled on the boulevard Raspail and we would go and see them to-morrow.

In the meanwhile Gertrude Stein had received a letter from Fernande, very dignified, written with the reticence of a frenchwoman. She said that she wished to tell Gertrude Stein that she understood perfectly that the friendship had always been with Pablo and that although Gertrude had always shown her every mark of sympathy and affection now that she and Pablo were separated, it was naturally impossible that in the future there should be any intercourse between them because the friendship having been with Pablo there could of course be no question of a choice. That she would always remember their intercourse with pleasure and that she would permit herself, if ever she were in need, to throw herself upon Gertrude's generosity.

And so Picasso left Montmartre never to return.

When I first came to the rue de Fleurus Gertrude Stein was correcting the proofs of Three Lives. I was soon helping her with this and before very long the book was published. I asked her to let me subscribe to Romeike's clipping bureau, the advertisement for Romeike in the San Francisco Argonaut having been one of the romances of my childhood. Soon the clippings began to come in.

It is rather astonishing the number of newspapers that noticed this book, printed privately and by a perfectly unknown person. The notice that pleased Gertrude Stein most was in the Kansas City Star. She often asked then and in later years who it was who might have written it but she never found out. It was a very sympathetic and a very understanding review. Later on when she was discouraged by what others said she would refer to it as having given her at that time great comfort. She says in Composition and Explanation, when you write a thing it is perfectly clear and then you begin to be doubtful about it, but then you read it again and you lose yourself in it again as when you wrote it.

The other thing in connection with this her first book that gave her pleasure was a very enthusiastic note from H. G. Wells. She kept this for years apart, it had meant so much to her. She wrote to him at that time and they were often to meet but as it happened they never did. And they are not likely to now.

Gertrude Stein was at that time writing The Making of Americans. It had changed from being a history of a family to being a history of everybody the family knew and then it became the history of every kind and of every individual human being. But in spite of all this there was a hero and he was to die. The day he died I met Gertrude Stein at Mildred Aldrich's apartment. Mildred was very fond of Gertrude Stein and took a deep interest in the book's ending. It was over a thousand pages long and I was typewriting it.

I always say that you cannot tell what a picture really is or what an object

A good many years later Jane Heap said

really is until you dust it every day and you cannot tell what a book is until you type it or proof-read it. It then does something to you that only reading never can do. A good many years later Jane Heap said that she had never appreciated the quality of Gertrude Stein's work until she proof-read it.

When The Making of Americans was finished, Gertrude Stein began another which also was to be long and which she called A Long Gay Book but it did not turn out to be long, neither that nor one begun at the same time Many Many Women because they were both interrupted by portrait writing. This is how portrait writing began.

Hélène used to stay at home with her husband Sunday evening, that is to say she was always willing to come but we often told her not to bother. I like cooking, I am an extremely good five-minute cook, and beside, Gertrude Stein liked from time to time to have me make american dishes. One Sunday evening I was very busy preparing one of these and then I called Gertrude Stein to come in from the atelier for supper. She came in much excited and would not sit down. Here I want to show you something, she said. No I said it has to be eaten hot. No, she said, you have to see this first. Gertrude Stein never likes her food hot and I do like mine hot, we never agree about this. She admits that one can wait to cool it but one cannot heat it once it is on a plate so it is agreed that I have it served as hot as I like. In spite of my protests and the food cooling I had to read. I can still see the little tiny pages of the note-book written forward and back. It was the portrait called Ada, the first in Geography and Plays. I began it and I thought she was making fun of me and I protested, she says I protest now about my autobiography. Finally I read it all and was terribly pleased with it. And then we ate our supper.

This was the beginning of the long series of portraits. She has written portraits of practically everybody she has known, and written them in all manners and in all styles.

Ada was followed by portraits of Matisse and Picasso, and Stieglitz who was much interested in them and in Gertrude Stein printed them in a special number of Camera Work.

She then began to do short portraits of everybody who came in and out.

She did one of Arthur Frost, the son of A. B. Frost the american illustrator. Frost was a Matisse pupil and his pride when he read his portrait and found that it was three full pages longer than either the portrait of Matisse or the portrait of Picasso was something to hear.

A. B. Frost complained to Pat Bruce who had led Frost to Matisse that it was a pity that Arthur could not see his way to becoming a conventional artist and so earning fame and money. You can lead a horse to water but you cannot make him drink said Pat Bruce. Most horses drink, Mr. Bruce, said A. B. Frost.

Bruce, Patrick Henry Bruce, was one of the early and most ardent Matisse pupils and soon he made little Matisses, but he was not happy. In explaining his unhappiness he told Gertrude Stein, they talk about the sorrows of great artists, the tragic unhappiness of great artists but after all they are great artists. A little artist has all the tragic unhappiness and the sorrows of a great artist and he is not a great artist.

She did portraits of Nadelman, also of the protégés of the sculptress Mrs. Whitney, Lee and Russell also of Harry Phelan Gibb, her first and best english friend. She did portraits of Manguin and Roché and Purrmann and David Edstrom, the fat swedish sculptor who married the head of the Christian Science Church in Paris and destroyed her. And Brenner, Brenner the sculptor who never finished anything. He had an admirable technique and a great many obsessions which kept him from work. Gertrude Stein was very fond of him and still is. She once posed to him for weeks and he did a fragmentary portrait of her that is very fine. He and Cody later published some numbers of a little review called Soil and they were among the very early ones to print something of Gertrude Stein. The only little magazine that preceded it was one called Rogue, printed by Allan Norton and which printed her description of the Galérie Lafayette. This was of course all much later and happened through Carl Van Vechten.

She also did portraits of Miss Etta Cone and her sister Doctor Claribel Cone. She also did portraits of Miss Mars and Miss Squires under the title of Miss Furr and Miss Skeene. There were portraits of Mildred Aldrich and her sister. Everybody was given their portrait to read and they were all pleased and it was all very amusing. All this occupied a great deal of that winter and then we went to Spain.

In Spain Gertrude Stein began to write the things that led to Tender Buttons.

I liked Spain immensely. We went several times to Spain and I always liked it more and more. Gertrude Stein says that I am impartial on every subject except that of Spain and spaniards.

We went straight to Avila and I immediately lost my heart to Avila, I must stay in Avila forever I insisted. Gertrude Stein was very upset, Avila was alright but, she insisted, she needed Paris. I felt that I needed nothing but Avila. We were both very violent about it. We did however stay there for ten days and as Saint Theresa was a heroine of Gertrude Stein's youth we thoroughly enjoyed it. In the opera Four Saints written a few years ago she describes the landscape that so profoundly moved me.

We went on to Madrid and there we met Georgiana King of Bryn Mawr, an old friend of Gertrude Stein from Baltimore days. Georgiana King wrote some of the most interesting of the early criticisms of Three Lives. She was then re-editing Street on the cathedrals of Spain and in connection with this she had wandered all over Spain. She gave us a great deal of very good advice.

In these days Gertrude Stein wore a brown corduroy suit, jacket and skirt, a small straw cap, always crocheted for her by a woman in Fiesole, sandals, and she often carried a cane. That summer the head of the cane was of amber. It is more or less this costume without the cap and the cane that Picasso has painted in his portrait of her. This costume was ideal for Spain, they all thought of her as belonging to some religious order and we were always treated with the most absolute respect. I remember that once a nun was showing us the treasures in a convent church in Toledo. We were near the steps of the altar. All of a sudden there was a crash, Gertrude Stein had dropped her cane. The nun paled, the worshippers startled. Gertrude Stein picked up her cane and turning to the frightened nun said reassuringly, no it is not broken.

I used in those days of spanish travelling to wear what I was wont to call my spanish disguise. I always wore a black silk coat, black gloves and a black hat, the only pleasure I allowed myself were lovely artificial flowers on my hat. These always enormously interested the peasant women and they used to very courteously ask my permission to touch them, to realise for themselves that they were artificial.

We went to Cuenca that summer, Harry Gibb the english painter had told us about it. Harry Gibb is a strange case of a man who foresaw everything. He had been a successful animal painter in his youth in England, he came from the north of England, he had married and gone to Germany, there he had become dissatisfied with what he had been doing and heard about the new school of painting in Paris. He came to Paris and was immediately influenced by Matisse. He then became interested in Picasso and he did some very remarkable painting under their combined influences. Then all this together threw him into something else something that fairly completely achieved what the surréalists after the war tried to do. The only thing he lacked is what the french call saveur, what may be called the graciousness of a picture. Because of this lack it was impossible for him to find a french audience. Naturally in those days there was no english audience. Harry Gibb fell on bad days. He was always falling upon bad days. He and his wife Bridget one of the pleasantest of the wives of a genius I have sat with were full of courage and they faced everything admirably, but there were always very difficult days. And then things were a little better. He found a couple of patrons who believed in him and it was at this time, 1912-1913, that he went to Dublin and had rather an epoch-making show of his pictures there. It was at that time that he took with him several copies of the portrait of Mabel Dodge at the Villa Curonia, Mabel Dodge had had it printed in Florence, and it was then that the Dublin writers in the cafés heard Gertrude Stein read aloud. Doctor Gogarty, Harry Gibb's host and admirer, loved to read it aloud himself and have others read it aloud.

After that there was the war and eclipse for poor Harry, and since then a long sad struggle. He has had his ups and downs, more downs than up, but only recently there was a new turn of the wheel. Gertrude Stein who loved them both dearly always was convinced that the two painters of her

The only pleasure I allowed myself were
lovely artificial flowers on my hat.

generation who would be discovered after they were dead, they being pre-destined to a life of tragedy, were Juan Gris and Harry Gibb. Juan Gris dead these five years is beginning to come into his own. Harry Gibb still alive is still unknown. Gertrude Stein and Harry Gibb have always been very loyal and very loving friends. One of the very good early portraits she did she did of him, it was printed in the Oxford Review and then in Geography and Plays.

So Harry Gibb told us about Cuenca and we went on a little railroad that turned around curves and ended in the middle of nowhere and there was Cuenca.

We delighted in Cuenca and the population of Cuenca delighted in us. It delighted in us so much that it was getting uncomfortable. Then one day when we were out walking, all of a sudden the population, particularly the children, kept their distance. Soon a uniformed man came up and saluting said that he was a policeman of the town and that the governor of the province had detailed him to always hover in the distance as we went about the country to prevent our being annoyed by the population and that he hoped that this would not inconvenience us. It did not, he was charming and he took us to lovely places in the country where we could not very well have gone by ourselves. Such was Spain in the old days.

We finally came back to Madrid again and there we discovered the Argentina and bull-fights. The young journalists of Madrid had just discovered her. We happened upon her in a music hall, we went to them to see spanish dancing, and after we saw her the first time we went every afternoon and every evening. We went to the bull-fights. At first they upset me and Gertrude Stein used to tell me, now look, now don't look, until finally I was able to look all the time.

We finally came to Granada and stayed there for some time and there Gertrude Stein worked terrifically. She was always very fond of Granada. It was there she had her first experience of Spain when still at college just after the spanish-american war when she and her brother went through Spain. They had a delightful time and she always tells of sitting in the dining room talking to a bostonian and his daughter when suddenly there was

We happened upon her in a music hall.

a terrific noise, the hee-haw of a donkey. What is it, said the young bostonian trembling. Ah, said the father, it is the last sigh of the Moor.

We enjoyed Granada, we met many amusing people english and spanish and it was there and at that time that Gertrude Stein's style gradually changed. She says hitherto she had been interested only in the insides of people, their character and what went on inside them, it was during that summer that she first felt a desire to express the rhythm of the visible world.

It was a long tormenting process, she looked, listened and described. She always was, she always is, tormented by the problem of the external and the internal. One of the things that always worries her about painting is the difficulty that the artist feels and which sends him to painting still lifes, that after all the human being essentially is not paintable. Once again and very recently she has thought that a painter has added something to the solution of this problem. She is interested in Picabia in whom hitherto she has never been interested because he at least knows that if you do not solve your painting problem in painting human beings you do not solve it at all. There is also a follower of Picabia's, who is facing the problem, but will he solve it. Perhaps not. Well anyway it is that of which she is always talking and now her own struggle with it was to begin.

These were the days in which she wrote Susie Asado and Preciocilla and Gypsies in Spain. She experimented with everything in trying to describe. She tried a bit inventing words but she soon gave that up. The english language was her medium and with the english language the task was to be achieved, the problem solved. The use of fabricated words offended her, it was an escape into imitative emotionalism.

No, she stayed with her task, although after the return to Paris she described objects, she described rooms and objects, which joined with her first experiments done in Spain, made the volume Tender Buttons.

She always however made her chief study people and therefore the never ending series of portraits.

We came back to the rue de Fleurus as usual.

One of the people who had impressed me very much when I first came to the rue de Fleurus was Mildred Aldrich.

Mildred Aldrich was then in her early fifties, a stout vigorous woman with a George Washington face, white hair and admirably clean fresh clothes and gloves. A very striking figure and a very satisfying one in the crowd of mixed nationalities. She was indeed one of whom Picasso could say and did say, c'est elle qui fera la glorie de l'Amérique. She made one very satisfied with one's country, which had produced her.

Her sister having left for America she lived alone on the top floor of a building on the corner of the boulevard Raspail and the half street, rue Boissonade. There she had at the window an enormous cage filled with canaries. We always thought it was because she loved canaries. Not at all. A friend had once left her a canary in a cage to take care of during her absence. Mildred as she did everything else, took excellent care of the canary in the cage. Some friend seeing this and naturally concluding that Mildred was fond of canaries gave her another canary. Mildred of course took excellent care of both canaries and so the canaries increased and the size of the cage grew until in 1914 she moved to Huiry to the Hilltop on the Marne and gave her canaries away. Her excuse was that in the country cats would eat the canaries. But her real reason she once told me was that she really could not bear canaries.

Mildred was an excellent housekeeper. I was very surprised, having had a very different impression of her, going up to see her one afternoon, finding her mending her linen and doing it beautifully.

Mildred adored cablegrams, she adored being hard up, or rather she adored spending money and as her earning capacity although great was limited, Mildred was chronically hard up. In those days she was making contracts to put Maeterlinck's Blue Bird on the american stage. The arrangements demanded endless cablegrams, and my early memories of Mildred were of her coming to our little apartment in the rue Notre-Dame-des-Champs late in the evening and asking me to lend her the money for a long cable. A few days later the money was returned with a lovely azalea worth five times the money. No wonder she was always hard up. But everybody listened to her. No one in the world could tell stories like Mildred. I can still see her at the rue de Fleurus sitting in one of the big armchairs and gradually the audience increasing around her as she talked.

She was very fond of Gertrude Stein, very interested in her work, enthusiastic about Three Lives, deeply impressed but slightly troubled by The Making of Americans, quite upset by Tender Buttons, but always loyal and convinced that if Gertrude Stein did it it had something in it that was worth while.

Her joy and pride when in nineteen twenty-six Gertrude Stein gave her lecture at Cambridge and Oxford was touching. Gertrude Stein must come out and read it to her before leaving. Gertrude Stein did, much to their mutual pleasure.

Mildred Aldrich liked Picasso and even liked Matisse, that is personally, but she was troubled. One day she said to me, Alice, tell me is it alright, are they really alright, I know Gertrude thinks so and Gertrude knows, but really is it not all fumisterie, is it not all false.

In spite of these occasional doubtful days Mildred Aldrich liked it all. She liked coming herself and she liked bringing other people. She brought a great many. It was she who brought Henry McBride who was then writing on the New York Sun. It was Henry McBride who used to keep Gertrude Stein's name before the public all those tormented years. Laugh if you like, he used to say to her detractors, but laugh with and not at her, in that way you will enjoy it all much better.

Henry McBride did not believe in worldly success. It ruins you, it ruins you, he used to say. But Henry, Gertrude Stein used to answer dolefully, don't you think I will ever have any success, I would like to have a little, you know. Think of my unpublished manuscripts. But Henry McBride was firm, the best that I can wish you, he always said, is to have no success. It is the only good thing. He was firm about that.

He was however enormously pleased when Mildred was successful and he now says he thinks the time has come when Gertrude Stein could indulge in a little success. He does not think that now it would hurt her.

It was about this time that Roger Fry first came to the house. He brought Clive Bell and Mrs. Clive Bell and later there were many others. In these days Clive Bell went along with the other two. He was rather complainful that his wife and Roger Fry took too much interest in capital works of art. He was quite funny about it. He was very amusing, later when he became a real art critic he was less so.

Roger Fry was always charming, charming as a guest and charming as a host; later when we went to London we spent a day with him in the country.

He was filled with excitement at the sight of the portrait of Gertrude Stein by Picasso. He wrote an article about it in the Burlington Review and illustrated it by two photographs side by side, one the photograph of this portrait and the other a photograph of a portrait by Raphael. He insisted that these two pictures were equal in value. He brought endless people to the house. Very soon there were throngs of englishmen, Augustus John and Lamb, Augustus John amazing looking and not too sober, Lamb rather strange and attractive.

It was about this time that Roger Fry had many young disciples. Among them was Wyndham Lewis, Wyndham Lewis, tall and thin, looked rather like a young frenchman on the rise, perhaps because his feet were very french, or at least his shoes. He used to come and sit and measure pictures. I can not say that he actually measured with a measuring-rod but he gave all the effect of being in the act of taking very careful measurement of the canvas, the lines within the canvas and everything that might be of use. Gertrude Stein rather liked him. She particularly liked him one day when he came and told all about his quarrel with Roger Fry. Roger Fry had come in not many days before and had already told all about it. They told exactly the same story only it was different, very different.

This was about the time too that Prichard of the Museum of Fine Arts, Boston and later of the Kensington Museum began coming. Prichard brought a great many young Oxford men. They were very nice in the room, and they thought Picasso wonderful. They felt and indeed in a way it was true that he had a halo. With these Oxford men came Thomas Whittemore of Tufts College. He was fresh and engaging and later to Gertrude Stein's great delight he one day said, all blue is precious.

Everybody brought somebody. As I said the character of the Saturday evenings was gradually changing, that is to say, the kind of people who came had changed. Somebody brought the Infanta Eulalia and brought her several times. She was delighted and with the flattering memory of royalty she always remembered my name even some years after when we met quite by accident in the place Vendôme. When she first came into the room she was a little frightened. It seemed a strange place but gradually she liked it very much.

Lady Cunard brought her daughter Nancy, then a little girl, and very solemnly bade her never forget the visit.

Who else came. There were so many. The bavarian minister brought quantities of people. Jacques-Emile Blanche brought delightful people, so did Alphonse Kann. There was Lady Otoline Morrell looking like a marvellous feminine version of Disraeli and tall and strange shyly hesitating at the door. There was a dutch near royalty who was left by her escort who had to go and find a cab and she looked during this short interval badly frightened.

There was a roumanian princess, and her cabman grew impatient. Hélène came in to announce violently that the cabman would not wait. And then after a violent knock, the cabman himself announced that he would not wait.

It was an endless variety. And everybody came and no one made any difference. Gertrude Stein sat peacefully in a chair and those who could did the same, the rest stood. There were the friends who sat around the stove and talked and there were the endless strangers who came and went. My memory of it is very vivid.

As I say everybody brought people. William Cook brought a great many from Chicago, very wealthy stout ladies and equally wealthy tall good-looking thin ones. That summer having found the Balearic Islands on the map, we went to the island of Mallorca and on the little boat going over was Cook. He too had found it on the map. We stayed only a little while but he settled down for the summer, and then later he went back and was the

we went to the island of Mallorca.

solitary first of all the big crowd of americans who have discovered Palma since. We all went back again during the war.

It was during this summer that Picasso gave us a letter to a friend of his youth one Raventos in Barcelona. But does he talk french, asked Gertrude Stein, Pablo giggled, better than you do Gertrude, he answered.

Raventos gave us a good time, he and a descendant of de Soto took us about for two long days, the days were long because so much of them were night. They had an automobile, even in those early days, and they took us up into the hills to see early churches. We would rush up a hill and then happily come down a little slower and every two hours or so we ate a dinner. When we finally came back to Barcelona about ten o'clock in the evening they said, now we will have an apéritif and then we will eat dinner. It was exhausting eating so many dinners but we enjoyed ourselves.

Later on much later on indeed only a few years ago Picasso introduced us to another friend of his youth.

Sabartes and he have known each other ever since they were fifteen years old but as Sabartes had disappeared into South America, Montevideo, Uruguay, before Gertrude Stein met Picasso, she had never heard of him. One day a few years ago Picasso sent word that he was bringing Sabartes to the house. Sabartes, in Uruguay, had read some things of Gertrude Stein in various magazines and he had conceived a great admiration for her work. It never occurred to him that Picasso would know her. Having come back for the first time in all these years to Paris he went to see Picasso and he told him about this Gertrude Stein. But she is my only friend, said Picasso, it is the only home I go to. Take me, said Sabartes, and so they came.

Gertrude Stein and spaniards are natural friends and this time too the friendship grew.

It was about this time that the futurists, the italian futurists, had their big show in Paris and it made a great deal of noise. Everybody was excited and this show being given in a very well known gallery everybody went. Jacques-Emile Blanche was terribly upset by it. We found him wandering tremblingly in the garden of the Tuileries and he said, it looks alright but is it. No it isn't, said Gertude Stein. You do me good, said Jacques-Emile Blanche.

The futurists all of them led by Severini thronged around Picasso. He brought them all to the house. Marinetti came by himself later as I remember. In any case everybody found the futurists very dull.

Epstein the sculptor came to the rue de Fleurus one evening. When Gertrude Stein first came to Paris in nineteen hundred and four, Epstein was a thin rather beautiful rather melancholy ghost who used to slip in and out among the Rodin statues in the Luxembourg museum. He had illustrated Hutchins Hapgood's studies of the ghetto and with the funds he came to Paris and was very poor. Now when I first saw him, he had come to Paris to place his sphynx statue to Oscar Wilde over Oscar Wilde's grave. He was a large rather stout man, not unimpressive but not beautiful. He had an english wife who had a very remarkable pair of brown eyes, of a shade of brown I had never before seen in eyes.

Doctor Claribel Cone of Baltimore came majestically in and out. She loved to read Gertrude Stein's work out loud and she did read it out loud extraordinarily well. She liked ease and graciousness and comfort. She and her sister Etta Cone were traveling. The only room in the hotel was not comfortable. Etta bade her sister put up with it as it was only for one night. Etta, answered Doctor Claribel, one night is as important as any other night in my life and I must be comfortable. When the war broke out she happened to be in Munich engaged in scientific work. She could never leave because it was never comfortable to travel. Everybody delighted in Doctor Claribel. Much later Picasso made a drawing of her.

Emily Chadbourne came, it was she who brought Lady Otoline Morrell and she also brought many bostonians.

Mildred Aldrich once brought a very extraordinary person Myra Edgerly. I remembered very well that when I was quite young and went to a fancy-dress ball, a Mardi Gras ball in San Francisco, I saw a very tall and very beautiful and very brilliant woman there. This was Myra Edgerly young. Genthe, the well known photographer did endless photographs of her, mostly with a cat. She had come to London as a miniaturist and she had had one of those phenomenal successes that americans do have in Europe. She had miniatured everybody, and the royal family, and she had maintained her earnest gay careless outspoken San Francisco way through it all. She now came to Paris to study a little. She met Mildred Aldrich and became very devoted to her. Indeed it was Myra who in nineteen thirteen, when Mildred's earning capacity was rapidly dwindling secured an annuity for her and made it possible for Mildred to retire to the Hilltop on the Marne.

Myra Edgerly was very earnestly anxious that Gertrude Stein's work should be more widely known. When Mildred told her about all those unpublished manuscripts Myra said something must be done. And of course something was done.

She knew John Lane slightly and she said Gertrude Stein and I must go to London. But first Myra must write letters and then I must write letters to everybody for Gertrude Stein. She told me the formula I must employ. I remember it began, Miss Gertrude Stein as you may or may not know, is, and then you went on and said everything you had to say.

Under Myra's strenuous impulsion we went to London in the winter of nineteen twelve, thirteen, for a few weeks. We did have an awfully good time.

Myra took us with her to stay with Colonel and Mrs. Rogers at Riverhill in Surrey. This was in the vicinity of Knole and of Ightham Mote, beautiful houses and beautiful parks. This was my first experience of country-house visiting in England since, as a small child, I had only been in the nursery. I enjoyed every minute of it. The comfort, the open fires, the tall maids who were like annunciation angels, the beautiful gardens, the children, the ease of it all. And the quantity of objects and of beautiful things. What is that, I would ask Mrs. Rogers, ah that I know nothing about, it was here when I came. It gave me a feeling that there had been so many lovely brides in that house who had found all these things there when they came.

Gertrude Stein liked country-house visiting less than I did. The continuous pleasant hesitating flow of conversation, the never ceasing sound of the human voice speaking in english, bothered her.

On our next visit to London and when because of being caught by the war we stayed in country houses with our friends a very long time, she managed to isolate herself for considerable parts of the day and to avoid at least one of the three or four meals, and so she liked it better.

We did have a good time in England. Gertrude Stein completely forgot her early dismal memory of London and has liked visiting there immensely ever since.

We went to Roger Fry's house in the country and were charmingly entertained by his quaker sister. We went to Lady Otoline Morrell and met everybody. We went to Clive Bell's. We went about all the time, we went shopping and ordered things. I still have my bag and jewel box. We had an extremely good time. And we went very often to see John Lane. In fact we were supposed to go every Sunday afternoon to his house for tea and Gertrude Stein had several interviews with him in his office. How well I knew all the things in all the shops near the Bodley Head because while Gertrude Stein was inside with John Lane while nothing happened and then when finally something happened I waited outside and looked at everything.

The Sunday afternoons at John Lane's were very amusing. As I remember during that first stay in London we went there twice.

John Lane was very interested. Mrs. John Lane was a Boston woman and very kind.

Tea at the John Lane's Sunday afternoons was an experience. John Lane had copies of Three Lives and The Portrait of Mabel Dodge. One did not know why he selected the people he did to show it to. He did not give either book to any one to read. He put it into their hands and took it away again and inaudibly he announced that Gertrude Stein was here. Nobody was introduced to anybody. From time to time John Lane would take Gertrude Stein into various rooms and show her his pictures, odd pictures of English schools of all periods, some of them very pleasing. Sometimes he told a story about how he had come to get it. He never said anything else about a picture. He also showed her a great many Beardsley drawings and they talked about Paris.

The second Sunday he asked her to come again to the Bodley Head. This was a long interview. He said that Mrs. Lane had read Three Lives and thought very highly of it and that he had the greatest confidence in her

This was in the vicinity of Knole.

judgment. He asked Gertrude Stein when she was coming back to London. She said she probably was not coming back to London. Well, he said, when you come in July I imagine we will be ready to arrange something. Perhaps, he added, I may see you in Paris in the early spring.

And so we left London. We were on the whole very pleased with ourselves. We had had a very good time and it was the first time that Gertrude Stein had ever had a conversation with a publisher.

Mildred Aldrich often brought a whole group of people to the house Saturday evening. One evening a number of people came in with her and among them was Mabel Dodge. I remember my impression of her very well.

She was a stoutish woman with a very sturdy fringe of heavy hair over her forehead, heavy long lashes and very pretty eyes and a very old fashioned coquetry. She had a lovely voice. She reminded me of a heroine of my youth, the actress Georgia Cayvan. She asked us to come to Florence to stay with her. We were going to spend the summer as was then our habit in Spain but we were going to be back in Paris in the fall and perhaps we then would. When we came back there were several urgent telegrams from Mabel Dodge asking us to come to the Villa Curonia and we did.

We had a very amusing time. We liked Edwin Dodge and we liked Mabel Dodge but we particularly liked Constance Fletcher whom we met there.

Constance Fletcher came a day or so after we arrived and I went to the station to meet her. Mabel Dodge had described her to me as a very large woman who would wear a purple robe and who was deaf. As a matter of fact she was dressed in green and was not deaf but very short sighted, and she was delightful.

Her father and mother came from and lived in Newburyport, Massachusetts. Edwin Dodge's people came from the same town and this was a strong bond of union. When Constance was twelve years old her mother fell in love with the english tutor of Constance's younger brother. Constance knew that her mother was about to leave her home. For a week Constance laid on her bed and wept and then accompanied her mother and her future step-father to Italy. Her step-father being an englishman Constance became passionately an english woman. The step-father was a painter who had a local reputation among the english residents in Italy.

When Constance Fletcher was eighteen years old she wrote a best-seller called Kismet and was engaged to be married to Lord Lovelace the descendant of Byron.

She did not marry him and thereafter lived always in Italy. Finally she became permanently fixed in Venice. This was after the death of her mother and father. I always liked as a californian her description of Joaquin Miller in Rome, in her younger days.

Now in her comparative old age she was attractive and impressive. I am very fond of needlework and I was fascinated by her fashion of embroidering wreaths of flowers. There was nothing drawn upon her linen, she just held it in her hands, from time to time bringing it closely to one eye, and eventually the wreath took form. She was very fond of ghosts. There were two of them in the Villa Curonia and Mabel was very fond of frightening visiting americans with them which she did in her suggestive way very effectively. Once she drove a house party consisting of Jo and Yvonne Davidson, Florence Bradley, Mary Foote and a number of others quite mad with fear. And at last to complete the effect she had the local priest in to exorcise the ghosts. You can imagine the state of mind of her guests. But Constance Fletcher was fond of ghosts and particularly attached to the later one, who was a wistful ghost of an english governess who had killed herself in the house.

One morning I went in to Constance Fletcher's bedroom to ask her how she was, she had not been very well the night before.

I went in and closed the door. Constance Fletcher very large and very white was lying in one of the vast renaissance beds with which the villa was furnished. Near the door was a very large renaissance cupboard. I had a delightful night, said Constance Fletcher, the gentle ghost visited me all night, indeed she has just left me. I imagine she is still in the cupboard, will you open it please. I did. Is she there, asked Constance Fletcher. I said I saw nothing. Ah yes, said Constance Fletcher.

We had a delightful time and Gertrude Stein at that time wrote The Portrait of Mabel Dodge. She also wrote the portrait of Constance Fletcher that was later printed in Geography and Plays. Many years later indeed after the war in London I met Siegfried Sassoon at a party given by Edith Sitwell for Gertrude Stein. He spoke of Gertrude Stein's portrait of Constance Fletcher which he had read in Geography and Plays and said that he had first become interested in Gertrude Stein's work because of this portrait. And he added, and did you know her and if you did can you tell me about her marvellous voice. I said, very much interested, then you did not know her. No, he said, I never saw her but she ruined my life. How, I asked excitedly. Because, he answered, she separated my father from my mother.

Constance Fletcher had written one very successful play which had had a long run in London called Green Stockings but her real life had been in Italy. She was more italian than the italians. She admired her step-father and therefore was english but she was really dominated by the fine italian hand of Machiavelli. She could and did intrigue in the italian way better than even the italians and she was a disturbing influence for many years in Venice not only among the english but also among the italians.

André Gide turned up while we were at the Villa Curonia. It was rather a dull evening. It was then also that we first met Muriel Draper and Paul Draper. Gertrude Stein always liked Paul very much. She delighted in his american enthusiasm, and explanation of all things musical and human. He had had a great deal of adventure in the West and that was another bond between them. When Paul Draper left to return to London Mabel Dodge received a telegram saying, pearls missing suspect the second man. She came to Gertrude Stein in great agitation asking what she should do about it. Don't wake me, said Gertrude Stein, do nothing. And then sitting up, but that is a nice thing to say, suspect the second man, that is charming, but who and what is the second man. Mabel explained that the last time they had a robbery in the villa the police said that they could do nothing because nobody suspected any particular person and this time Paul to avoid that complication suspected the second man servant. While this explanation was being given another telegram came, pearls found. The second man had put the pearls in the collar box.

Haweis and his wife, later Mina Loy were also in Florence. Their home had been dismantled as they had had workmen in it but they put it all in order to give us a delightful lunch. Both Haweis and Mina were among the very earliest to be interested in the work of Gertrude Stein. Haweis had been fascinated with what he had read in manuscript of The Making of Americans. He did however plead for commas. Gertrude Stein said commas were unnecessary, the sense should be intrinsic and not have to be explained by commas and otherwise commas were only a sign that one should pause and take breath but one should know of oneself when one wanted to pause and take breath. However, as she liked Haweis very much and he had given her a delightful painting for a fan, she gave him two commas. It must however be added that on rereading the manuscript she took the commas out.

Mina Loy equally interested was able to understand without the commas. She has always been able to understand.

Gertrude Stein having written The Portrait of Mabel Dodge, Mabel Dodge immediately wanted it printed. She had three hundred copies struck off and bound in Florentine paper. Constance Fletcher corrected the proofs and we were all awfully pleased. Mabel Dodge immediately conceived the idea that Gertrude Stein should be invited from one country house to another and do portraits and then end up doing portraits of american millionaires which would be a very exciting and lucrative career. Gertrude Stein laughed. A little later we went back to Paris.

It was during this winter that Gertrude Stein began to write plays. They began with the one entitled, It Happened a Play. This was written about a dinner party given by Harry and Bridget Gibb. She then wrote Ladies' Voices. Her interest in writing plays continues. She says a landscape is such a natural arrangement for a battle-field or a play that one must write plays.

Florence Bradley, a friend of Mabel Dodge, was spending a winter in Paris. She had had some stage experience and had been interested in planning a little theatre. She was vitally interested in putting these plays on the stage. Demuth was in Paris too at this time. He was then more interested in writing than in painting and particularly interested in these plays. He and Florence Bradley were always talking them over together.

Gertrude Stein has never seen Demuth since. When she first heard that he was painting she was much interested. They never wrote to each other but they often sent messages by mutual friends. Demuth always sent word that some day he would do a little picture that would thoroughly please him and then he would send it to her. And sure enough after all these years, two years ago some one left at the rue de Fleurus during our absence a little picture with a message that this was the picture that Demuth was ready to give to Gertrude Stein. It is a remarkable little landscape in which the roofs and windows are so subtle that they are as mysterious and as alive as the roofs and windows of Hawthorne or Henry James.

It was not long after this that Mabel Dodge went to America and it was the winter of the armoury show which was the first time the general public had a chance to see any of these pictures. It was there that Marcel Duchamp's Nude Descending the Staircase was shown.

It was about this time that Picabia and Gertrude Stein met. I remember going to dinner at the Picabias' and a pleasant dinner it was, Gabrielle Picabia full of life and gaiety, Picabia dark and lively, and Marcel Duchamp looking like a young norman crusader.

I was always perfectly able to understand the enthusiasm that Marcel Duchamp aroused in New York when he went there in the early years of the war. His brother had just died from the effect of his wounds, his other brother was still at the front and he himself was inapt for military service. He was very depressed and he went to America. Everybody loved him. So much so that it was a joke in Paris that when any american arrived in Paris the first thing he said was, and how is Marcel. Once Gertrude Stein went to see Braque, just after the war, and going into the studio in which there happened just then to be three young americans, she said to Braque, and how is Marcelle. The three young americans came up to her breathlessly and said, have you seen Marcel. She laughed, and having become accustomed

Everybody loved him.

to the inevitableness of the american belief that there was only one Marcel, she explained that Braque's wife was named Marcelle and it was Marcelle Braque about whom she was enquiring.

In those days Picabia and Gertrude Stein did not get to be very good friends. He annoyed her with his incessantness and what she called the vulgarity of his delayed adolescence. But oddly enough in this last year they have gotten to be very fond of each other. She is very much interested in his drawing and in his painting. It began with his show just a year ago. She is now convinced that although he has in a sense not a painter's gift he has an idea that has been and will be of immense value to all time. She calls him the Leonardo da Vinci of the movement. And it is true, he understands and invents everything.

As soon as the winter of the armoury show was over Mabel Dodge came back to Europe and she brought with her what Jacques-Emile Blanche called her collection des jeunes gens assortis, a mixed assortment of young men. In the lot were Carl Van Vechten, Robert Jones and John Reed. Carl Van Vechten did not come to the rue de Fleurus with her. He came later in the spring by himself. The other two came with her. I remember the evening they all came. Picasso was there too. He looked at John Reed critically and said, le genre de Braque mais beaucoup moins rigolo, Braque's kind but much less diverting. I remember also that Reed told me about his trip through Spain. He told me he had seen many strange sights there, that he had seen witches chased through the street of Salamanca. As I had been spending months in Spain and he only weeks I neither liked his stories nor believed them.

Robert Jones was very impressed by Gertrude Stein's looks. He said he would like to array her in cloth of gold and he wanted to design it then and there. It did not interest her.

Among the people that we had met at John Lane's in London was Gordon Caine and her husband. Gordon Caine had been a Wellesley girl who played the harp with which she always travelled, and who always rearranged the furniture in the hotel room completely, even if she was only to stay one night. She was tall, rosy-haired and very good-looking. Her husband was a well known humorous english writer and one of John Lane's authors. They had entertained us very pleasantly in London and we asked them to dine with us their first night in Paris. I don't know quite what happened but Hélène cooked a very bad dinner. Only twice in all her long service did Hélène fail us. This time and when about two weeks later Carl Van Vechten turned up. That time too she did strange things, her dinner consisting of a series of hors d'oeuvres. However that is later.

During dinner Mrs. Caine said that she had taken the liberty of asking her very dear friend and college mate Mrs. Van Vechten to come in after dinner because she was very anxious that she should meet Gertrude Stein as she was very depressed and unhappy and Gertrude Stein could undoubtedly have an influence for the good in her life. Gertrude Stein said that she had a vague association with the name of Van Vechten but could not remember what it was. She has a bad memory for names. Mrs. Van Vechten came. She too was a very tall woman, it would appear that a great many tall ones go to Wellesley, and she too was good-looking. Mrs. Van Vechten told the story of the tragedy of her married life but Gertrude Stein was not particularly interested.

It was about a week later that Florence Bradley asked us to go with her to see the second performance of the Sacre du Printemps. The russian ballet had just given the first performance of it and it had made a terrible uproar. All Paris was excited about it. Florence Bradley had gotten three tickets in a box, the box held four, and asked us to go with her. In the meantime there had been a letter from Mabel Dodge introducing Carl Van Vechten, a young New York journalist. Gertrude Stein invited him to dine the following Saturday evening.

We went early to the russian ballet, these were the early great days of the russian ballet with Nijinsky as the great dancer. And a great dancer he was. Dancing excites me tremendously and it is a thing I know a great deal about. I have seen three very great dancers. My geniuses seem to run in threes, but that is not my fault, it happens to be a fact. The three really great dancers I have seen are the Argentina, Isadora Duncan and Nijinsky. Like the three geniuses I have known they are each one of a different nationality.

The three really great dancers I have seen are

the Argentina, Isadora Duncan and Nijinsky.

Nijinsky did not dance in the Sacre du Printemps but he created the dance of those who did dance.

We arrived in the box and sat down in the three front chairs leaving one chair behind. Just in front of us in the seats below was Guillaume Apollinaire. He was dressed in evening clothes and he was industriously kissing various important looking ladies' hands. He was the first one of his crowd to come out into the great world wearing evening clothes and kissing hands. We were very amused and very pleased to see him do it. It was the first time we had seen him doing it. After the war they all did these things but he was the only one to commence before the war.

Just before the performance began the fourth chair in our box was occupied. We looked around and there was a tall well-built young man, he might have been a dutchman, a scandinavian or an american and he wore a soft evening shirt with the tiniest pleats all over the front of it. It was impressive, we had never even heard that they were wearing evening shirts like that. That evening when we got home Gertrude Stein did a portrait of the unknown called a Portrait of One.

The performance began. No sooner had it commenced when the excitement began. The scene now so well known with its brilliantly coloured background now not at all extraordinary, outraged the Paris audience. No sooner did the music begin and the dancing than they began to hiss. The defenders began to applaud. We could hear nothing, as a matter of fact I never did hear any of the music of the Sacre du Printemps because it was the only time I ever saw it and one literally could not, throughout the whole performance, hear the sound of music. The dancing was very fine and that we could see although our attention was constantly distracted by a man in the box next to us flourishing his cane, and finally in a violent altercation with an enthusiast in the box next to him, his cane came down and smashed the opera hat the other had just put on in defiance. It was all incredibly fierce.

The next Saturday evening Carl Van Vechten was to come to dinner. He came and he was the young man of the soft much-pleated evening shirt

Stravinsky   Nijinsky

and it was the same shirt. Also of course he was the hero or villain of Mrs. Van Vechten's tragic tale.

As I said Hélène did for the second time in her life make an extraordinarily bad dinner. For some reason best known to herself she gave us course after course of hors d'oeuvres finishing up with a sweet omelet. Gertrude Stein began to tease Carl Van Vechten by dropping a word here and there of intimate knowledge of his past life. He was naturally bewildered. It was a curious evening.

Gertrude Stein and he became dear friends.

He interested Allan and Louise Norton in her work and induced them to print in the little magazine they founded, The Rogue, the first thing of Gertrude Stein's ever printed in a little magazine, The Galérie Lafayette. In another number of this now rare little magazine, he printed a little essay on the work of Gertrude Stein. It was he who in one of his early books printed as a motto the device on Gertrude Stein's note-paper, a rose is a rose is a rose is a rose. Just recently she has had made for him by our local potter at the foot of the hill at Belley some plates in the yellow clay of the country and around the border is a rose is a rose is a rose is a rose and in the centre is to Carl.

In season and out he kept her name and her work before the public. When he was beginning to be well known and they asked him what he thought the most important book of the year he replied Three Lives by Gertrude Stein. His loyalty and his effort never weakened. He tried to make Knopf publish The Making of Americans and he almost succeeded but of course they weakened.

Speaking of the device of rose is a rose is a rose is a rose, it was I who found it in one of Gertrude Stein's manuscripts and insisted upon putting it as a device on the letter paper, on the table linen and anywhere that she would permit that I would put it. I am very pleased with myself for having done so.

Carl Van Vechten has had a delightful habit all these years of giving letters of introduction to people who he thought would amuse Gertrude Stein. This he has done with so much discrimination that she has liked them all.

The first and perhaps the one she has liked the best was Avery Hopwood. The friendship lasted until Avery's death a few years ago. When Avery came to Paris he always asked Gertrude Stein and myself to dine with him. This custom began in the early days of the acquaintance. Gertrude Stein is not a very enthusiastic diner-out but she never refused Avery. He always had the table charmingly decorated with flowers and the menu most carefully chosen. He sent us endless petits bleus, little telegrams, arranging this affair and we always had a good time. In these early days, holding his head a little on one side and with his tow-coloured hair, he looked like a lamb. Sometimes in the latter days as Gertrude Stein told him the lamb turned into a wolf. Gertrude Stein would I know at this moment say, dear Avery. They were very fond of each other. Not long before his death he came into the room one day and said I wish I could give you something else beside just dinner, he said, perhaps I could give you a picture. Gertrude Stein laughed, it is alright, she said to him, Avery, if you will always come here and take just tea. And then in the future beside the petit bleu in which he proposed our dining with him he would send another petit bleu saying that he would come one afternoon to take just tea. Once he came and brought with him Gertrude Atherton. He said so sweetly, I want the two Gertrudes whom I love so much to know each other. It was a perfectly delightful afternoon. Every one was pleased and charmed and as for me a californian, Gertrude Atherton had been my youthful idol and so I was very content.

The last time we saw Avery was on his last visit to Paris. He sent his usual message asking us to dinner and when he came to call for us he told Gertrude Stein that he had asked some of his friends to come because he was going to ask her to do something for him. You see, he said, you have never gone to Montmartre with me and I have a great fancy that you should to-night. I know it was your Montmartre long before it was mine but would you. She laughed and said, of course Avery.

We did after dinner go up to Montmartre with him. We went to a great many queer places and he was so proud and pleased. We were always going in a cab from one place to another and Avery Hopwood and Gertrude

Diaghilev

Stein went together and they had long talks and Avery must have had some premonition that it was the last time because he had never talked so openly and so intimately. Finally we left and he came out and put us into a cab and he told Gertrude Stein it had been one of the best evenings of his life. He left the next day for the south and we for the country. A little while after Gertrude Stein had a postal from him telling her how happy he had been to see her again and the same morning there was the news of his death in the Herald.

It was about nineteen twelve that Alvin Langdon Coburn turned up in Paris. He was a queer american who brought with him a queer english woman, his adopted mother. Alvin Langdon Coburn had just finished a series of photographs that he had done for Henry James. He had published a book of photographs of prominent men and he wished now to do a companion volume of prominent women. I imagine it was Roger Fry who had told him about Gertrude Stein. At any rate he was the first photographer to come and photograph her as a celebrity and she was nicely gratified. He did make some very good photographs of her and gave them to her and then he disappeared and though Gertrude Stein has often asked about him nobody seems ever to have heard of him since.

This brings us pretty well to the spring of nineteen fourteen. During this winter among the people who used to come to the house was the younger step-daughter of Bernard Berenson. She brought with her a young friend, Hope Mirlees and Hope said that when we went to England in the summer we must go down to Cambridge and stay with her people. We promised that we would.

During the winter Gertrude Stein's brother decided that he would go to Florence to live. They divided the pictures that they had bought together, between them. Gertrude Stein kept the Cézannes and Picassos and her brother the Matisses and Renoirs, with the exception of the original Femme au Chapeau.

We planned that we would have a little passage-way made between the studio and the little house and as that entailed cutting a door and plastering we decided that we would paint the atelier and repaper the house and put in electricity. We proceeded to have all this done. It was the end of June before this was accomplished and the house had not yet been put in order when Gertrude Stein received a letter from John Lane saying he would be in Paris the following day and would come to see her.

We worked very hard, that is I did and the concierge and Hélène and the room was ready to receive him.

He brought with him the first copy of Blast by Wyndham Lewis and he gave it to Gertrude Stein and wanted to know what she thought of it and would she write for it. She said she did not know.

John Lane then asked her if she would come to London in July as he had almost made up his mind to republish the Three Lives and would she bring another manuscript with her. She said she would and she suggested a collection of all the portraits she had done up to that time. The Making of Americans was not considered because it was too long. And so that having been arranged John Lane left.

In those days Picasso having lived rather sadly in the rue Schœlcher was to move a little further out to Montrouge. It was not an unhappy time for him but after the Montmartre days one never heard his high whinnying spanish giggle. His friends, a great many of them, had followed him to Montparnasse but it was not the same. The intimacy with Braque was waning and of his old friends the only ones he saw frequently were Guillaume Apollinaire and Gertrude Stein. It was in that year that he began to use ripolin paints instead of the usual colours used by painters. Just the other day he was talking a long time about the ripolin paints. They are, said he gravely, la santé des couleurs, that is they are the basis of good health for paints. In those days he painted pictures and everything with ripolin paints as he still does, and as so many of his followers young and old do.

He was at this time too making constructions in paper, in tin and in all sorts of things, the sort of thing that made it possible for him afterwards to do the famous stage setting for Parade.

It was in these days that Mildred Aldrich was preparing to retire to the Hilltop on the Marne. She too was not unhappy but rather sad. She wanted us often in those spring evenings to take a cab and have what she called our last ride together. She more often than ever dropped her house key all the way down the centre of the stairway while she called good-night to us from the top story of the apartment house on the rue Boissonade.

We often went out to the country with her to see her house. Finally she moved in. We went out and spent the day with her. Mildred was not unhappy but she was very sad. My curtains are all up, my books in order, everything is clean and what shall I do now, said Mildred. I told her that when I was a little girl, my mother said that I always used to say, what shall I do now, which was only varied by now what shall I do. Mildred said that the worst of it was that we were going to London and that she would not see us all summer. We assured her that we would only stay away a month, in fact we had return tickets, and so we had to, and as soon as we got home we would go out to see her. Anyway she was happy that at last Gertrude Stein was going to have a publisher who would publish her books. But look out for John Lane, he is a fox, she said, as we kissed her and left.

Hélène was leaving 27 rue de Fleurus because, her husband having recently been promoted to be foreman in his work shop he insisted that she must not work out any longer but must stay at home.

In short in this spring and early summer of nineteen fourteen the old life was over.

VI.

The War

AMERICANS LIVING IN Europe before the war never really believed that there was going to be war. Gertrude Stein always tells about the little janitor's boy who, playing in the court, would regularly every couple of years assure her that papa was going to the war. Once some cousins of hers were living in Paris, they had a country girl as a servant. It was the time of the russian-japanese war and they were all talking about the latest news. Terrified she dropped the platter and cried, and are the germans at the gates.

William Cook's father was an Iowan who at seventy years of age was making his first trip in Europe in the summer of nineteen fourteen. When the war was upon them he refused to believe it and explained that he could understand a family fighting among themselves, in short a civil war, but not a serious war with one's neighbours.

Gertrude Stein in 1913 and 1914 had been very interested reading the newspapers. She rarely read french newspapers, she never read anything in french, and she always read the Herald. That winter she added the Daily Mail. She liked to read about the suffragettes and she liked to read about Lord Roberts' campaign for compulsory military service in England. Lord Roberts had been a favourite hero of hers early in her life. His Forty-One Years in India was a book she often read and she had seen Lord Roberts when she and her brother, then taking a college vacation, had seen Edward the Seventh's coronation procession. She read the Daily Mail, although, as she said, she was not interested in Ireland.

We went to England July fifth and went according to programme to see John Lane at his house Sunday afternoon.

There were a number of people there and they were talking of many things but some of them were talking about war. One of them, some one told me he was an editorial writer on one of the big London dailies, was bemoaning the fact that he would not be able to eat figs in August in Provence as was his habit. Why not, asked some one. Because of the war, he answered. Some one else, Walpole or his brother I think it was, said that there was no hope of beating Germany as she had such an excellent system, all her railroad trucks were numbered in connection with locomotives and switches. But, said the eater of figs, that is all very well as long as the trucks remain in Germany on their own lines and switches, but in an aggressive war they will leave the frontiers of Germany and then, well I promise you then there will be a great deal of numbered confusion.

This is all I remember definitely of that Sunday afternoon in July.

As we were leaving, John Lane said to Gertrude Stein that he was going out of town for a week and he made a rendezvous with her in his office for the end of July, to sign the contract for Three Lives. I think, he said, in the present state of affairs I would rather begin with that than with something more entirely new. I have confidence in that book. Mrs. Lane is very enthusiastic and so are the readers.

Having now ten days on our hands we decided to accept the invitation of Mrs. Mirlees, Hope's mother, and spend a few days in Cambridge. We went there and thoroughly enjoyed ourselves.

It was a most comfortable house to visit. Gertrude Stein liked it, she could stay in her room or in the garden as much as she liked without hearing too much conversation. The food was excellent, scotch food, delicious and fresh, and it was very amusing meeting all the University of Cambridge dignitaries. We were taken into all the gardens and invited into many of the homes. It was lovely weather, quantities of roses, morris-dancing by all the students and girls and generally delightful. We were invited to lunch at Newnham, Miss Jane Harrison, who had been Hope Mirlees' pet enthusiasm, was much interested in meeting Gertrude Stein. We sat up on the dais with the faculty and it was very awe inspiring. The conversation was not however particularly amusing. Miss Harrison and Gertrude Stein did not particularly interest each other.

We had been hearing a good deal about Doctor and Mrs. Whitehead. They no longer lived in Cambridge. The year before Doctor Whitehead had left Cambridge to go to London University. They were to be in Cambridge shortly and they were to dine at the Mirlees'. They did and I met my third genius.

It was a pleasant dinner. I sat next to Housman, the Cambridge poet, and we talked about fishes and David Starr Jordan but all the time I was more interested in watching Doctor Whitehead. Later we went into the garden and he came and sat next to me and we talked about the sky in Cambridge.

Gertrude Stein and Doctor Whitehead and Mrs. Whitehead all became interested in each other. Mrs. Whitehead asked us to dine at her house in London and then to spend a week end, the last week end in July with them in their country home in Lockridge, near Salisbury Plain. We accepted with pleasure.

We went back to London and had a lovely time. We were ordering some comfortable chairs and a comfortable couch covered with chintz to replace some of the italian furniture that Gertrude Stein's brother had taken with him. This took a great deal of time. We had to measure ourselves into the chairs and into the couch and to choose chintz that would go with the pictures, all of which we successfully achieved. These chairs and this couch, and they are comfortable, in spite of war came to the door one day in January, nineteen fifteen at the rue de Fleurus and were greeted by us with the greatest delight. One needed such comforting and such comfort in those days. We dined with the Whiteheads and liked them more than ever and they liked us more than ever and were kind enough to say so.

Gertrude Stein kept her appointment with John Lane at the Bodley Head. They had a very long conversation, this time so long that I quite exhausted all the shop windows of that region for quite a distance, but finally Gertrude Stein came out with a contract. It was a gratifying climax.

Then we took the train to Lockridge to spend the week end with the Whiteheads. We had a week-end trunk, we were very proud of our week-end trunk, we had used it on our first visit and now we were actively using it again. As one of my friends said to me later, they asked you to spend the week end and you stayed six weeks. We did.

There was quite a house party when we arrived, some Cambridge people, some young men, the younger son of the Whiteheads, Eric, then fifteen years old but very tall and flower-like and the daughter Jessie just back from Newnham. There could not have been much serious thought of war because they were all talking of Jessie Whitehead's coming trip to Finland. Jessie always made friends with foreigners from strange places, she had a passion for geography and a passion for the glory of the British Empire. She had a friend, a finn, who had asked her to spend the summer with her people in Finland and had promised Jessie a possible uprising against Russia. Mrs. Whitehead was hesitating but had practically consented. There was an older son North who was away at the time.

Then suddenly, as I remember, there were the conferences to prevent the war, Lord Grey and the russian minister of foreign affairs. And then before anything further could happen the ultimatum to France. Gertrude Stein and I were completely miserable as was Evelyn Whitehead, who had french blood and who had been raised in France and had strong french sympathies. Then came the days of the invasion of Belgium and I can still hear Doctor Whitehead's gentle voice reading the papers out loud and then all of them talking about the destruction of Louvain and how they must help the brave little belgians. Gertrude Stein desperately unhappy said to me, where is Louvain. Don't you know, I said. No, she said, nor do I care, but where is it.

Our week end was over and we told Mrs. Whitehead that we must leave. But you cannot get back to Paris now, she said. No, we answered, but we can stay in London. Oh no, she said, you must stay with us until you can get back to Paris. She was very sweet and we were very unhappy and we liked them and they liked us and we agreed to stay. And then to our infinite relief England came into the war.

We had to go to London to get our trunks, to cable to people in America and to draw money, and Mrs. Whitehead wished to go in to see if she and her daughter could do anything to help the belgians. I remember that trip so well. There seemed so many people about everywhere, although the train was not overcrowded, but all the stations even little country ones, were filled with people, not people at all troubled but just a great many people. At the junction where we were to change trains we met Lady Astley, a friend of Myra Edgerly's whom we had met in Paris. Oh how do you do, she said in a cheerful loud voice, I am going to London to say goodbye to my son. Is he going away, we said politely. Oh yes, she said, he is in the guards you know, and is leaving tonight for France.

In London everything was difficult. Gertrude Stein's letter of credit was on a french bank but mine luckily small was on a California one. I say luckily small because the banks would not give large sums but my letter of credit was so small and so almost used up that they without hesitation gave me all that there was left of it.

Gertrude Stein cabled to her cousin in Baltimore to send her money, we gathered in our trunks, we met Evelyn Whitehead at the train and we went back with her to Lockridge. It was a relief to get back. We appreciated her kindness because to have been at a hotel in London at that moment would have been too dreadful.

Then one day followed another and it is hard to remember just what happened. North Whitehead was away and Mrs. Whitehead was terribly worried lest he should rashly enlist. She must see him. So they telegraphed to him to come at once. He came. She had been quite right. He had immediately gone to the nearest recruiting station to enlist and luckily there had been so many in front of him that the office closed before he was admitted.

She immediately went to London to see Kitchener. Doctor Whitehead's brother was a bishop in India and he had in his younger days known Kitchener very intimately. Mrs. Whitehead had this introduction and North was given a commission. She came home much relieved. North was to join in three days but in the meantime he must learn to drive a motor car. The three days passed very quickly and North was gone. He left immediately for France and without much equipment. And then came the time of waiting.

Evelyn Whitehead was very busy planning war work and helping every one and I as far as possible helped her. Gertrude Stein and Doctor Whitehead walked endlessly around the country. They talked of philosophy and history, it was during these days that Gertrude Stein realised how completely it was Doctor Whitehead and not Russell who had had the ideas for their great book. Doctor Whitehead, the gentlest and most simply generous of human beings never claimed anything for himself and enormously admired anyone who was brilliant, and Russell undoubtedly was brilliant.

Gertrude Stein used to come back and tell me about these walks and the country still the same as in the days of Chaucer, with the green paths of the early britons that could still be seen in long stretches, and the triple rainbows of that strange summer. They used, Doctor Whitehead and Gertrude Stein, to have long conversations with game-keepers and mole-catchers. The mole-catcher had said, but sir, England has never been in a war but that she has been victorious. Doctor Whitehead turned to Gertrude Stein with a gentle smile. I think we may say so, he said. The game-keeper, when Doctor Whitehead seemed discouraged said to him, but Doctor Whitehead, England is the predominant nation, is she not. I hope she is, yes I hope she is, replied Doctor Whitehead gently.

The germans were getting nearer and nearer Paris. One day Doctor Whitehead said to Gertrude Stein, they were just going through a rough little wood and he was helping her, have you any copies of your writings or are they all in Paris. They are all in Paris, she said. I did not like to ask, said Doctor Whitehead, but I have been worrying.

The germans were getting nearer and nearer Paris and the last day Gertrude Stein could not leave her room, she sat and mourned. She loved Paris, she thought neither of manuscripts nor of pictures, she thought only of Paris and she was desolate. I came up to her room, I called out, it is alright Paris is saved, the germans are in retreat. She turned away and said, don't tell me these things. But it's true, I said, it is true. And then we wept together.

The first description that any one we knew received in England of the battle of the Marne came in a letter to Gertrude Stein from Mildred Aldrich. It was practically the first letter of her book the Hilltop on the Marne. We were delighted to receive it, to know that Mildred was safe, and to know all about it. It was passed around and everybody in the neighbourhood read it.

Later when we returned to Paris we had two other descriptions of the battle of the Marne. I had an old school friend from California, Nellie Jacot who lived in Boulogne-sur-Seine and I was very worried about her. I telegraphed to her and she telegraphed back characteristically, Nullement en danger ne t'inquiète pas, there is no danger don't worry. It was Nellie who used to call Picasso in the early days a good-looking bootblack and used to say of Fernande, she is alright but I don't see why you bother about her. It was also Nellie who made Matisse blush by cross-questioning him about the different ways he saw Madame Matisse, how she looked to him as a wife and how she looked to him as a picture, and how he could change from one to the other. It was also Nellie who told the story which Gertrude Stein loved to quote, of a young man who once said to her, I love you Nellie, Nellie is your name, isn't it. It was also Nellie who when we came back from England and we said that everybody had been so kind, said, oh yes, I know that kind.

Nellie described the battle of the Marne to us. You know, she said, I always come to town once a week to shop and I always bring my maid. We come in in the street car because it is difficult to get a taxi in Boulogne and we go back in a taxi. Well we came in as usual and didn't notice anything and when we had finished our shopping and had had our tea we stood on a corner to get a taxi. We stopped several and when they heard where we wanted to go they drove on. I know that sometimes taxi drivers don't like to go out to Boulogne so I said to Marie tell them we will give them a big tip if they will go. So she stopped another taxi with an old driver and I said to him, I will give you a very big tip to take us out to Boulogne. Ah, said he laying his finger on his nose, to my great regret madame it is impossible, no taxi can leave the city limits to-day. Why, I asked. He winked in answer and drove off. We had to go back to Boulogne in a street car. Of course we understood later, when we heard about Gallieni and the taxis, said Nellie and added, and that was the battle of the Marne.

Another description of the battle of the Marne when we first came back to Paris was from Alfy Maurer. I was sitting, said Alfy at a café and Paris was pale, if you know what I mean, said Alfy, it was like a pale absinthe. Well I was sitting there and then I noticed lots of horses pulling lots of big trucks going slowly by and there were some soldiers with them and on the boxes was written Banque de France. That was the gold going away just like that, said Alfy, before the battle of the Marne.

In those dark days of waiting in England of course a great many things happened. There were a great many people coming and going in the White-heads' home and there was of course plenty of discussion. First there was Lytton Strachey. He lived in a little house not far from Lockridge.

He came one evening to see Mrs. Whitehead. He was a thin sallow man with a silky beard and a faint high voice. We had met him the year before when we had been invited to meet George Moore at the house of Miss Ethel Sands. Gertrude Stein and George Moore, who looked very like a prosperous Mellins Food baby, had not been interested in each other. Lytton Strachey and I talked together about Picasso and the russian ballet.

He came in this evening and he and Mrs. Whitehead discussed the possibility of rescuing Lytton Strachey's sister who was lost in Germany. She suggested that he apply to a certain person who could help him. But, said Lytton Strachey faintly, I have never met him. Yes, said Mrs. Whitehead, but you might write to him and ask to see him. Not, replied Lytton Strachey faintly, if I have never met him.

Another person who turned up during that week was Bertrand Russell.

He came to Lockridge the day North Whitehead left for the front. He was a pacifist and argumentative and although they were very old friends Doctor and Mrs. Whitehead did not think they could bear hearing his views just then. He came and Gertrude Stein, to divert everybody's mind from the burning question of war or peace, introduced the subject of education. This caught Russell and he explained all the weaknesses of the american system of education, particularly their neglect of the study of greek. Gertrude Stein replied that of course England which was an island needed Greece which was or might have been an island. At any rate greek was essentially an island culture, while America needed essentially the culture of a continent which was of necessity latin. This argument fussed Mr. Russell, he became very eloquent. Gertrude Stein then became very earnest and gave a long discourse on the value of greek to the english, aside from its being an island, and the lack of value of greek culture for the americans based upon the psychology of americans as different from the psychology of the english. She grew very eloquent on the disembodied abstract quality of the american character and cited examples, mingling automobiles with Emerson, and all proving that they did not need greek, in a way that fussed Russell more and more and kept everybody occupied until everybody went to bed.

There were many discussions in those days. The bishop, the brother of Doctor Whitehead and his family came to lunch. They all talked constantly about how England had come into the war to save Belgium. At last my nerves could bear it no longer and I blurted out, why do you say that, why do you not say that you are fighting for England, I do not consider it a disgrace to fight for one's country.

Mrs. Bishop, the bishop's wife was very funny on this occasion. She said solemnly to Gertrude Stein, Miss Stein you are I understand an important person in Paris. I think it would come very well from a neutral like yourself to suggest to the french government that they give us Pondichéry. It would be very useful to us. Gertrude Stein replied politely that to her great regret her importance such as it was was among painters and writers and not with politicians. But that, said Mrs. Bishop, would make no difference. You should I think suggest to the french government that they give us

Pondichéry. After lunch Gertrude Stein said to me under her breath, where the hell is Pondichéry.

Gertrude Stein used to get furious when the english all talked about german organisation. She used to insist that the germans had no organisation, they had method but no organisation. Don't you understand the difference, she used to say angrily, any two americans, any twenty americans, any millions of americans can organise themselves to do something but germans cannot organise themselves to do anything, they can formulate a method and this method can be put upon them but that isn't organisation. The germans, she used to insist, are not modern, they are a backward people who have made a method of what we conceive as organisation, can't you see. They cannot therefore possibly win this war because they are not modern.

Then another thing that used to annoy us dreadfully was the english statement that the germans in America would turn America against the allies. Don't be silly, Gertrude Stein used to say to any and all of them, if you do not realise that the fundamental sympathy in America is with France and England and could never be with a mediaeval country like Germany, you cannot understand America. We are republican, she used to say with energy, profoundly intensely and completely a republic and a republic can have everything in common with France and a great deal in common with England but whatever its form of government nothing in common with Germany. How often I have heard her then and since explain that americans are republicans living in a republic which is so much a republic that it could never be anything else.

The long summer wore on. It was beautiful weather and beautiful country, and Doctor Whitehead and Gertrude Stein never ceased wandering around in it and talking about all things.

From time to time we went to London. We went regularly to Cook's office to know when we might go back to Paris and they always answered not yet. Gertrude Stein went to see John Lane. He was terribly upset. He was passionately patriotic. He said of course he was doing nothing at present but publishing war-books but soon very soon things would be different or perhaps the war would be over.

Gertrude Stein's cousin and my father sent us money by the United States cruiser Tennessee. We went to get it. We were each one put on the scale and our heights measured and then they gave the money to us. How, said we to one another, can a cousin who has not seen you in ten years and a father who has not seen me for six years possibly know our heights and our weights. It had always been a puzzle. Four years ago Gertrude Stein's cousin came to Paris and the first thing she said to him was, Julian how did you know my weight and height when you sent me money by the Tennessee. Did I know it, he said. Well, she said, at any rate they had written it down that you did. I cannot remember of course, he said, but if any one were to ask me now I would naturally send to Washington for a copy of your passport and I probably did that then. And so was the mystery solved.

We also had to go to the american embassy to get temporary passports to go back to Paris. We had no papers, nobody had any papers in those days. Gertrude Stein as a matter of fact had what they called in Paris a papier de matriculation which stated that she was an american and a french resident.

The embassy was very full of not very american looking citizens waiting their turn. Finally we were ushered in to a very tired looking young american. Gertrude Stein remarked upon the number of not very american looking citizens that were waiting. The young american sighed. They are easier, he said, because they have papers, it is only the native born american who has no papers. Well what do you do about them, asked Gertrude Stein. We guess, he said, and we hope we guess right. And now, said he, will you take the oath. Oh dear, he said, I have said it so often I have forgotten it.

By the fifteenth of October Cook's said we could go back to Paris. Mrs. Whitehead was to go with us. North, her son, had left without an overcoat, and she had secured one and she was afraid he would not get it until much later if she sent it the ordinary way. She arranged to go to Paris and deliver it to him herself or find some one who would take it to him directly. She had papers from the war office and Kitchener and we started.

I remember the leaving London very little, I cannot even remember whether it was day-light or not but it must have been because when we were on the channel boat it was daylight. The boat was crowded. There were quantities of belgian soldiers and officers escaped from Antwerp, all with tired eyes. It was our first experience of the tired but watchful eyes of soldiers. We finally were able to arrange a seat for Mrs. Whitehead who had been ill and soon we were in France. Mrs. Whitehead's papers were so overpowering that there were no delays and soon we were in the train and about ten o'clock at night we were in Paris. We took a taxi and drove through Paris, beautiful and unviolated, to the rue de Fleurus. We were once more at home.

Everybody who had seemed so far away came to see us. Alfy Maurer described being on the Marne at his favourite village, he always fished the Marne, and the mobilisation locomotive coming and the germans were coming and he was so frightened and he tried to get a conveyance and finally after terrific efforts he succeeded and got back to Paris. As he left Gertrude Stein went with him to the door and came back smiling. Mrs. Whitehead said with some constraint, Gertrude you have always spoken so warmly of Alfy Maurer but how can you like a man who shows himself not only selfish but a coward and at a time like this. He thought only of saving himself and he after all was a neutral. Gertrude Stein burst out laughing. You foolish woman, she said, didn't you understand, of course Alfy had his girl with him and he was scared to death lest she should fall into the hands of the germans.

There were not many people in Paris just then and we liked it and we wandered around Paris and it was so nice to be there, wonderfully nice. Soon Mrs. Whitehead found means of sending her son's coat to him and went back to England and we settled down for the winter.

Gertrude Stein sent copies of her manuscripts to friends in New York to keep for her. We hoped that all danger was over but still it seemed better to do so and there were Zeppelins to come. London had been completely darkened at night before we left. Paris continued to have its usual street lights until January.

How it all happened I do not at all remember but it was through Carl Van Vechten and had something to do with the Nortons, but at any rate there was a letter from Donald Evans proposing to publish three manuscripts to make a small book and would Gertrude Stein suggest a title for them. Of these three manuscripts two had been written during our first trip into Spain and Food, Rooms etcetera, immediately on our return. They were the beginning, as Gertrude Stein would say, of mixing the outside with the inside. Hitherto she had been concerned with seriousness and the inside of things, in these studies she began to describe the inside as seen from the outside. She was awfully pleased at the idea of these three things being published, and immediately consented, and suggested the title of Tender Buttons. Donald Evans called his firm the Claire Marie and he sent over a contract just like any other contract. We took it for granted that there was a Claire Marie but there evidently was not. There were printed of this edition I forget whether it was seven hundred and fifty or a thousand copies but at any rate it was a very charming little book and Gertrude Stein was enormously pleased, and it, as every one knows, had an enormous influence on all young writers and started off columnists in the newspapers of the whole country on their long campaign of ridicule. I must say that when the columnists are really funny, and they quite often are, Gertrude Stein chuckles and reads them aloud to me.

In the meantime the dreary winter of fourteen and fifteen went on. One night, I imagine it must have been about the end of January, I had as was and is my habit gone to bed very early, and Gertrude Stein was down in the studio working, as was her habit. Suddenly I heard her call me gently. What is it, I said. Oh nothing, said she, but perhaps if you don't mind putting on something warm and coming downstairs I think perhaps it would be better. What is it, I said, a revolution. The concierges and the wives of the concierges were all always talking about a revolution. The french are so accustomed to revolutions, they have had so many, that when anything happens they immediately think and say, revolution. Indeed Gertrude Stein once said rather impatiently to some french soldiers when they said something about a revolution, you are silly, you have had one perfectly good revolution and several not quite so good ones; for an intelligent people it seems to me foolish to be always thinking of repeating yourselves. They looked very sheepish and said, bien sûr mademoiselle, in other words, sure you're right.

Well I too said when she woke me, is it a revolution and are there soldiers. No, she said, not exactly. Well what is it, said I impatiently. I don't quite know, she answered, but there has been an alarm. Anyway you had better come. I started to turn on the light. No, she said, you had better not. Give me your hand and I will get you down and you can go to sleep down stairs on the couch. I came. It was very dark. I sat down on the couch and then I said, I'm sure I don't know what is the matter with me but my knees are knocking together. Gertrude Stein burst out laughing, wait a minute, I will get you a blanket, she said. No don't leave me, I said. She managed to find something to cover me and then there was a loud boom, then several more. It was a soft noise and then there was the sound of horns blowing in the streets and then we knew it was all over. We lighted the lights and went to bed.

I must say I would not have believed it was true that knees knocked together as described in poetry and prose if it had not happened to me.

The next time there was a Zeppelin alarm and it was not very long after this first one, Picasso and Eve were dining with us. By this time we knew that the two-story building of the atelier was no more protection than the roof of the little pavillion under which we slept and the concierge had suggested that we should go into her room where at least we would have six stories over us. Eve was not very well these days and fearful so we all went into the concierge's room. Even Jeanne Poule the Breton servant who had succeeded Hélène, came too. Jeanne soon was bored with this precaution and so in spite of all remonstrance, she went back to her kitchen, lit her light, in spite of the regulations, and proceeded to wash the dishes. We soon too got bored with the concierge's loge and went back to the atelier. We put a candle under the table so that it would not make much light, Eve and I tried to sleep and Picasso and Gertrude Stein talked until two in the morning when the all's clear sounded and they went home.

Picasso and Eve were living these days on the rue Schœlcher in a rather sumptuous studio apartment that looked over the cemetery. It was not very gay. The only excitement were the letters from Guillaume Apollinaire who was falling off of horses in the endeavour to become an artilleryman. The only other intimates at that time were a russian whom they called G. Apostrophe and his sister the baronne. They bought all the Rousseaus that were in Rousseau's atelier when he died. They had an apartment in the boulevard Raspail above Victor Hugo's tree and they were not unamusing. Picasso learnt the russian alphabet from them and began putting it into some of his pictures.

It was not a very cheerful winter. People came in and out, new ones and old ones. Ellen La Motte turned up, she was very heroic but gun shy. She wanted to go to Serbia and Emily Chadbourne wanted to go with her but they did not go.

Gertrude Stein wrote a little novelette about this event.

Ellen La Motte collected a set of souvenirs of the war for her cousin Dupont de Nemours. The stories of how she got them were diverting. Everybody brought you souvenirs in those days, steel arrows that pierced horses' heads, pieces of shell, ink-wells made out of pieces of shell, helmets, some one even offered us a piece of a Zeppelin or an aeroplane, I forget which, but we declined. It was a strange winter and nothing and everything happened. If I remember rightly it was at this time that some one, I imagine it was Apollinaire on leave, gave a concert and a reading of Blaise Cendrars' poems. It was then that I first heard mentioned and first heard the music of Erik Satie. I remember this took place in some one's atelier and the place was crowded. It was in these days too that the friendship between Gertrude Stein and Juan Gris began. He was living in the rue Ravignan in the studio where Salmon had been shut up when he ate my yellow fantaisie.

We used to go there quite often. Juan was having a hard time, no one was buying pictures and the french artists were not in want because they were at the front and their wives or their mistresses if they had been together a certain number of years were receiving an allowance. There was one bad case, Herbin, a nice little man but so tiny that the army dismissed him. He said ruefully the pack he had to carry weighed as much as he did and it was

no use, he could not manage it. He was returned home inapt for service and he came near starving. I don't know who told us about him, he was one of the early simple earnest cubists. Luckily Gertrude Stein succeeded in interesting Roger Fry. Roger Fry took him and his painting over to England where he made and I imagine still has a considerable reputation.

Juan Gris' case was more difficult. Juan was in those days a tormented and not particularly sympathetic character. He was very melancholy and effusive and as always clear sighted and intellectual. He was at that time painting almost entirely in black and white and his pictures were very sombre. Kahnweiler who had befriended him was an exile in Switzerland, Juan's sister in Spain was able to help him only a little. His situation was desperate.

It was just at this time that the picture dealer who afterwards, as the expert in the Kahnweiler sale said he was going to kill cubism, undertook to save cubism and he made contracts with all the cubists who were still free to paint. Among them was Juan Gris and for the moment he was saved.

As soon as we were back in Paris we went to see Mildred Aldrich. She was within the military area so we imagined we would have to have a special permit to go and see her. We went to the police station of our quarter and asked them what we should do. He said what papers have you. We have american passports, french matriculation papers, said Gertrude Stein taking out a pocket full. He looked at them all and said and what is this, of another yellow paper. That, said Gertrude Stein, is a receipt from my bank for the money I have just deposited. I think, said he solemnly, I would take that along too. I think, he added, with all those you will not have any trouble.

We did not as a matter of fact have to show any one any papers. We stayed with Mildred several days.

She was much the most cheerful person we knew that winter. She had been through the battle of the Marne, she had had the Uhlans in the woods below her, she had watched the battle going on below her and she had become part of the country-side. We teased her and told her she was beginning to look like a french peasant and she did, in a funny kind of way,

the friendship between gertrude Stein
and Juan Gris began.

born and bred new englander that she was. It was always astonishing that the inside of her little french peasant house with french furniture, french paint and a french servant and even a french poodle, looked completely american. We saw her several times that winter.

At last the spring came and we were ready to go away for a bit. Our friend William Cook after nursing a while in the american hospital for french wounded had gone again to Palma de Mallorca. Cook who had always earned his living by painting was finding it difficult to get on and he had retired to Palma where in those days when the spanish exchange was very low one lived extremely well for a few francs a day.

We decided we would go to Palma too and forget the war a little. We had only the temporary passports that had been given to us in London so we went to the embassy to get permanent ones with which we might go to Spain. We were first interviewed by a kindly old gentleman most evidently not in the diplomatic service. Impossible, he said, why, said he, look at me, I have lived in Paris for forty years and come of a long line of americans and I have no passport. No, he said, you can have a passport to go to America or you can stay in France without a passport. Gertrude Stein insisted upon seeing one of the secretaries of the embassy. We saw a flushed reddish-headed one. He told us exactly the same thing. Gertrude Stein listened quietly. She then said, but so and so who is exactly in my position, a native born american, has lived the same length of time in Europe, is a writer and has no intention of returning to America at present, has just received a regular passport from your department. I think, said the young man still more flushed, there must be some error. It is very simple, replied Gertrude Stein, to verify it by looking the matter up in your records. He disappeared and presently came back and said, yes you are quite correct but you see it was a very special case. There can be, said Gertrude Stein severely, no privilege extended to one american citizen which is not to be, given similar circumstances, accorded to any other american citizen. He once more disappeared and came back and said, yes yes now may I go through the preliminaries. He then explained that they had orders to give out as few passports as possible but if any one really wanted one why of course it was quite alright. We got ours in record time.

And we went to Palma thinking to spend only a few weeks but we stayed the winter. First we went to Barcelona. It was extraordinary to see so many men on the streets. I did not imagine there could be so many men left in the world. One's eyes had become so habituated to menless streets, the few men one saw being in uniform and therefore not being men but soldiers, that to see quantities of men walking up and down the Ramblas was bewildering. We sat in the hotel window and looked. I went to bed early and got up early and Gertrude Stein went to bed late and got up late and so in a way we overlapped but there was not a moment when there were not quantities of men going up and down the Ramblas.

We arrived in Palma once again and Cook met us and arranged every thing for us. William Cook could always be depended upon. In those days he was poor but later when he had inherited money and was well to do and Mildred Aldrich had fallen upon very bad ways and Gertrude Stein was not able to help any more, William Cook gave her a blank cheque and said, use that as much as you need for Mildred, you know my mother loved to read her books.

William Cook often disappeared and one knew nothing of him and then when for one reason or another you needed him there he was. He went into the american army later and at that time Gertrude Stein and myself were doing war work for the American Fund for French Wounded and I had often to wake her up very early. She and Cook used to write the most lugubrious letters to each other about the unpleasantness of sunrises met suddenly. Sunrises were, they contended, alright when approached slowly from the night before, but when faced abruptly from the same morning they were awful. It was William Cook too who later on taught Gertrude Stein how to drive a car by teaching her on one of the old battle of the Marne tanks. Cook being hard up had become a taxi driver in Paris, that was in sixteen and Gertrude Stein was to drive a car for the American Fund for French Wounded. So on dark nights they went out beyond the fortifications and the two of them sitting solemnly on the driving seat of one of those old two-cylinder before-the-war Renault taxis, William Cook taught Gertrude Stein how to drive. It was William Cook who inspired the only movie Gertrude Stein ever wrote in english, I have just published it in Operas and Plays in the Plain Edition. The only other one she ever wrote, also in Operas and Plays, many years later and in french, was inspired by her white poodle dog called Basket.

But to come back to Palma de Mallorca. We had been there two summers before and had liked it and we liked it again. A great many americans seem to like it now but in those days Cook and ourselves were the only americans to inhabit the island. There were a few english, about three families there. There was a descendant of one of Nelson's captains, a Mrs. Penfold, a sharp-tongued elderly lady and her husband. It was she who said to young Mark Gilbert, an english boy of sixteen with pacifist tendencies who had at tea at her house refused cake, Mark you are either old enough to fight for your country or young enough to eat cake. Mark ate cake.

There were several french families there, the french consul, Monsieur Marchand with a charming italian wife whom we soon came to know very well. It was he who was very much amused at a story we had to tell him of Morocco. He had been attached to the french residence at Tangiers at the moment the french induced Moulai Hafid the then sultan of Morocco to abdicate. We had been in Tangiers at that time for ten days, it was during that first trip to Spain when so much happened that was important to Gertrude Stein.

We had taken on a guide Mohammed and Mohammed had taken a fancy to us. He became a pleasant companion rather than a guide and we used to take long walks together and he used to take us to see his cousins' wonderfully clean arab middle class homes and drink tea. We enjoyed it all. He also told us all about politics. He had been educated in Moulai Hafid's palace and he knew everything that was happening. He told us just how much money Moulai Hafid would take to abdicate and just when he would be ready to do it. We liked these stories as we liked all Mohammed's stories always ending up with, and when you come back there will be street cars and then we won't have to walk and that will be nice. Later in Spain we read in the papers that it had all happened exactly as Mohammed had said it would and we paid no further attention. Once in talking of our only visit to Morocco we told Monsieur Marchand this story. He said, yes that is diplomacy, probably the only people in the world who were not arabs who knew what the french government wanted so desperately to know were you two and you knew it quite by accident and to you it was of no importance.

Life in Palma was pleasant and so instead of travelling any more that summer we decided to settle down in Palma. We sent for our french servant Jeanne Poule and with the aid of the postman we found a little house on the calle de Dos de Mayo in Terreno, just outside of Palma, and we settled down. We were very content. Instead of spending only the summer we stayed until the following spring.

We had been for some time members of Mudie's Library in London and wherever we went Mudie's Library books came to us. It was at this time that Gertrude Stein read aloud to me all of Queen Victoria's letters and she herself became interested in missionary autobiographies and diaries. There were a great many in Mudie's Library and she read them all.

It was during this stay at Palma de Mallorca that most of the plays afterwards published in Geography and Plays were written. She always says that a certain kind of landscape induces plays and the country around Terreno certainly did.

We had a dog, a mallorcan hound, the hounds slightly crazy, who dance in the moonlight, striped, not all one colour as the spanish hound of the continent. We called this dog Polybe because we were pleased with the articles in the Figaro signed Polybe. Polybe was, as Monsieur Marchand said, like an arab, bon accueil à tout le monde et fidèle à personne. He had an incurable passion for eating filth and nothing would stop him. We muzzled him to see if that would cure him, but this so outraged the russian servant of the english consul that we had to give it up. Then he took to annoying sheep. We even took to quarrelling with Cook about Polybe. Cook had a fox terrier called Marie-Rose and we were convinced that Marie-Rose led Polybe into mischief and then virtuously withdrew and let him take the blame. Cook was convinced that we did not know how to bring up Polybe. Polybe had one nice trait. He would sit in a chair and gently smell large bunches of tube-roses with which I always filled a vase in the centre of the room on the floor. He never tried to eat them, he just gently smelled them. When we left we left Polybe behind us in the care of one of the guardians of the old fortress of Belver. When we saw him a week after he did not know us or his name. Polybe comes into many of the plays Gertrude Stein wrote at that time.

The feelings of the island at that time were very mixed as to the war. The thing that impressed them the most was the amount of money it cost. They could discuss by the hour, how much it cost a year, a month, a week, a day, an hour and even a minute. We used to hear them of a summer evening, five million pesetas, a million pesetas, two million pesetas, good-night, good-night, and know they were busy with their endless calculations of the cost of the war. As most of the men even those of the better middle classes read wrote and ciphered with difficulty and the women not at all, it can be imagined how fascinating and endless a subject the cost of the war was.

One of our neighbours had a german governess and whenever there was a german victory she hung out a german flag. We responded as well as we could, but alas just then there were not many allied victories. The lower classes were strong for the allies. The waiter at the hotel was always looking forward to Spain's entry into the war on the side of the allies. He was certain that the spanish army would be of great aid as it could march longer on less food than any army in the world. The maid at the hotel took great interest in my knitting for the soldiers. She said, of course madame knits very slowly, all ladies do. But, said I hopefully, if I knit for years may I not come to knit quickly, not as quickly as you but quickly. No, said she firmly, ladies knit slowly. As a matter of fact I did come to knit very quickly and could even read and knit quickly at the same time.

We led a pleasant life, we walked a great deal and ate extremely well, and were well amused by our Breton servant.

She was patriotic and always wore the tricolour ribbon around her hat. She once came home very excited. She had just been seeing another french servant and she said, imagine, Marie has just had news that her brother was drowned and has had a civilian funeral. How did that happen, I asked also much excited. Why, said Jeanne, he had not yet been called to the army. It was a great honour to have a brother have a civilian funeral during the war. At any rate it was rare. Jeanne was content with spanish newspapers, she had no trouble reading them, as she said, all the important words were in french.

Jeanne told endless stories of french village life and Gertrude Stein could listen a long time and then all of a sudden she could not listen any more.

Life in Mallorca was pleasant until the attack on Verdun began. Then we all began to be very miserable. We tried to console each other but it was difficult. One of the frenchmen, an engraver who had palsy and in spite of the palsy tried every few months to get the french consul to accept him for the army, used to say we must not worry if Verdun is taken, it is not an entry into France, it is only a moral victory for the germans. But we were all desperately unhappy. I had been so confident and now I had an awful feeling that the war had gotten out of my hands.

In the port of Palma was a german ship called the Fangturm which sold pins and needles to all the Mediterranean ports before the war and further, presumably, because it was a very big steamer. It had been caught in Palma when the war broke out and had never been able to leave. Most of the officers and sailors had gotten away to Barcelona but the big ship remained in the harbour. It looked very rusty and neglected and it was just under our windows. All of a sudden as the attack on Verdun commenced, they began painting the Fangturm. Imagine our feelings. We were all pretty unhappy and this was despair. We told the french consul and he told us and it was awful.

Day by day the news was worse and one whole side of the Fangturm was painted and then they stopped painting. They knew it before we did. Verdun was not going to be taken. Verdun was safe. The germans had given up hoping to take it.

When it was all over we none of us wanted to stay in Mallorca any longer, we all wanted to go home. It was at this time that Cook and Gertrude Stein spent all their time talking about automobiles. They neither of them had ever driven but they were getting very interested. Cook also began to wonder how he was going to earn his living when he got to Paris. His tiny income did for Mallorca but it would not keep him long in Paris. He thought of driving horses for Félix Potin's delivery wagons, he said after all he liked horses better than automobiles. Anyway he went back to Paris and when we got there, we went a longer way, by way of Madrid, he was driving a Paris taxi. Later on he became a trier-out of cars for the Renault works and I can remember how exciting it was when he described how the wind blew out his cheeks when he made eighty kilometres an hour. Then later he joined the american army.

We went home by way of Madrid. There we had a curious experience. We went to the american consul to have our passports visaed. He was a great big flabby man and he had a filipino as an assistant. He looked at our passports, he measured them, weighed them, looked at them upside down and finally said that he supposed they were alright but how could he tell. He then asked the filipino what he thought. The filipino seemed inclined to agree that the consul could not tell. I tell you what you do, he said ingratiatingly, you go to the french consul since you are going to France and you live in Paris and if the french consul says they are alright, why the consul will sign. The consul sagely nodded.

We were furious. It was an awkward position that a french consul, not an american one should decide whether american passports were alright. However there was nothing else to do so we went to the french consul.

When our turn came the man in charge took our passports and looked them over and said to Gertrude Stein, when were you last in Spain. She stopped to think, she never can remember anything when anybody asks her suddenly, and she said she did not remember but she thought it was such and such a date. He said no, and mentioned another year. She said very likely he was right. Then he went on to give all the dates of her various visits to Spain and finally he added a visit when she was still at college when she was in Spain with her brother just after the spanish war. It was all in a way rather frightening to me standing by but Gertrude Stein and the assistant consul seemed to be thoroughly interested in fixing dates. Finally he said, you see I was for many years in the letter of credit department of the Crédit Lyonnais in Madrid and I have a very good memory and I remember, of course I remember you very well. We were all very pleased. He signed the passports and told us to go back and tell our consul to do so also.

At the time we were furious with our consul but now I wonder if it was not an arrangement between the two offices that the american consul should not sign any passport to enter France until the french consul had decided whether its owner was or was not desirable.

We came back to an entirely different Paris. It was no longer gloomy. It was no longer empty. This time we did not settle down, we decided to get into the war. One day we were walking down the rue des Pyramides and there was a ford car being backed up the street by an american girl and on the car it said, American Fund for French Wounded. There, said I, that is what we are going to do. At least, said I to Gertrude Stein, you will drive the car and I will do the rest. We went over and talked to the american girl and then interviewed Mrs. Lathrop, the head of the organisation. She was enthusiastic, she was always enthusiastic and she said, get a car. But where, we asked. From America, she said. But how, we said. Ask somebody, she said, and Gertrude Stein did, she asked her cousin and in a few months the ford car came. In the meanwhile Cook had taught her to drive his taxi.

As I said it was a changed Paris. Everything was changed, and everybody was cheerful.

During our absence Eve had died and Picasso was now living in a little home in Montrouge. We went out to see him. He had a marvellous rose pink silk counterpane on his bed. Where did that come from Pablo, asked Gertrude Stein. Ah ça, said Picasso with much satisfaction, that is a lady. It was a well known chilean society woman who had given it to him. It was a marvel. He was very cheerful. He was constantly coming to the house, bringing Paquerette a girl who was very nice or Irene a very lovely woman who came from the mountains and wanted to be free. He brought Erik Satie and the Princesse de Polignac and Blaise Cendrars.

It was a great pleasure to know Erik Satie. He was from Normandy and very fond of it. Marie Laurencin comes from Normandy, so also does Braque. Once when after the war Satie and Marie Laurencin were at the house for lunch they were delightfully enthusiastic about each other as being normans. Erik Satie liked food and wine and knew a lot about both. We had at that time some very good eau de vie that the husband of Mildred Aldrich's servant had given us and Erik Satie, drinking his glass slowly and with appreciation, told stories of the country in his youth.

Only once in the half dozen times that Erik Satie was at the house did he talk about music. He said that it had always been his opinion and he was glad that it was being recognised that modern french music owed nothing to modern Germany. That after Debussy had led the way french musicians had either followed him or found their own french way.

He told charming stories, usually of Normandy, he had a playful wit which was sometimes very biting. He was a charming dinner-guest. It was many years later that Virgil Thomson, when we first knew him in his tiny room near the Gare Saint-Lazare, played for us the whole of Socrate. It was then that Gertrude Stein really became a Satie enthusiast.

Ellen La Motte and Emily Chadbourne, who had not gone to Serbia, were still in Paris. Ellen La Motte, who was an ex Johns Hopkins nurse, wanted to nurse near the front. She was still gun shy but she did want to nurse at the front, and they met Mary Borden-Turner who was running a hospital at the front and Ellen La Motte did for a few months nurse at the front. After that she and Emily Chadbourne went to China and after that became leaders of the anti-opium campaign.

Mary Borden-Turner had been and was going to be a writer. She was very enthusiastic about the work of Gertrude Stein and travelled with what she had of it and volumes of Flaubert to and from the front. She had taken a house near the Bois and it was heated and during that winter when the rest of us had no coal it was very pleasant going to dinner there and being warm. We liked Turner. He was a captain in the British army and was doing contre-espionage work very successfully. Although married to Mary Borden he did not believe in millionaires. He insisted upon giving his own Christmas party to the women and children in the village in which he

It was a great pleasure to know Erik Satie.

After Debussy had led the way French musicians had

either followed him or found their own French way.

was billeted and he always said that after the war he would be collector of customs for the British in Düsseldorf or go out to Canada and live simply. After all, he used to say to his wife, you are not a millionaire, not a real one. He had british standards of millionairedom. Mary Borden was very Chicago. Gertrude Stein always says that chicagoans spent so much energy losing Chicago that often it is difficult to know what they are. They have to lose the Chicago voice and to do so they do many things. Some lower their voices, some raise them, some get an english accent, some even get a german accent, some drawl, some speak in a very high tense voice, and some go chinese or spanish and do not move the lips. Mary Borden was very Chicago and Gertrude Stein was immensely interested in her and in Chicago.

All this time we were waiting for our ford truck which was on its way and then we waited for its body to be built. We waited a great deal. It was then that Gertrude Stein wrote a great many little war poems, some of them have since been published in the volume Useful Knowledge which has in it only things about America.

Stirred by the publication of Tender Buttons many newspapers had taken up the amusement of imitating Gertrude Stein's work and making fun of it. Life began a series that were called after Gertrude Stein.

Gertrude Stein suddenly one day wrote a letter to Masson who was then editor of Life and said to him that the real Gertrude Stein was as Henry McBride had pointed out funnier in every way than the imitations, not to say much more interesting, and why did they not print the original. To her astonishment she received a very nice letter from Mr. Masson saying that he would be glad to do so. And they did. They printed two things that she sent them, one about Wilson and one longer thing about war work in France. Mr. Masson had more courage than most.

This winter Paris was bitterly cold and there was no coal. We finally had none at all. We closed up the big room and stayed in a little room but at last we had no more coal. The government was giving coal away to the needy but we did not feel justified in sending our servant to stand in line to get it. One afternoon it was bitterly cold, we went out and on a street corner was a policeman and standing with him was a sergeant of police. Gertrude Stein went up to them. Look here, she said to them, what are we to do. I live in a pavillon on the rue de Fleurus and have lived there many years. Oh yes, said they nodding their heads, certainly madame we know you very well. Well, she said, I have no coal not even enough to heat one small room. I do not want to send my servant to get it for nothing, that does not seem right. Now, she said, it is up to you to tell me what to do. The policeman looked at his sergeant and the sergeant nodded. Alright, they said.

We went home. That evening the policeman in civilian clothes turned up with two sacks of coal. We accepted thankfully and asked no questions. The policeman, a stalwart breton became our all in all. He did everything for us, he cleaned our home, he cleaned our chimneys, he got us in and he got us out and on dark nights when Zeppelins came it was comfortable to know that he was somewhere outside.

There were Zeppelin alarms from time to time, but like everything else we had gotten used to them. When they came at dinner time we went on eating and when they came at night Gertrude Stein did not wake me, she said I might as well stay where I was if I was asleep because when asleep it took more than even the siren that they used then to give the signal, to wake me.

Our little ford was almost ready. She was later to be called Auntie after Gertrude Stein's aunt Pauline who always behaved admirably in emergencies and behaved fairly well most times if she was properly flattered.

One day Picasso came in and with him and leaning on his shoulder was a slim elegant youth. It is Jean, announced Pablo, Jean Cocteau and we are leaving for Italy.

Picasso had been excited at the prospect of doing the scenery for a russian ballet, the music to be by Satie, the drama by Jean Cocteau. Everybody was at the war, life in Montparnasse was not very gay, Montrouge with even a faithful servant was not very lively, he too needed a change. He was very lively at the prospect of going to Rome. We all said goodbye and we all went our various ways.

The little ford car was ready. Gertrude Stein had learned to drive a

french car and they all said it was the same. I have never driven any car, but it would appear that it is not the same. We went outside of Paris to get it when it was ready and Gertrude Stein drove it in. Of course the first thing she did was to stop dead on the track between two street cars. Everybody got out and pushed us off the track. The next day when we started off to see what would happen we managed to get as far as the Champs Elysées and once more stopped dead. A crowd shoved us to the side walk and then tried to find out what was the matter. Gertrude Stein cranked, the whole crowd cranked, nothing happened. Finally an old chauffeur said, no gasoline. We said proudly, oh yes at least a gallon, but he insisted on looking and of course there was none. Then the crowd stopped a whole procession of military trucks that were going up the Champs Elysées. They all stopped and a couple of them brought over an immense tank of gasoline and tried to pour it into the little ford. Naturally the process was not successful. Finally getting into a taxi I went to a store in our quarter where they sold brooms and gasoline and where they knew me and I came back with a tin of gasoline and we finally arrived at the Alcazar d'Eté, the then headquarters of the American Fund for French Wounded.

Mrs. Lathrop was waiting for one of the cars to take her to Montmartre. I immediately offered the service of our car and went out and told Gertrude Stein. She quoted Edwin Dodge to me. Once Mabel Dodge's little boy said he would like to fly from the terrace to the lower garden. Do, said Mabel. It is easy, said Edwin Dodge, to be a spartan mother.

However Mrs. Lathrop came and the car went off. I must confess to being terribly nervous until they came back but come back they did.

We had a consultation with Mrs. Lathrop and she sent us off to Perpignan, a region with a good many hospitals that no american organisation had ever visited. We started. We had never been further from Paris than Fontainbleau in the car and it was terribly exciting.

We had a few adventures, we were caught in the snow and I was sure

Tzara came to the house. One day Picasso came in and with him and leaning on his shoulder was a slim elegant youth.

that we were on the wrong road and wanted to turn back. Wrong or right, said Gertrude Stein, we are going on. She could not back the car very successfully and indeed I may say even to this day when she can drive any kind of a car anywhere she still does not back a car very well. She goes forward admirably, she does not go backwards successfully. The only violent discussions that we have had in connection with her driving a car have been on the subject of backing.

On this trip South we picked up our first military god-son. We began the habit then which we kept up all through the war of giving any soldier on the road a lift. We drove by day and we drove by night and in very lonely parts of France and we always stopped and gave a lift to any soldier, and never had we any but the most pleasant experiences with these soldiers. And some of them were as we sometimes found out pretty hard characters. Gertrude Stein once said to a soldier who was doing something for her, they were always doing something for her, whenever there was a soldier or a chauffeur or any kind of a man anywhere, she never did anything for herself, neither changing a tyre, cranking the car or repairing it. Gertrude Stein said to this soldier, but you are tellement gentil, very nice and kind. Madame, said he quite simply, all soldiers are nice and kind.

This faculty of Gertrude Stein of having everybody do anything for her puzzled the other drivers of the organisation. Mrs. Lathrop who used to drive her own car said that nobody did those things for her. It was not only soldiers, a chauffeur would get off the seat of a private car in the place Vendôme and crank Gertrude Stein's old ford for her. Gertrude Stein said that the others looked so efficient, of course nobody would think of doing anything for them. Now as for herself she was not efficient, she was good humoured, she was democratic, one person was as good as another, and she knew what she wanted done. If you are like that she says, anybody will do anything for you. The important thing, she insists, is that you must have deep down as the deepest thing in you a sense of equality. Then anybody will do anything for you.

It was not far from Saulieu that we picked up our first military god-son. He was a butcher in a tiny village not far from Saulieu. Our taking him up was a good example of the democracy of the french army. There were three of them walking along the road. We stopped and said we could take one of them on the step. They were all three going home on leave and walking into the country to their homes from the nearest big town. One was a lieutenant, one was a sergeant and one a soldier. They thanked us and then the lieutenant said to each one of them, how far have you to go. They each one named the distance and then they said, and you my lieutenant, how far have you to go. He told them. Then they all agreed that it was the soldier who had much the longest way to go and so it was his right to have the lift. He touched his cap to his sergeant and officer and got in.

As I say he was our first military god son. We had a great many afterwards and it was quite an undertaking to keep them all going. The duty of a military god-mother was to write a letter as often as she received one and to send a package of comforts or dainties about once in ten days. They liked the packages but they really liked letters even more. And they answered so promptly. It seemed to me, no sooner was my letter written than there was an answer. And then one had to remember all their family histories and once I did a dreadful thing, I mixed my letters and so I asked a soldier whose wife I knew all about and whose mother was dead to remember me to his mother, and the one who had the mother to remember me to his wife. Their return letters were quite mournful. They each explained that I had made a mistake and I could see that they had been deeply wounded by my error.

The most delightful god-son we ever had was one we took on in Nîmes. One day when we were in the town I dropped my purse. I did not notice the loss until we returned to the hotel and then I was rather bothered as there had been a good deal of money in it. While we were eating our dinner the waiter said some one wanted to see us. We went out and there was a man holding the purse in his hand. He said he had picked it up in the street and as soon as his work was over had come to the hotel to give it to us. There was a card of mine in the purse and he took it for granted that a stranger would be at the hotel, beside by that time we were very well known in Nîmes. I naturally offered him a considerable reward from the contents of the purse but he said no. He said however that he had a favour to ask. They were refugees from the Marne and his son Abel now seventeen years old had just volunteered and was at present in the garrison at Nîmes, would I be his god-mother. I said I would, and I asked him to tell his son to come to see me his first free evening. The next evening the youngest, the sweetest, the smallest soldier imaginable came in. It was Abel.

We became very attached to Abel. I always remember his first letter from the front. He began by saying that he was really not very much surprised by anything at the front, it was exactly as it had been described to him and as he had imagined it, except that there being no tables one was compelled to write upon one's knees.

The next time we saw Abel he was wearing the red fourragère, his regiment as a whole had been decorated with the legion of honour and we were very proud of our filleul. Still later when we went into Alsace with the french army, after the armistice, we had Abel come and stay with us a few days and a proud boy he was when he climbed to the top of the Strasbourg cathedral.

When we finally returned to Paris, Abel came and stayed with us a week. We took him to see everything and he said solemnly at the end of his first day, I think all that was worth fighting for. Paris in the evening however frightened him and we always had to get somebody to go out with him. The front had not been scareful but Paris at night was.

Some time later he wrote and said that the family were moving into a different department and he gave me his new address. By some error the address did not reach him and we lost him.

We did finally arrive at Perpignan and began visiting hospitals and giving away our stores and sending word to headquarters if we thought they needed more than we had. At first it was a little difficult but soon we were doing all we were to do very well. We were also given quantities of comfort-bags and distributing these was a perpetual delight, it was like a continuous Christmas. We always had permission from the head of the hospital to distribute these to the soldiers themselves which was in itself a great pleasure but also it enabled us to get the soldiers to immediately write postal cards of thanks and these we used to send off in batches to Mrs. Lathrop who sent them to America to the people who had sent the comfort-bags. And so everybody was pleased.

Then there was the question of gasoline. The American Fund for French Wounded had an order from the french government giving them the privilege of buying gasoline. But there was no gasoline to buy. The french army had plenty of it and were ready to give it to us but they could not sell it and we were privileged to buy it but not to receive it for nothing. It was necessary to interview the officer in command of the commissary department.

Gertrude Stein was perfectly ready to drive the car anywhere, to crank the car as often as there was nobody else to do it, to repair the car, I must say she was very good at it, even if she was not ready to take it all down and put it back again for practice as I wanted her to do in the beginning, she was even resigned to getting up in the morning, but she flatly refused to go inside of any office and interview any official. I was officially the delegate and she was officially the driver but I had to go and interview the major.

He was a charming major. The affair was very long drawn out, he sent me here and he sent me there but finally the matter was straightened out. All this time of course he called me Mademoiselle Stein because Gertrude Stein's name was on all the papers that I presented to him, she being the driver. And so now, he said, Mademoiselle Stein, my wife is very anxious to make your acquaintance and she has asked me to ask you to dine with us. I was very confused. I hesitated. But I am not Mademoiselle Stein, I said. He almost jumped out of his chair. What, he shouted, not Mademoiselle Stein. Then who are you. It must be remembered this was war time and Perpignan almost at the spanish frontier. Well, said I, you see Mademoiselle Stein. Where is Mademoiselle Stein, he said. She is downstairs, I said feebly, in the automobile. Well what does all this mean, he said. Well, I said, you see Mademoiselle Stein is the driver and I am the delegate and Mademoiselle Stein has no patience she will not go into offices and wait and interview people and explain, so I do it for her while she sits in the automobile. But what, said he sternly, would you have done if I had asked you to sign something. I would have told you, I said, as I am telling you now. Indeed, he said, let us go downstairs and see this Mademoiselle Stein.

We went downstairs and Gertrude Stein was sitting in the driver's seat of the little ford and he came up to her. They immediately became friends and he renewed his invitation and we went to dinner. We had a good time. Madame Dubois came from Bordeaux, the land of food and wine. And what food above all the soup. It still remains to me the standard of comparison with all the other soups in the world. Sometimes some approach it, a very few have equalled it but none have surpassed it.

Perpignan is not far from Rivesaltes and Rivesaltes is the birthplace of Joffre. It had a little hospital and we got it extra supplies in honour of Papa Joffre. We had also the little ford car showing the red cross and the A.F.F.W. sign and ourselves in it photographed in front of the house in the little street where Joffre was born and had this photograph printed and sent to Mrs. Lathrop. The postal cards were sent to America and sold for the benefit of the fund. In the meantime the U.S. had come into the war and we had some one send us a lot of ribbon with the stars and stripes printed on it and we cut this up and gave it to all the soldiers and they and we were pleased.

Which reminds me of a french peasant. Later in Nîmes we had an american ambulance boy in the car with us and we were out in the country. The boy had gone off to visit a waterfall and I had gone off to see a hospital and Gertrude Stein stayed with the car. She told me when I came back that an old peasant had come up to her and asked her what uniform the young man was wearing. That, she had said proudly, is the uniform of the american army, your new ally. Oh, said the old peasant. And then contemplatively, I ask myself what will we accomplish together, je me demande je me demande qu'est-ce que nous ferons ensemble.

Our work in Perpignan being over we started back to Paris. On the way

Our little ford was almost Ready. She was later to be called Auntie.

everything happened to the car. Perhaps it had been too hot even for a ford car in Perpignan. Perpignan is below sea level near the Mediterranean and it is hot. Gertrude Stein who had always wanted it hot and hotter has never been really enthusiastic about heat after this experience. She said she had been just like a pancake, the heat above and the heat below and cranking a car beside. I do not know how often she used to swear and say, I am going to scrap it, that is all there is about it I am going to scrap it. I encouraged and remonstrated until the car started again.

It was in connection with this that Mrs. Lathrop played a joke on Gertrude Stein. After the war was over we were both decorated by the french government, we received the Reconnaissance Française. They always in giving you a decoration give you a citation telling why you have been given it. The account of our valour was exactly the same, except in my case they said that my devotion was sans relâche, with no abatement, and in her case they did not put in the words sans relâche.

On the way back to Paris we, as I say had everything happen to the car but Gertrude Stein with the aid of an old tramp on the road who pushed and shoved at the critical moments managed to get it to Nevers where we met the first piece of the american army. They were the quartermasters department and the marines, the first contingent to arrive in France. There we first heard what Gertrude Stein calls the sad song of the marines, which tells how everybody else in the american army has at sometime mutinied, but the marines never.

Immediately on entering Nevers, we saw Tarn McGrew, a californian and parisian whom we had known very slightly but he was in uniform and we called for help. He came. We told him our troubles. He said, alright get the car into the garage of the hotel and to-morrow some of the soldiers will put it to rights. We did so.

That evening we spent at Mr. McGrew's request at the Y. M. C. A. and saw for the first time in many years americans just americans, the kind that would not naturally ever have come to Europe. It was quite a thrilling experience. Gertrude Stein of course talked to them all, wanted to know what state and what city they came from, what they did, how old they were and how they liked it. She talked to the french girls who were with the american boys and the french girls told her what they thought of the american boys and the american boys told her all they thought about the french girls.

The next day she spent with California and Iowa in the garage, as she called the two soldiers who were detailed to fix up her car. She was pleased with them when every time there was a terrific noise anywhere, they said solemnly to each other, that french chauffeur is just changing gears. Gertrude Stein, Iowa and California enjoyed themselves so thoroughly that I am sorry to say the car did not last out very well after we left Nevers, but at any rate we did get to Paris.

It was at this time that Gertrude Stein conceived the idea of writing a history of the United States consisting of chapters wherein Iowa differs from Kansas, and wherein Kansas differs from Nebraska etcetera. She did do a little of it which also was printed in the book, Useful Knowledge.

We did not stay in Paris very long. As soon as the car was made over we left for Nîmes, we were to do the three departments the Gard, the Bouches-du-Rhône and the Vaucluse.

We arrived in Nîmes and settled down to a very comfortable life there. We went to see the chief military doctor in the town, Doctor Fabre and through his great kindness and that of his wife we were soon very much at home in Nîmes, but before we began our work there, Doctor Fabre asked a favour of us. There were no automobile ambulances left in Nîmes. At the military hospital was a pharmacist, a captain in the army, who was very ill, certain to die, and wanted to die in his own home. His wife was with him and would sit with him and we were to have no responsibility for him except to drive him home. Of course we said we would and we did.

It had been a long hard ride up into the mountains and it was dark long before we were back. We were still some distance from Nîmes when suddenly on the road we saw a couple of figures. The old ford car's lights did not light up much of anything on the road, and nothing along the side of the road and we did not make out very well who it was. However we stopped as we always did when anybody asked us to give them a lift. One man, he was evidently an officer said, my automobile has broken down and

I must get back to Nîmes. Alright we said, both of you climb into the back, you will find a mattress and things, make yourselves comfortable. We went on to Nîmes. As we came into the city I called through the little window, where do you want to get down, where are you going, a voice replied. To the Hôtel Luxembourg, I said. That will do alright, the voice replied. We arrived in front of the Hôtel Luxembourg and stopped. Here there was plenty of light. We heard a scramble in the back and then a little man, very fierce with the cap and oak leaves of a full general and the legion of honour medal at his throat, appeared before us. He said, I wish to thank you but before I do so I must ask you who you are. We, I replied cheerfully are the delegates of the American Fund for French Wounded and we are for the present stationed at Nîmes. And I, he retorted, am the general who commands here and as I see by your car that you have a french military number you should have reported to me immediately. Should we, I said, I did not know, I am most awfully sorry. It is alright, he said aggressively, if you should ever want or need anything let me know.

We did let him know very shortly because of course there was the eternal gasoline question and he was kindness itself and arranged everything for us.

The little general and his wife came from the north of France and had lost their home and spoke of themselves as refugees. When later the big Bertha began to fire on Paris and one shell hit the Luxembourg gardens very near the rue de Fleurus, I must confess I began to cry and said I did not want to be a miserable refugee. We had been helping a good many of them. Gertrude Stein said, General Frotier's family are refugees and they are not miserable. More miserable than I want to be, I said bitterly.

Soon the american army came to Nîmes. One day Madame Fabre met us and said that her cook had seen some american soldiers. She must have mistaken some english soldiers for them, we said. Not at all, she answered, she is very patriotic. At any rate the american soldiers came, a regiment of them of the S. O. S. the service of supply, how well I remember how they used to say it with the emphasis on the of.

We soon got to know them all well and some of them very well. There was Duncan, a southern boy with such a very marked southern accent that when he was well into a story I was lost. Gertrude Stein whose people all come from Baltimore had no difficulty and they used to shout with laughter together, and all I could understand was that they had killed him as if he was a chicken. The people in Nîmes were as much troubled as I was. A great many of the ladies in Nîmes spoke english very well. There had always been english governesses in Nîmes, and they, the nîmoises had always prided themselves on their knowledge of english but as they said not only could they not understand these americans but these americans could not understand them when they spoke english. I had to admit that it was more or less the same with me.

The soldiers were all Kentucky, South Carolina etcetera and they were hard to understand.

Duncan was a dear. He was supply-sergeant to the camp and when we began to find american soldiers here and there in french hospitals we always took Duncan along to give the american soldier pieces of his lost uniform and white bread. Poor Duncan was miserable because he was not at the front. He had enlisted as far back as the expedition to Mexico and here he was well in the rear and no hope of getting away because he was one of the few who understood the complicated system of army book-keeping and his officers would not recommend him for the front. I will go, he used to say bitterly, they can bust me if they like I will go. But as we told him there were plenty of A.W.O.L. absent without leave the south was full of them, we were always meeting them and they would say, say any military police around here. Duncan was not made for that life. Poor Duncan. Two days before the armistice, he came in to see us and he was drunk and bitter. He was usually a sober boy but to go back and face his family never having been to the front was too awful. He was with us in a little sitting-room and in the front room were some of his officers and it would not do for them to see him in that state and it was time for him to get back to the camp. He had fallen half asleep with his head on the table. Duncan, said Gertrude Stein sharply, yes, he said. She said to him, listen Duncan. Miss Toklas is going to stand up, you stand up too and fix your eyes right on the back of her head, do you understand. Yes, he said. Well then she will start to walk and you follow her and don't you for a moment move your eyes from the back of her head until you are in my car. Yes, he said. And he did and Gertrude Stein drove him to the camp.

Dear Duncan. It was he who was all excited by the news that the americans had taken forty villages at Saint-Mihiel. He was to go with us that afternoon to Avignon to deliver some cases. He was sitting very straight on the step and all of a sudden his eye was caught by some houses. What are they, he asked. Oh just a village, Gertrude Stein said. In a minute there were some more houses. And what are those houses, he asked. Oh just a village. He fell very silent and he looked at the landscape as he had never looked at it before. Suddenly with a deep sigh, forty villages ain't so much, he said.

We did enjoy the life with these doughboys. I would like to tell nothing but doughboy stories. They all got on amazingly well with the french. They worked together in the repair sheds of the railroad. The only thing that bothered the americans were the long hours. They worked too concentratedly to keep it up so long. Finally an arrangement was made that they should have their work to do in their hours and the french in theirs. There was a great deal of friendly rivalry. The american boys did not see the use of putting so much finish on work that was to be shot up so soon again, the french said they could not complete work without finish. But both lots thoroughly liked each other.

Gertrude Stein always said the war was so much better than just going to America. Here you were with America in a kind of way that if you only went to America you could not possibly be. Every now and then one of the american soldiers would get into the hospital at Nîmes and as Doctor Fabre knew that Gertrude Stein had had a medical education he always wanted her present with the doughboy on these occasions. One of them fell off the train. He did not believe that the little french trains could go fast but they did, fast enough to kill him.

This was a tremendous occasion. Gertrude Stein in company with the wife of the préfet, the governmental head of the department and the wife of the general were the chief mourners. Duncan and two others blew on the bugle and everybody made speeches. The Protestant pastor asked Gertrude Stein about the dead man and his virtues and she asked the doughboys. It was difficult to find any virtue. Apparently he had been a fairly hard citizen. But can't you tell me something good about him, she said despairingly. Finally Taylor, one of his friends, looked up solemnly and said, I tell you he had a heart as big as a washtub.

I often wonder, I have often wondered if any of all these doughboys who knew Gertrude Stein so well in those days ever connected her with the Gertrude Stein of the newspapers.

We led a very busy life. There were all the americans, there were a great many in the small hospitals round about as well as in the regiment in Nîmes and we had to find them all and be good to them, then there were all the french in the hospitals, we had them to visit as this was really our business, and then later came the spanish grippe and Gertrude Stein and one of the military doctors from Nîmes used to go to all the villages miles around to bring into Nîmes the sick soldiers and officers who had fallen ill in their homes while on leave.

It was during these long trips that she began writing a great deal again. The landscape, the strange life stimulated her. It was then that she began to love the valley of the Rhône, the landscape that of all landscapes means the most to her. We are still here in Bilignin in the valley of the Rhône.

She wrote at that time the poem of The Deserter, printed almost immediately in Vanity Fair. Henry McBride had interested Crowninshield in her work.

One day when we were in Avignon we met Braque. Braque had been badly wounded in the head and had come to Sorgues near Avignon to recover. It was there that he had been staying when the mobilisation orders came to him. It was awfully pleasant seeing the Braques again. Picasso had just written to Gertrude Stein announcing his marriage to a jeune fille, a real young lady, and he had sent Gertrude Stein a wedding present of a lovely little painting and a photograph of a painting of his wife.

That lovely little painting he copied for me many years later on tapestry canvas and I embroidered it and that was the beginning of my tapestrying.

I did not think it possible to ask him to draw me something to work but when I told Gertrude Stein she said, alright, I'll manage. And so one day when he was at the house she said, Pablo, Alice wants to make a tapestry of that little picture and I said I would trace it for her. He looked at her with kindly contempt, if it is done by anybody, he said, it will be done by me. Well, said Gertrude Stein, producing a piece of tapestry canvas, go to it, and he did. And I have been making tapestry of his drawings ever since and they are very successful and go marvellously with old chairs. I have done two small Louis fifteenth chairs in this way. He is kind enough now to make me drawings on my working canvas and to colour them for me.

Braque also told us that Apollinaire too had married a real young lady. We gossiped a great deal together. But after all there was little news to tell.

Time went on, we were very busy and then came the armistice. We were the first to bring the news to many small villages. The french soldiers in the hospitals were relieved rather than glad. They seemed not to feel that it was going to be such a lasting peace. I remember one of them saying to Gertrude Stein when she said to him, well here is peace, at least for twenty years, he said.

The next morning we had a telegram from Mrs. Lathrop. Come at once want you to go with the french armies to Alsace. We did not stop on the way. We made it in a day. Very shortly after we left for Alsace.

We left for Alsace and on the road had our first and only accident. The roads were frightful, mud, ruts, snow, slush, and covered with the french armies going into Alsace. As we passed, two horses dragging an army kitchen kicked out of line and hit our ford, the mud-guard came off and the tool-chest, and worst of all the triangle of the steering gear was badly bent. The army picked up our tools and our mud-guard but there was nothing to do about the bent triangle. We went on, the car wandering all over the muddy road, up hill and down hill, and Gertrude Stein sticking to the wheel. Finally after about forty kilometres, we saw on the road some american ambulance men. Where can we get our car fixed. Just a little farther, they said. We went a little farther and there found an american ambulance outfit. They had no extra mud-guard but they could give us a new triangle. I told our troubles to the sergeant, he grunted and said a word in an undertone to a mechanic. Then turning to us he said gruffly, run-her-in. Then the mechanic took off his tunic and threw it over the radiator. As Gertrude Stein said when any american did that the car was his.

We had never realised before what mud-guards were for but by the time we arrived in Nancy we knew. The french military repair shop fitted us out with a new mud-guard and tool-chest and we went on our way.

Soon we came to the battle-fields and the lines of trenches of both sides. To any one who did not see it as it was then it is impossible to imagine it. It was not terrifying it was strange. We were used to ruined houses and even ruined towns but this was different. It was a landscape. And it belonged to no country.

I remember hearing a french nurse once say and the only thing she did say of the front was, c'est un paysage passionant, an absorbing landscape. And that was what it was as we saw it. It was strange. Camouflage, huts, everything was there. It was wet and dark and there were a few people, one did not know whether they were chinamen or europeans. Our fanbelt had stopped working. A staff car stopped and fixed it with a hairpin, we still wore hairpins.

Another thing that interested us enormously was how different the camouflage of the french looked from the camouflage of the germans, and then once we came across some very very neat camouflage and it was american. The idea was the same but as after all it was different nationalities who did it the difference was inevitable. The colour schemes were different, the designs were different, the way of placing them was different, it made plain the whole theory of art and its inevitability.

Finally we came to Strasbourg and then went on to Mulhouse. Here we stayed until well into May.

Our business in Alsace was not hospitals but refugees. The inhabitants were returning to their ruined homes all over the devastated country and it was the aim of the A.F.F.W. to give a pair of blankets, underclothing and children's and babies' woollen stockings and babies' booties to every family. There was a legend that the quantity of babies' booties sent to us came from the gifts sent to Mrs. Wilson who was supposed at that time to be about to produce a little Wilson. There were a great many babies' booties but not too many for Alsace.

Our headquarters was the assembly-room of one of the big school-buildings in Mulhouse. The german school teachers had disappeared and french school teachers who happened to be in the army had been put in temporarily to teach. The head of our school was in despair, not about the docility of his pupils nor their desire to learn french, but on account of their clothes. French children are all always neatly clothed. There is no such thing as a ragged child, even orphans farmed out in country villages are neatly dressed, just as all french women are neat, even the poor and the aged. They may not always be clean but they are always neat. From this standpoint the parti-coloured rags of even the comparatively prosperous alsatian children were deplorable and the french schoolmasters suffered. We did our best to help him out with black children's aprons but these did not go far, beside we had to keep them for the refugees.

We came to know Alsace and the alsatians very well, all kinds of them. They were astonished at the simplicity with which the french army and french soldiers took care of themselves. They had not been accustomed to that in the german army. On the other hand the french soldiers were rather mistrustful of the alsatians who were too anxious to be french and yet were not french. They are not frank, the french soldiers said. And it is quite true. The french whatever else they may be are frank. They are very polite, they are very adroit but sooner or later they always tell you the truth. The alsatians are not adroit, they are not polite and they do not inevitably tell you the truth. Perhaps with renewed contact with the french they will learn these things.

We distributed. We went into all the devastated villages. We usually asked the priest to help us with the distribution. One priest who gave us a great deal of good advice and with whom we became very friendly had only one large room left in his house. Without any screens or partitions he had made himself three rooms, the first third had his parlour furniture, the second third his dining room furniture and the last third his bedroom furniture. When we lunched with him and we lunched well and his alsatian wines were very good, he received us in his parlour, he then excused himself and withdrew into his bedroom to wash his hands, and then he invited us very formally to come into the dining room, it was like an old-fashioned stage setting.

We distributed, we drove around in the snow we talked to everybody and everybody talked to us and by the end of May it was all over and we decided to leave.

We went home by way of Metz, Verdun and Mildred Aldrich.

We once more returned to a changed Paris. We were restless. Gertrude Stein began to work very hard, it was at this time that she wrote her Accents in Alsace and other political plays, the last plays in Geography and Plays. We were still in the shadow of war work and we went on doing some of it, visiting hospitals and seeing the soldiers left in them, now pretty well neglected by everybody. We had spent a great deal of our money during the war and we were economising, servants were difficult to get if not impossible, prices were high. We settled down for the moment with a femme de ménage for only a few hours a day. I used to say Gertrude Stein was the chauffeur and I was the cook. We used to go over early in the morning to the public markets and get in our provisions. It was a confused world.

Jessie Whitehead had come over with the peace commission as secretary to one of the delegations and of course we were very interested in knowing all about the peace. It was then that Gertrude Stein described one of the young men of the peace commission who was holding forth, as one who knew all about the war, he had been here ever since the peace. Gertrude Stein's cousins came over, everybody came over, everybody was dissatisfied and every one was restless. It was a restless and disturbed world.

Gertrude Stein and Picasso quarrelled. They neither of them ever quite knew about what. Anyway they did not see each other for a year and then they met by accident at a party at Adrienne Monnier's. Picasso said, how do you do to her and said something about her coming to see him. No I will not, she answered gloomily. Picasso came to me and said, Gertrude says she won't come to see me, does she mean it. I am afraid if she says it she means it. They did not see each other for another year and in the meantime Picasso's little boy was born and Max Jacob was complaining that he had not been named god-father. A very little while after this we were somewhere at some picture gallery and Picasso came up and put his hand on Gertrude Stein's shoulder and said, oh hell, let's be friends. Sure, said Gertrude Stein and they embraced. When can I come to see you, said Picasso, let's see, said Gertrude Stein, I am afraid we are busy but come to dinner the end of the week. Nonsense, said Picasso, we are coming to dinner to-morrow, and they came.

It was a changed Paris. Guillaume Apollinaire was dead. We saw a tremendous number of people but none of them as far as I can remember that we had ever known before. Paris was crowded. As Clive Bell remarked, they say that an awful lot of people were killed in the war but it seems to me that an extraordinary large number of grown men and women have suddenly been born.

As I say we were restless and we were economical and all day and all evening we were seeing people and at last there was the defile, the procession under the Arc de Triomphe, of the allies.

The members of the American Fund for French Wounded were to have seats on the benches that were put up the length of the Champs Elysées but quite rightly the people of Paris objected as these seats would make it impossible for them to see the parade and so Clemenceau promptly had them taken down. Luckily for us Jessie Whitehead's room in her hotel looked right over the Arc de Triomphe and she asked us to come to it to see the parade. We accepted gladly. It was a wonderful day.

We got up at sunrise, as later it would have been impossible to cross Paris in a car. This was one of the last trips Auntie made. By this time the red cross was painted off it but it was still a truck. Very shortly after it went its honourable way and was succeeded by Godiva, a two-seated runabout, also a little ford. She was called Godiva because she had come naked into the world and each of our friends gave us something with which to bedeck her.

Auntie then was making practically her last trip. We left her near the river and walked up to the hotel. Everybody was on the streets, men, women, children, soldiers, priests, nuns, we saw two nuns being helped into a tree from which they would be able to see. And we ourselves were admirably placed and we saw perfectly.

We saw it all, we saw first the few wounded from the Invalides in their wheeling chairs wheeling themselves. It is an old french custom that a military procession should always be preceded by the veterans from the Invalides. They all marched past through the Arc de Triomphe. Gertrude Stein remembered that when as a child she used to swing on the chains that were around the Arc de Triomphe her governess had told her that no one must walk underneath since the german armies had marched under it after 1870. And now everybody except the germans were passing through.

All the nations marched differently, some slowly, some quickly, the french carry their flags the best of all, Pershing and his officer carrying the flag behind him were perhaps the most perfectly spaced. It was this scene that Gertrude Stein described in the movie she wrote about this time that I have published in Operas and Plays in the Plain Edition,

However it all finally came to an end. We wandered up and we wandered down the Champs Elysées and the war was over and the piles of captured cannon that had made two pyramids were being taken away and peace was upon us.

VII.

After the War

1919-1932

WE WERE, IN these days as I look back at them, constantly seeing people.

It is a confused memory those first years after the war and very difficult to think back and remember what happened before or after something else. Picasso once said, I have already told, when Gertrude Stein and he were discussing dates, you forget that when we were young an awful lot happened in a year. During the years just after the war as I look in order to refresh my memory over the bibliography of Gertrude Stein's work, I am astonished when I realise how many things happened in a year. Perhaps we were not so young then but there were a great many young in the world and perhaps that comes to the same thing.

The old crowd had disappeared. Matisse was now permanently in Nice and in any case although Gertrude Stein and he were perfectly good friends when they met, they practically never met. This was the time when Gertrude Stein and Picasso were not seeing each other. They always talked with the tenderest friendship about each other to any one who had known them both but they did not see each other. Guillaume Apollinaire was dead. Braque and his wife we saw from time to time, he and Picasso by this time were fairly bitterly on the outs. I remember one evening Man Ray brought a photograph that he had made of Picasso to the house and Braque happened to be there. The photograph was being passed around and when it came to Braque he looked at it and said, I ought to know who that gentleman is, je dois connaître ce monsieur. It was a period this and a very considerable time afterward that Gertrude Stein celebrated under the title, Of Having for a Long Time Not Continued to be Friends.

Juan Gris was ill and discouraged. He had been very ill and was never really well again. Privation and discouragement had had their effect. Kahnweiler came back to Paris fairly early after the war but all his old crowd with the exception of Juan were too successful to have need of him. Mildred Aldrich had had her tremendous success with the Hilltop on the Marne, in Mildred's way she had spent royally all she had earned royally and was now still spending and enjoying it although getting a little uneasy. We used to go out and see her about once a month, in fact all the rest of her life we always managed to get out to see her regularly. Even in the days of her very greatest glory she loved a visit from Gertrude Stein better than a visit from anybody else. In fact it was largely to please Mildred that Gertrude Stein tried to get the Atlantic Monthly to print something of hers. Mildred always felt and said that it would be a blue ribbon if the Atlantic Monthly consented, which of course it never did. Another thing used to annoy Mildred dreadfully. Gertrude Stein's name was never in Who's Who in America. As a matter of fact it was in english authors' bibliographies before it ever entered an american one. This troubled Mildred very much. I hate to look at Who's Who in America, she said to me, when I see all those insignificant people and Gertrude's name not in. And then she would say, I know it's alright but I wish Gertrude were not so outlawed. Poor Mildred. And now just this year for reasons best known to themselves Who's Who has added Gertrude Stein's name to their list. The Atlantic Monthly needless to say has not.

The Atlantic Monthly story is rather funny.

As I said Gertrude Stein sent the Atlantic Monthly some manuscripts, not with any hope of their accepting them, but if by any miracle they should, she would be pleased and Mildred delighted. An answer came back, a long and rather argumentative answer from the editorial office. Gertrude Stein thinking that some Boston woman in the editorial office had written, answered the arguments lengthily to Miss Ellen Sedgwick. She received an almost immediate answer meeting all her arguments and at the same time admitting that the matter was not without interest but that of course Atlantic Monthly readers could not be affronted by having these manuscripts presented in the review, but it might be possible to have them introduced by somebody in the part of the magazine, if I remember rightly, called the Contributors' Club. The letter ended by saying that the writer was not Ellen but Ellery Sedgwick.

Gertrude Stein of course was delighted with its being Ellery and not Ellen and accepted being printed in the Contributors' Club, but equally of course the manuscripts did not appear even in the part called Contributors' Club.

We began to meet new people all the time.

Some one told us, I have forgotten who, that an american woman had started a lending library of english books in our quarter. We had in those days of economy given up Mudie's, but there was the American Library which supplied us a little, but Gertrude Stein wanted more. We investigated and we found Sylvia Beach. Sylvia Beach was very enthusiastic about Gertrude Stein and they became friends. She was Sylvia Beach's first annual subscriber and Sylvia Beach was proportionately proud and grateful. Her little place was in a little street near the Ecole de Médecine. It was not then much frequented by americans. There was the author of Beebie the Beebeist and there was the niece of Marcel Schwob and there were a few stray irish poets. We saw a good deal of Sylvia those days, she used to come to the house and also go out into the country with us in the old car. We met Adrienne Monnier and she brought Valéry Larbaud to the house and they were all very interested in Three Lives and Valéry Larbaud, so we understood, meditated translating it. It was at this time that Tristan Tzara first appeared in Paris. Adrienne Monnier was much excited by his advent.

Sylvia Beach was very enthusiastic about

Gertrude Stein and they became friends.

Picabia had found him in Switzerland during the war and they had together created dadaism, and out of dadaism, with a great deal of struggle and quarrelling came surréalisme.

Tzara came to the house, I imagine Picabia brought him but I am not quite certain. I have always found it very difficult to understand the stories of his violence and his wickedness, at least I found it difficult then because Tzara when he came to the house sat beside me at the tea table and talked to me like a pleasant and not very exciting cousin.

Adrienne Monnier wanted Sylvia to move to the rue de l'Odéon and Sylvia hesitated but finally she did so and as a matter of fact we did not see her very often afterward. They gave a party just after Sylvia moved in and we went and there Gertrude Stein first discovered that she had a young Oxford following. There were several young Oxford men there and they were awfully pleased to meet her and they asked her to give them some manuscripts and they published them that year nineteen twenty, in the Oxford Magazine.

Sylvia Beach from time to time brought groups of people to the house, groups of young writers and some older women with them. It was at that time that Ezra Pound came, no that was brought about in another way. She later ceased coming to the house but she sent word that Sherwood Anderson had come to Paris and wanted to see Gertrude Stein and might he come. Gertrude Stein sent back word that she would be very pleased and he came with his wife and Rosenfeld, the musical critic.

For some reason or other I was not present on this occasion, some domestic complication in all probability, at any rate when I did come home Gertrude Stein was moved and pleased as she has very rarely been. Gertrude Stein was in those days a little bitter, all her unpublished manuscripts, and no hope of publication or serious recognition. Sherwood Anderson came and quite simply and directly as is his way told her what he thought of her work and what it had meant to him in his development. He told it to her then and what was even rarer he told it in print immediately after. Gertrude Stein and Sherwood Anderson have always been the best of friends but I do not believe even he realises how much his visit meant to her. It was he who thereupon wrote the introduction to Geography and Plays.

In those days you met anybody anywhere. The Jewetts were an american couple who owned a tenth century château near Perpignan. We had met them there during the war and when they came to Paris we went to see them. There we met first Man Ray and later Robert Coates, how either of them happened to get there I do not know.

There were a lot of people in the room when we came in and soon Gertrude Stein was talking to a little man who sat in the corner. As we went out she made an engagement with him. She said he was a photographer and seemed interesting, and reminded me that Jeanne Cook, William Cook's wife, wanted her picture taken to send to Cook's people in America. We all three went to Man Ray's hotel. It was one of the little, tiny hotels in the rue Delambre and Man Ray had one of the small rooms, but I have never seen any space, not even a ship's cabin, with so many things in it and the things so admirably disposed. He had a bed, he had three large cameras, he had several kinds of lighting, he had a window screen, and in a little closet he did all his developing. He showed us pictures of Marcel Duchamp and a lot of other people and he asked if he might come and take photographs of the studio and of Gertrude Stein. He did and he also took some of me and we were very pleased with the result. He has at intervals taken pictures of Gertrude Stein and she is always fascinated with his way of using lights. She always comes home very pleased. One day she told him that she liked his photographs of her better than any that had ever been taken except one snap shot I had taken of her recently. This seemed to bother Man Ray. In a little while he asked her to come and pose and she did. He said, move all you like, your eyes, your head, it is to be a pose but it is to have in it all the qualities of a snap shot. The poses were very long, she, as he requested, moved, and the result, the last photographs he made of her, are extraordinarily interesting.

Robert Coates we also met at the Jewetts' in those early days just after the war. I remember the day very well. It was a cold, dark day, on an upper floor of a hotel. There were a number of young men there and suddenly

This seemed to bother Man Ray.

Gertrude Stein said she had forgotten to put the light on her car and she did not want another fine, we had just had one because I had blown the klaxon at a policeman trying to get him out of our way and she had received one by going the wrong way around a post. Alright, said a red-haired young man and immediately he was down and back. The light is on, he announced. How did you know which my car was, asked Gertrude Stein. Oh I knew, said Coates. We always liked Coates. It is extraordinary in wandering about Paris how very few people you know you meet, but we often met Coates hatless and red-headed in the most unexpected places. This was just about the time of Broom, about which I will tell very soon, and Gertrude Stein took a very deep interest in Coates' work as soon as he showed it to her. She said he was the one young man who had an individual rhythm, his words made a sound to the eyes, most people's words do not. We also liked Coates' address, the City Hotel, on the island, and we liked all his ways.

Gertrude Stein was delighted with the scheme of study that he prepared for the Guggenheim prize. Unfortunately, the scheme of study, which was a most charming little novel, with Gertrude Stein as a backer, did not win a prize.

As I have said there was Broom.

Before the war we had known a young fellow, not known him much but a little; Elmer Harden, who was in Paris studying music. During the war we heard that Elmer Harden had joined the french army and had been badly wounded. It was rather an amazing story. Elmer Harden had been nursing french wounded in the american hospital and one of his patients, a captain with an arm fairly disabled, was going back to the front. Elmer Harden could not content himself any longer nursing. He said to Captain Peter, I am going with you. But it is impossible, said Captain Peter. But I am, said Elmer stubbornly. So they took a taxi and they went to the war office and to a dentist and I don't know where else, but by the end of the week Captain Peter had rejoined and Elmer Harden was in his regiment as a soldier. He fought well and was wounded. After the war we met him again and then we met often. He and the lovely flowers he used to send us were a great comfort in those days just after the peace. He and I always say that he and

I will be the last people of our generation to remember the war. I am afraid we both of us have already forgotten it a little. Only the other day though Elmer announced that he had had a great triumph, he had made Captain Peter and Captain Peter is a breton admit that it was a nice war. Up to this time when he had said to Captain Peter, it was a nice war, Captain Peter had not answered, but this time when Elmer said, it was a nice war, Captain Peter said, yes Elmer, it was a nice war.

Kate Buss came from the same town as Elmer, from Medford, Mass. She was in Paris and she came to see us. I do not think Elmer introduced her but she did come to see us. She was much interested in the writings of Gertrude Stein and owned everything that up to that time could be bought. She brought Kreymborg to see us. Kreymborg had come to Paris with Harold Loeb to start Broom. Kreymborg and his wife came to the house frequently. He wanted very much to run The Long Gay Book, the thing Gertrude Stein had written just after The Making of Americans, as a serial. Of course Harold Loeb would not consent to that. Kreymborg used to read out the sentences from this book with great gusto. He and Gertrude Stein had a bond of union beside their mutual liking because the Grafton Press that had printed Three Lives had printed his first book and about the same time.

Kate Buss brought lots of people to the house. She brought Djuna Barnes and Mina Loy and they had wanted to bring James Joyce but they didn't. We were glad to see Mina whom we had known in Florence as Mina Haweis. Mina brought Glenway Wescott on his first trip to Europe. Glenway impressed us greatly by his english accent. Hemingway explained. He said, when you matriculate at the University of Chicago you write down just what accent you will have and they give it to you when you graduate. You can have a sixteenth century or modern, whatever you like. Glenway left behind him a silk cigarette case with his initials, we kept it until he came back again and then gave it to him.

Mina also brought Robert McAlmon. McAlmon was very nice in those days, very mature and very good-looking. It was much later that he published The Making of Americans in the Contact press and that everybody quarrelled. But that is Paris, except that as a matter of fact Gertrude Stein and he never became friends again.

Kate Buss brought Ernest Walsh, he was very young then and very feverish and she was very worried about him. We met him later with Hemingway and then in Belley, but we never knew him very well.

We met Ezra Pound at Grace Lounsbery's house, he came home to dinner with us and he stayed and he talked about japanese prints among other things. Gertrude Stein liked him but did not find him amusing. She said he was a village explainer, excellent if you were a village, but if you were not, not. Ezra also talked about T. S. Eliot. It was the first time any one had talked about T.S. at the house. Pretty soon everybody talked about T.S. Kitty Buss talked about him and much later Hemingway talked about him as the Major. Considerably later Lady Rothermere talked about him and invited Gertrude Stein to come and meet him. They were founding the Criterion. We had met Lady Rothermere through Muriel Draper whom we had seen again for the first time after many years. Gertrude Stein was not particularly anxious to go to Lady Rothermere's and meet T. S. Eliot, but we all insisted she should, and she gave a doubtful yes. I had no evening dress to wear for this occasion and started to make one. The bell rang and in walked Lady Rothermere and T.S.

Eliot and Gertrude Stein had a solemn conversation, mostly about split infinitives and other grammatical solecisms and why Gertrude Stein used them. Finally Lady Rothermere and Eliot rose to go and Eliot said that if he printed anything of Gertrude Stein's in the Criterion it would have to be her very latest thing. They left and Gertrude Stein said, don't bother to finish your dress, now we don't have to go, and she began to write a portrait of T. S. Eliot and called it the fifteenth of November, that being this day and so there could be no doubt but that it was her latest thing. It was all about wool is wool and silk is silk or wool is woollen and silk is silken. She sent it to T. S. Eliot and he accepted it but naturally he did not print it.

Then began a long correspondence, not between Gertrude Stein and T. S. Eliot, but between T. S. Eliot's secretary and myself. We each addressed the other as Sir, I signing myself A. B. Toklas and she signing initials. It was only considerably afterwards that I found out that his secretary was not a young man. I don't know whether she ever found out that I was not.

In spite of all this correspondence nothing happened and Gertrude Stein mischievously told the story to all the english people coming to the house and at that moment there were a great many english coming in and out. At any rate finally there was a note, it was now early spring, from the Criterion asking would Miss Stein mind if her contribution appeared in the October number. She replied that nothing could be more suitable than the fifteenth of November on the fifteenth of October.

Once more a long silence and then this time came proof of the article. We were surprised but returned the proof promptly. Apparently a young man had sent it without authority because very shortly came an apologetic letter saying that there had been a mistake, the article was not to be printed just yet. This was also told to the passing english with the result that after all it was printed. Thereafter it was reprinted in the Georgian Stories. Gertrude Stein was delighted when later she was told that Eliot had said in Cambridge that the work of Gertrude Stein was very fine but not for us.

But to come back to Ezra. Ezra did come back and he came back with the editor of The Dial. This time it was worse than japanese prints, it was much more violent. In his surprise at the violence Ezra fell out of Gertrude Stein's favourite little armchair, the one I have since tapestried with Picasso designs, and Gertrude Stein was furious. Finally Ezra and the editor of The Dial left, nobody too well pleased. Gertrude Stein did not want to see Ezra again. Ezra did not quite see why. He met Gertrude Stein one day near the Luxembourg gardens and said, but I do want to come to see you. I am so sorry, answered Gertrude Stein, but Miss Toklas has a bad tooth and beside we are busy picking wild flowers. All of which was literally true, like all of Gertrude Stein's literature, but it upset Ezra, and we never saw him again.

During these months after the war we were one day going down a little street and saw a man looking in at a window and going backwards and forwards and right and left and otherwise behaving strangely. Lipschitz, said Gertrude Stein. Yes, said Lipschitz, I am buying an iron cock. Where is it, we asked. Why in there, he said, and in there it was. Gertrude Stein had known Lipschitz very slightly at one time but this incident made them friends and soon he asked her to pose. He had just finished a bust of Jean Cocteau and he wanted to do her. She never minds posing, she likes the calm of it and although she does not like sculpture and told Lipschitz so, she began to pose. I remember it was a very hot spring and Lipschitz's studio was appallingly hot and they spent hours there.

Lipschitz is an excellent gossip and Gertrude Stein adores the beginning and middle and end of a story and Lipschitz was able to supply several missing parts of several stories.

And then they talked about art and Gertrude Stein rather liked her portrait and they were very good friends and the sittings were over.

One day we were across town at a picture show and somebody came up to Gertrude Stein and said something. She said, wiping her forehead, it is hot. He said he was a friend of Lipschitz and she answered, yes it was hot there. Lipschitz was to bring her some photographs of the head he had done but he did not and we were awfully busy and Gertrude Stein sometimes wondered why Lipschitz did not come. Somebody wanted the photos so she wrote to him to bring them. He came. She said why did you not come before. He said he did not come before because he had been told by some one to whom she had said it, that she was bored sitting for him. Oh hell, she said, listen I am fairly well known for saying things about any one and anything, I say them about people, I say them to people, I say them when I please and how I please but as I mostly say what I think, the least that you or anybody else can do is to rest content with what I say to you. He seemed very content and they talked happily and pleasantly and they said à bientôt, we will meet soon. Lipschitz left and we did not see him for several years.

Then Jane Heap turned up and wanted to take some of Lipschitz's things to America and she wanted Gertrude Stein to come and choose them. But how can I, said Gertrude Stein, when Lipschitz is very evidently angry, I am sure I have not the slightest idea why or how but he is. Jane Heap said that Lipschitz said that he was fonder of Gertrude Stein than he was of almost anybody and was heart broken at not seeing her. Oh, said

Gertrude Stein, I am very fond of him. Sure I will go with you. She went, they embraced tenderly and had a happy time and her only revenge was in parting to say to Lipschitz, à très bientôt. And Lipschitz said, comme vous êtes méchante. They have been excellent friends ever since and Gertrude Stein has done of Lipschitz one of her most lovely portraits but they have never spoken of the quarrel and if he knows what happened the second time she does not.

It was through Lipschitz that Gertrude Stein again met Jean Cocteau. Lipschitz had told Gertrude Stein a thing which she did not know, that Cocteau in his Potomak had spoken of and quoted The Portrait of Mabel Dodge. She was naturally very pleased as Cocteau was the first french writer to speak of her work. They met once or twice and began a friendship that consists in their writing to each other quite often and liking each other immensely and having many young and old friends in common, but not in meeting.

Jo Davidson too sculptured Gertrude Stein at this time. There, all was peaceful, Jo was witty and amusing and he pleased Gertrude Stein. I cannot remember who came in and out, whether they were real or whether they were sculptured but there were a great many. There were among others Lincoln Steffens and in some queer way he is associated with the beginning of our seeing a good deal of Janet Scudder but I do not well remember just what happened.

I do however remember very well the first time I ever heard Janet Scudder's voice. It was way back when I first came to Paris and my friend and I had a little apartment in the rue Notre-Dame-des-Champs. My friend in the enthusiasm of seeing other people enthusiastic had bought a Matisse and it had just been hung on the wall. Mildred Aldrich was calling on us, it was a warm spring afternoon and Mildred was leaning out of the window. I suddenly heard her say, Janet, Janet come up here. What is it, said a very lovely drawling voice. I want you to come up here and meet my friends Harriet and Alice and I want you to come up and see their new apartment. Oh, said the voice. And then Mildred said, and they have a new big Matisse. Come up and see it. I don't think so, said the voice.

The Miss Etta Cones as Pablo Picasso

used to call her and her sister.

Janet did later see a great deal of Matisse when he lived out in Clamart. And Gertrude Stein and she had always been friends, at least ever since the period when they first began to see a good deal of each other.

Like Doctor Claribel Cone, Janet, always insisting that she understands none of it, reads and feels Gertrude Stein's work and reads it aloud understandingly.

We were going to the valley of the Rhône for the first time since the war and Janet and a friend in a duplicate Godiva were to come too. I will tell about this very soon.

During all these restless months we were also trying to get Mildred Aldrich the legion of honour. After the war was over a great many war-workers were given the legion of honour but they were all members of organisations and Mildred Aldrich was not. Gertrude Stein was very anxious that Mildred Aldrich should have it. In the first place she thought she ought, no one else had done as much propaganda for France as she had by her books which everybody in America read, and beside she knew Mildred would like it. So we began the campaign. It was not a very easy thing to accomplish as naturally the organisations had the most influence. We started different people going. We began to get lists of prominent americans and asked them to sign. They did not refuse, but a list in itself helps, but does not accomplish results. Mr. Jaccacci who had a great admiration for Miss Aldrich was very helpful but all the people that he knew wanted things for themselves first. We got the American Legion interested at least two of the colonels, but they also had other names that had to pass first. We had seen and talked to and interested everybody and everybody promised and nothing happened. Finally we met a senator. He would be helpful but then senators were busy and then one afternoon we met the senator's secretary. Gertrude Stein drove the senator's secretary home in Godiva.

As it turned out the senator's secretary had tried to learn to drive a car and had not succeeded. The way in which Gertrude Stein made her way through Paris traffic with the ease and indifference of a chauffeur, and was at the same time a well known author impressed her immensely. She said she would get Mildred Aldrich's papers out of the pigeon hole in which they were probably reposing and she did. Very shortly after the mayor of Mildred's village called upon her one morning on official business. He presented her with the preliminary papers to be signed for the legion of honour. He said to her, you must remember, Mademoiselle, these matters often start but do not get themselves accomplished. So you must be prepared for disappointment. Mildred answered quietly, monsieur le maire, if my friends have started a matter of this kind they will see to it that it is accomplished. And it was. When we arrived at Avignon on our way to Saint-Rémy there was a telegram telling us that Mildred had her decoration. We were delighted and Mildred Aldrich to the day of her death never lost her pride and pleasure in her honour.

During these early restless years after the war Gertrude Stein worked a great deal. Not as in the old days, night after night, but anywhere, in between visits, in the automobile while she was waiting in the street while I did errands, while posing. She was particularly fond in these days of working in the automobile while it stood in the crowded streets.

It was then that she wrote Finer Than Melanctha as a joke. Harold Loeb, at that time editing Broom all by himself, said he would like to have something of hers that would be as fine as Melanctha, her early negro story in Three Lives.

She was much influenced by the sound of the streets and the movement of the automobiles. She also liked then to set a sentence for herself as a sort of tuning fork and metronome and then write to that time and tune. Mildred's Thoughts, published in The American Caravan, was one of these experiments she thought most successful. The Birthplace of Bonnes, published in The Little Review, was another one. Moral Tales of 1920-1921, American Biography, and One Hundred Prominent Men, when as she said she created out of her imagination one hundred men equally men and all equally prominent were written then. These two were later printed in Useful Knowledge.

It was also about this time that Harry Gibb came back to Paris for a short while. He was very anxious that Gertrude Stein should publish a book of her work showing what she had been doing in those years. Not a little book, he kept saying, a big book, something they can get their teeth into. You must do it, he used to say. But no publisher will look at it now that John Lane is no longer active, she said. It makes no difference, said Harry Gibb violently, it is the essence of the thing that they must see and you must have a lot of things printed, and then turning to me he said, Alice you do it. I knew he was right and that it had to be done. But how.

I talked to Kate Buss about it and she suggested the Four Seas Company who had done a little book for her. I began a correspondence with Mr. Brown, Honest to God Brown as Gertrude Stein called him in imitation of William Cook's phrase when everything was going particularly wrong. The arrangements with Honest to God having finally been made we left for the south in July, nineteen twenty-two.

We started off in Godiva, the runabout ford and followed by Janet Scudder in a second Godiva accompanied by Mrs. Lane. They were going to Grasse to buy themselves a home, they finally bought one near Aix-en-Provence. And we were going to Saint-Rémy to visit in peace the country we had loved during the war.

We were only a hundred or so kilometers from Paris when Janet Scudder tooted her horn which was the signal agreed upon for us to stop and wait. Janet came alongside. I think, said she solemnly, Gertrude Stein always called her The Doughboy, she always said there were only two perfectly solemn things on earth, the doughboy and Janet Scudder. Janet had also, Gertrude Stein always said, all the subtlety of the doughboy and all his nice ways and all his lonesomeness. Janet came alongside, I think, she said solemnly, we are not on the right road, it says Paris-Perpignan and I want to go to Grasse.

Anyway at the time we got no further than Lorne and there we suddenly realised how tired we were. We were just tired.

We suggested that the others should move on to Grasse but they said they too would wait and we all waited. It was the first time we had just stayed still since Palma de Mallorca, since 1916. Finally we moved slowly on to Saint-Rémy and they went further to Grasse and then came back. They asked us what we were going to do and we answered, nothing just stay here. So they went off again and bought a property in Aix-en-Provence.

Janet Scudder, as Gertrude Stein always said, had the real pioneer's passion for buying useless real estate. In every little town we stopped on the way Janet would find a piece of property that she considered purchasable and Gertrude Stein, violently protesting, got her away. She wanted to buy property everywhere except in Grasse where she had gone to buy property. She finally did buy a house and grounds in Aix-en-Provence after insisting on Gertrude Stein's seeing it who told her not to and telegraphed no and telephoned no. However Janet did buy it but luckily after a year she was able to get rid of it. During that year we stayed quietly in Saint-Rémy.

We had intended staying only a month or two but we stayed all winter. With the exception of an occasional interchange of visits with Janet Scudder we saw no one except the people of the country. We went to Avignon to shop, we went now and then into the country we had known so well but for the most part we wandered around Saint-Rémy, we went up into the Alpilles, the little hills that Gertrude Stein described over and over again in the writing of that winter, we watched the enormous flocks of sheep going up into the mountains led by the donkeys and their water bottles, we sat above the roman monuments and we went often to Les Baux. The hotel was not very comfortable but we stayed on. The valley of the Rhône was once more exercising its spell over us.

It was during this winter that Gertrude Stein meditated upon the use of grammar, poetical forms and what might be termed landscape plays.

It was at this time that she wrote Elucidation, printed in transition in nineteen twenty-seven. It was her first effort to state her problems of expression and her attempts to answer them. It was her first effort to realise clearly just what her writing meant and why it was as it was. Later on much later she wrote her treatises on grammar, sentences, paragraphs, vocabulary etcetera, which I have printed in Plain Edition under the title of How To Write.

It was in Saint-Rémy and during this winter that she wrote the poetry that has so greatly influenced the younger generation. Her Capital Capitals, Virgil Thomson has put to music. Lend a Hand or Four Religions has been printed in Useful Knowledge. This play has always interested her immensely, it was the first attempt that later made her Operas and Plays, the first conception of landscape as a play. She also at that time wrote the Valentine to Sherwood Anderson, also printed in the volume Useful Knowledge, Indian Boy, printed later in the Reviewer, (Carl Van Vechten sent Hunter Stagg to us a young Southerner as attractive as his name), and Saints In Seven, which she used to illustrate her work in her lectures at Oxford and Cambridge, and Talks to Saints in Saint-Rémy.

She worked in those days with slow care and concentration, and was very preoccupied.

Finally we received the first copies of Geography and Plays, the winter was over and we went back to Paris.

This long winter in Saint-Rémy broke the restlessness of the war and the after war. A great many things were to happen, there were to be friendships and there were to be enmities and there were to be a great many other things but there was not to be any restlessness.

Gertrude Stein always says that she only has two real distractions, pictures and automobiles. Perhaps she might now add dogs.

Immediately after the war her attention was attracted by the work of a young french painter, Fabre, who had a natural feeling for objects on a table and landscapes but he came to nothing. The next painter who attracted her attention was André Masson. Masson was at that time influenced by Juan Gris in whom Gertrude Stein's interest was permanent and vital. She was interested in André Masson as a painter particularly as a painter of white and she was interested in his composition in the wandering line in his compositions. Soon Masson fell under the influence of the surréalistes.

The surréalistes are the vulgarisation of Picabia as Delaunay and his followers and the futurists were the vulgarisation of Picasso. Picabia had conceived and is struggling with the problem that a line should have the vibration of a musical sound and that this vibration should be the result of conceiving the human form and the human face in so tenuous a fashion that it would induce such vibration in the line forming it. It is his way of achieving the disembodied. It was this idea that conceived mathematically influenced Marcel Duchamp and produced his The Nude Descending the Staircase.

All his life Picabia has struggled to dominate and achieve this conception. Gertrude Stein thinks that perhaps he is now approaching the solution of his problem. The surréalistes taking the manner for the matter as is the way of the vulgarisers, accept the line as having become vibrant and as therefore able in itself to inspire them to higher flights. He who is going to be the creator of the vibrant line knows that it is not yet created and if it were it would not exist by itself, it would be dependent upon the emotion of the object which compels the vibration. So much for the creator and his followers.

Gertrude Stein, in her work, has always been possessed by the intellectual passion for exactitude in the description of inner and outer reality. She has produced a simplification by this concentration, and as a result the destruction of associational emotion in poetry and prose. She knows that beauty, music, decoration, the result of emotion should never be the cause, even events should not be the cause of emotion nor should they be the material of poetry and prose. Nor should emotion itself be the cause of poetry or prose. They should consist of an exact reproduction of either an outer or an inner reality.

It was this conception of exactitude that made the close understanding between Gertrude Stein and Juan Gris.

Juan Gris also conceived exactitude but in him exactitude had a mystical basis. As a mystic it was necessary for him to be exact. In Gertrude Stein the necessity was intellectual, a pure passion for exactitude. It is because of this that her work has often been compared to that of mathematicians and by a certain french critic to the work of Bach.

Picasso by nature the most endowed had less clarity of intellectual purpose. He was in his creative activity dominated by spanish ritual, later by negro ritual expressed in negro sculpture (which has an arab basis the basis also of spanish ritual) and later by russian ritual. His creative activity being tremendously dominant, he made these great rituals over into his own image.

Juan Gris was the only person whom Picasso wished away. The relation between them was just that.

In the days when the friendship between Gertrude Stein and Picasso had become if possible closer than before, (it was for his little boy, born February fourth to her February third, that she wrote her birthday book with a line for each day in the year) in those days her intimacy with Juan Gris displeased him. Once after a show of Juan's pictures at the Galérie Simon he said to her with violence, tell me why you stand up for his work, you know you do not like it; and she did not answer him.

Later when Juan died and Gertrude Stein was heart broken Picasso came to the house and spent all day there. I do not know what was said but I do know that at one time Gertrude Stein said to him bitterly, you have no right to mourn, and he said, you have no right to say that to me. You never realised his meaning because you did not have it, she said angrily. You know very well I did, he replied.

The most moving thing Gertrude Stein has ever written is The Life and Death of Juan Gris. It was printed in transition and later on translated in german for his retrospective show in Berlin.

Picasso never wished Braque away. Picasso said once when he and Gertrude Stein were talking together, yes, Braque and James Joyce, they are the incomprehensibles whom anybody can understand. Les incompréhensibles que tout le monde peut comprendre.

The first thing that happened when we were back in Paris was Hemingway with a letter of introduction from Sherwood Anderson.

I remember very well the impression I had of Hemingway that first afternoon. He was an extraordinarily good-looking young man, twenty-three years old. It was not long after that that everybody was twenty-six. It became the period of being twenty-six. During the next two or three years all the young men were twenty-six years old. It was the right age apparently for that time and place. There were one or two under twenty, for example George Lynes but they did not count as Gertrude Stein carefully explained to them. If they were young men they were twenty-six. Later on, much later on they were twenty-one and twenty-two.

So Hemingway was twenty-three, rather foreign looking, with passionately interested, rather than interesting eyes. He sat in front of Gertrude Stein and listened and looked.

They talked then, and more and more, a great deal together. He asked her to come and spend an evening in their apartment and look at his work. Hemingway had then and has always a very good instinct for finding apartments in strange but pleasing localities and good femmes de ménage and good food. This his first apartment was just off the place du Tertre. We spent the evening there and he and Gertrude Stein went over all the writing he had done up to that time. He had begun the novel that it was inevitable he would begin and there were the little poems afterwards printed by McAlmon in the Contract Edition. Gertrude Stein rather liked the poems, they were direct, Kiplingesque, but the novel she found wanting. There is a great deal of description in this, she said, and not particularly good description. Begin over again and concentrate, she said.

Hemingway was at this time Paris correspondent for a canadian newspaper. He was obliged there to express what he called the canadian viewpoint.

He and Gertrude Stein used to walk together and talk together a great deal. One day she said to him, look here, you say you and your wife have a little money between you. Is it enough to live on if you live quietly. Yes, he said. Well, she said, then do it. If you keep on doing newspaper work you will never see things, you will only see words and that will not do, that is of course if you intend to be a writer. Hemingway said he undoubtedly intended to be a writer. He and his wife went away on a trip and shortly after Hemingway turned up alone. He came to the house about ten o'clock in the morning and he stayed, he stayed for lunch, he stayed all afternoon, he stayed for dinner and he stayed until about ten o'clock at night and then all of a sudden he announced that his wife was enceinte and then with great bitterness, and I, I am too young to be a father. We consoled him as best we could and sent him on his way.

When they came back Hemingway said that he had made up his mind. They would go back to America and he would work hard for a year and with what he would earn and what they had they would settle down and he would give up newspaper work and make himself a writer. They went away and well within the prescribed year they came back with a new born baby. Newspaper work was over.

The first thing to do when they came back was as they thought to get the baby baptised. They wanted Gertrude Stein and myself to be god-mothers and an english war comrade of Hemingway was to be god-father. We were all born of different religions and most of us were not practising any, so it was rather difficult to know in what church the baby could be baptised. We spent a great deal of time that winter, all of us, discussing the matter. Finally it was decided that it should be baptised episcopalian and episcopalian it was. Just how it was managed with the assortment of god-parents I am sure I do not know, but it was baptised in the episcopalian chapel.

Writer or painter god-parents are notoriously unreliable. That is, there is certain before long to be a cooling of friendship. I know several cases of this, poor Paulot Picasso's god-parents have wandered out of sight and just as naturally it is a long time since any of us have seen or heard of our Hemingway god-child.

However in the beginning we were active god-parents, I particularly. I embroidered a little chair and I knitted a gay coloured garment for the god-child. In the meantime the god-child's father was very earnestly at work making himself a writer.

Gertrude Stein never corrects any detail of anybody's writing, she sticks strictly to general principles, the way of seeing what the writer chooses to see, and the relation between that vision and the way it gets down. When the vision is not complete the words are flat, it is very simple, there can be no mistake about it, so she insists. It was at this time that Hemingway began the short things that afterwards were printed in a volume called In Our Time.

One day Hemingway came in very excited about Ford Madox Ford and the Transatlantic. Ford Madox Ford had started the Transatlantic some months before. A good many years before, indeed before the war, we had met Ford Madox Ford who was at that time Ford Madox Hueffer. He was

It was not long after that
that everybody was twenty-six.

married to Violet Hunt and Violet Hunt and Gertrude Stein were next to each other at the tea table and talked a great deal together. I was next to Ford Madox Hueffer and I liked him very much and I liked his stories of Mistral and Tarascon and I liked his having been followed about in that land of the french royalist, on account of his resemblance to the Bourbon claimant. I had never seen the Bourbon claimant but Ford at that time undoubtedly might have been a Bourbon.

We had heard that Ford was in Paris, but we had not happened to meet. Gertrude Stein had however seen copies of the Transatlantic and found it interesting but had thought nothing further about it.

Hemingway came in then very excited and said that Ford wanted something of Gertrude Stein's for the next number and he, Hemingway, wanted The Making of Americans to be run in it as a serial and he had to have the first fifty pages at once. Gertrude Stein was of course quite overcome with her excitement at this idea, but there was no copy of the manuscript except the one that we had had bound. That makes no difference, said Hemingway, I will copy it. And he and I between us did copy it and it was printed in the next number of the Transatlantic. So for the first time a piece of the monumental work which was the beginning, really the beginning of modern writing, was printed, and we were very happy. Later on when things were difficult between Gertrude Stein and Hemingway, she always remembered with gratitude that after all it was Hemingway who first caused to be printed a piece of The Making of Americans. She always says, yes sure I have a weakness for Hemingway. After all he was the first of the young men to knock at my door and he did make Ford print the first piece of The Making of Americans.

I myself have not so much confidence that Hemingway did do this. I have never known what the story is but I have always been certain that there was some other story behind it all. That is the way I feel about it.

Gertrude Stein and Sherwood Anderson are very funny on the subject of Hemingway. The last time that Sherwood was in Paris they often talked

However in the beginning
we were active god-parents.

about him. Hemingway had been formed by the two of them and they were both a little proud and a little ashamed of the work of their minds. Hemingway had at one moment, when he had repudiated Sherwood Anderson and all his works, written him a letter in the name of american literature which he, Hemingway, in company with his contemporaries was about to save, telling Sherwood just what he, Hemingway thought about Sherwood's work, and, that thinking, was in no sense complimentary. When Sherwood came to Paris Hemingway naturally was afraid. Sherwood as naturally was not.

As I say he and Gertrude Stein were endlessly amusing on the subject. They admitted that Hemingway was yellow, he is, Gertrude Stein insisted, just like the flat-boat men on the Mississippi river as described by Mark Twain. But what a book, they both agreed, would be the real story of Hemingway, not those he writes but the confessions of the real Ernest Hemingway. It would be for another audience than the audience Hemingway now has but it would be very wonderful. And then they both agreed that they have a weakness for Hemingway because he is such a good pupil. He is a rotten pupil, I protested. You don't understand, they both said, it is so flattering to have a pupil who does it without understanding it, in other words he takes training and anybody who takes training is a favourite pupil. They both admit it to be a weakness. Gertrude Stein added further, you see he is like Derain. You remember Monsieur de Tuille said, when I did not understand why Derain was having the success he was having that it was because he looks like a modern and he smells of the museums. And that is Hemingway, he looks like a modern and he smells of the museums. But what a story that of the real Hem, and one he should tell himself but alas he never will. After all, as he himself once murmured, there is the career, the career.

But to come back to the events that were happening.

Hemingway did it all. He copied the manuscript and corrected the proof. Correcting proofs is, as I said before, like dusting, you learn the values of the thing as no reading suffices to teach it to you. In correcting these proofs Hemingway learned a great deal and he admired all that he learned. It was at this time that he wrote to Gertrude Stein saying that it was she who had done the work in writing The Making of Americans and he and all his had but to devote their lives to seeing that it was published.

He had hopes of being able to accomplish this. Some one, I think by the name of Sterne, said that he could place it with a publisher. Gertrude Stein and Hemingway believed that he could, but soon Hemingway reported that Sterne had entered into his period of unreliability. That was the end of that.

In the meantime and sometime before this Mina Loy had brought McAlmon to the house and he came from time to time and he brought his wife and brought William Carlos Williams. And finally he wanted to print The Making of Americans in the Contact Edition and finally he did. I will come to that.

In the meantime McAlmon had printed the three poems and ten stories of Hemingway and William Bird had printed In Our Time and Hemingway was getting to be known. He was coming to know Dos Passos and Fitzgerald and Bromfield and George Antheil and everybody else and Harold Loeb was once more in Paris. Hemingway had become a writer. He was also a shadow-boxer, thanks to Sherwood, and he heard about bull-fighting from me. I have always loved spanish dancing and spanish bull-fighting and I loved to show the photographs of bull-fighters and bull-fighting. I also loved to show the photograph where Gertrude Stein and I were in the front row and had our picture taken there accidentally. In these days Hemingway was teaching some young chap how to box. The boy did not know how, but by accident he knocked Hemingway out. I believe this sometimes happens. At any rate in these days Hemingway although a sportsman was easily tired. He used to get quite worn out walking from his house to ours. But then he had been worn by the war. Even now he is, as Hélène says all men are, fragile. Recently a robust friend of his said to Gertrude Stein, Ernest is very fragile, whenever he does anything sporting something breaks, his arm, his leg, or his head.

In those early days Hemingway liked all his contemporaries except Cummings. He accused Cummings of having copied everything, not from anybody but from somebody. Gertrude Stein who had been much impressed by The Enormous Room said that Cummings did not copy, he was the natural heir of the New England tradition with its aridity and its sterility, but also with its individuality. They disagreed about this. They also disagreed about Sherwood Anderson. Gertrude Stein contended that Sherwood Anderson had a genius for using a sentence to convey a direct emotion, this was in the great american tradition, and that really except Sherwood there was no one in America who could write a clear and passionate sentence. Hemingway did not believe this, he did not like Sherwood's taste. Taste has nothing to do with sentences, contended Gertrude Stein. She also added that Fitzgerald was the only one of the younger writers who wrote naturally in sentences.

Gertrude Stein and Fitzgerald are very peculiar in their relation to each other. Gertrude Stein had been very much impressed by This Side of Paradise. She read it when it came out and before she knew any of the young american writers. She said of it that it was this book that really created for the public the new generation. She has never changed her opinion about this. She thinks this equally true of The Great Gatsby. She thinks Fitzgerald will be read when many of his well known contemporaries are forgotten. Fitzgerald always says that he thinks Gertrude Stein says these things just to annoy him by making him think that she means them, and he adds in his favourite way, and her doing it is the cruellest thing I ever heard. They always however have a very good time when they meet. And the last time they met they had a good time with themselves and Hemingway.

Then there was McAlmon. McAlmon had one quality that appealed to Gertrude Stein, abundance, he could go on writing, but she complained that it was dull.

There was also Glenway Wescott but Glenway Wescott at no time interested Gertrude Stein. He has a certain syrup but it does not pour.

So then Hemingway's career was begun. For a little while we saw less of him and then he began to come again. He used to recount to Gertrude Stein the conversations that he afterwards used in The Sun Also Rises and they talked endlessly about the character of Harold Loeb. At this time Hemingway was preparing his volume of short stories to submit to publishers in America. One evening after we had not seen him for a while he turned up with Shipman. Shipman was an amusing boy who was to inherit a few thousand dollars when he came of age. He was not of age. He was to buy the Transatlantic Review when he came of age, so Hemingway said. He was to support a surrealist review when he came of age, André Masson said. He was to buy a house in the country when he came of age, Josette Gris said. As a matter of fact when he came of age nobody who had known him then seemed to know what he did do with his inheritance. Hemingway brought him with him to the house to talk about buying the Transatlantic and incidentally he brought the manuscript he intended sending to America. He handed it to Gertrude Stein. He had added to his stories a little story of meditations and in these he said that The Enormous Room was the greatest book he had ever read. It was then that Gertrude Stein said, Hemingway, remarks are not literature.

After this we did not see Hemingway for quite a while and then we went to see some one, just after The Making of Americans was printed, and Hemingway who was there came up to Gertrude Stein and began to explain why he would not be able to write a review of the book. Just then a heavy hand fell on his shoulder and Ford Madox Ford said young man it is I who wish to speak to Gertrude Stein. Ford then said to her, I wish to ask your permission to dedicate my new book to you. May I. Gertrude Stein and I were both awfully pleased and touched.

For some years after this Gertrude Stein and Hemingway did not meet. And then we heard that he was back in Paris and telling a number of people how much he wanted to see her. Don't you come home with Hemingway on your arm, I used to say when she went out for a walk. Sure enough one day she did come back bringing him with her.

They sat and talked a long time. Finally I heard her say, Hemingway, after all you are ninety percent Rotarian. Can't you, he said, make it eighty percent. No, said she regretfully, I can't. After all, as she always says, he did, and I may say, he does have moments of disinterestedness.

After that they met quite often. Gertrude Stein always says she likes to see him, he is so wonderful. And if he could only tell his own story. In their last conversation she accused him of having killed a great many of his rivals and put them under the sod. I never, said Hemingway, seriously killed anybody but one man and he was a bad man and, he deserved it, but if I killed anybody else I did it unknowingly, and so I am not responsible.

It was Ford who once said of Hemingway, he comes and sits at my feet and praises me. It makes me nervous. Hemingway also said once, I turn my flame which is a small one down and down and then suddenly there is a big explosion. If there were nothing but explosions my work would be so exciting nobody could bear it.

However, whatever I say, Gertrude Stein always says, yes I know but I have a weakness for Hemingway.

Jane Heap turned up one afternoon. The Little Review had printed the Birthplace of Bonnes and The Valentine to Sherwood Anderson. Jane Heap sat down and we began to talk. She stayed to dinner and she stayed the evening and by dawn the little ford car Godiva which had been burning its lights all night waiting to be taken home could hardly start to take Jane home. Gertrude Stein then and always liked Jane Heap immensely, Margaret Anderson interested her much less.

It was now once more summer and this time we went to the Côte d'Azur and joined the Picassos at Antibes. It was there I first saw Picasso's mother. Picasso looks extraordinarily like her. Gertrude Stein and Madame Picasso had difficulty in talking not having a common language but they talked enough to amuse themselves. They were talking about Picasso when Gertrude Stein first knew him. He was remarkably beautiful then, said Gertrude Stein, he was illuminated as if he wore a halo. Oh, said Madame Picasso, if you thought him beautiful then I assure you it was nothing compared to his looks when he was a boy. He was an angel and a devil in beauty, no one could cease looking at him. And now, said Picasso a little resentfully. Ah now, said they together, ah now there is no such beauty left. But, added his mother, you are very sweet and as a son very perfect. So he had to be satisfied with that.

It was at this time that Jean Cocteau who prides himself on being eternally thirty was writing a little biography of Picasso, and he sent him a telegram asking him to tell him the date of his birth. And yours, telegraphed back Picasso.

There are so many stories about Picasso and Jean Cocteau. Picasso like Gertrude Stein is easily upset if asked to do something suddenly and Jean Cocteau does this quite successfully. Picasso resents it and revenges himself at greater length. Not long ago there was a long story.

Picasso was in Spain, in Barcelona, and a friend of his youth who was editor of a paper printed, not in spanish but in catalan, interviewed him. Picasso knowing that the interview to be printed in catalan was probably never going to be printed in spanish, thoroughly enjoyed himself. He said that Jean Cocteau was getting to be very popular in Paris, so popular that you could find his poems on the table of any smart coiffeur.

As I say he thoroughly enjoyed himself in giving this interview and then returned to Paris.

Some catalan in Barcelona sent the paper to some catalan friend in Paris and the catalan friend in Paris translated it to a french friend and the french friend printed the interview in a french paper.

Picasso and his wife told us the story together of what happened then. As soon as Jean saw the article, he tried to see Pablo. Pablo refused to see him, he told the maid to say that he was always out and for days they could not answer the telephone. Cocteau finally stated in an interview given to the french press that the interview which had wounded him so sorely had turned out to be an interview with Picabia and not an interview with Picasso, his friend. Picabia of course denied this. Cocteau implored Picasso to give a public denial. Picasso remained discreetly at home.

The first evening the Picassos went out they went to the theatre and there in front of them seated was Jean Cocteau's mother. At the first intermission they went up to her, and surrounded by all their mutual friends she said, my dear, you cannot imagine the relief to me and to Jean to know that it was not you that gave out that vile interview, do tell me that it was not.

And as Picasso's wife said, I as a mother could not let a mother suffer and I said of course it was not Picasso and Picasso said, yes yes of course it was not, and so the public retraction was given.

It was this summer that Gertrude Stein, delighting in the movement of the tiny waves on the Antibes shore, wrote the Completed Portrait of Picasso, the Second Portrait of Carl Van Vechten, and The Book of Concluding With As A Wife Has A Cow A Love Story this afterwards beautifully illustrated by Juan Gris.

Robert McAlmon had definitely decided to publish The Making of Americans, and we were to correct proofs that summer. The summer before we had intended as usual to meet the Picassos at Antibes. I had been reading the Guide des Gourmets and I had found among other places where one ate well, Pernollet's Hôtel in the town of Belley. Belley is its name and Belley is its nature, as Gertrude Stein's elder brother remarked. We arrived there about the middle of August. On the map it looked as if it were high up in the mountains and Gertrude Stein does not like precipices and as we drove through the gorge I was nervous and she protesting, but finally the country opened out delightfully and we arrived in Belley. It was a pleasant hotel although it had no garden and we had intended that it should have a garden. We stayed on for several days.

Then Madame Pernollet, a pleasant round faced woman said to us that since we were evidently staying on why did we not make rates by the day or by the week. We said we would. In the meanwhile the Picassos wanted to know what had become of us. We replied that we were in Belley. We found that Belley was the birthplace of Brillat-Savarin. We now in Bilignin are enjoying using the furniture from the house of Brillat-Savarin which house belongs to the owner of this house.

We also found that Lamartine had been at school in Belley and Gertrude Stein says that wherever Lamartine stayed any length of time one eats well. Madame Récamier also comes from this region and the place is full of descendants of her husband's family. All these things we found out gradually but for the moment we were comfortable and we stayed on and left late. The following summer we were to correct proofs of The Making of Americans and so we left Paris early and came again to Belley. What a summer it was.

The Making of Americans is a book one thousand pages long, closely printed on large pages. Darantière has told me it has five hundred and sixty-five thousand words. It was written in nineteen hundred and six to nineteen hundred and eight, and except for the sections printed in Transatlantic it was all still in manuscript.

The sentences as the book goes on get longer and longer, they are sometimes pages long and the compositors were french, and when they made mistakes and left out a line the effort of getting it back again was terrific.

We used to leave the hotel in the morning with camp chairs, lunch and proof, and all day we struggled with the errors of French compositors. Proof had to be corrected most of it four times and finally I broke my glasses, my eyes gave out, and Gertrude Stein finished alone.

We used to change the scene of our labours and we found lovely spots but there were always to accompany us those endless pages of printers' errors. One of our favourite hillocks where we could see Mont Blanc in the distance we called Madame Mont Blanc.

Another place we went to often was near a little pool made by a small stream near a country cross-road. This was quite like the middle ages, so many things used to happen there, in a very simple middle age way. I remember once a country-man came up to us leading his oxen. Very politely he said, ladies is there anything the matter with me. Why yes, we replied, your face is covered with blood. Oh, he said, you see my oxen were slipping down the hill and I held them back and I too slipped and I wondered if anything had happened to me. We helped him wash the blood off and he went on.

It was during this summer that Gertrude Stein began two long things, A Novel and the Phenomena of Nature which was to lead later to the whole series of meditations on grammar and sentences.

It led first to An Acquaintance With Description, afterwards printed by the Seizin Press. She began at this time to describe landscape as if anything she saw was a natural phenomenon, a thing existent in itself, and

we were young then and we did

a great deal in a year.

she found it, this exercise, very interesting and it finally led her to the later series of Operas and Plays. I am trying to be as commonplace as I can be, she used to say to me. And then sometimes a little worried, it is not too commonplace. The last thing that she had finished, Stanzas of Meditation, and which I am now typewriting, she considers her real achievement of the commonplace.

But to go back. We returned to Paris, the proofs almost done, and Jane Heap was there. She was very excited. She had a wonderful plan, I have now quite forgotten what it was, but Gertrude Stein was enormously pleased with it. It had something to do with a plan for another edition of The Making of Americans in America.

At any rate in the various complications connected with this matter McAlmon became very angry and not without reason, and The Making of Americans appeared but McAlmon and Gertrude Stein were no longer friends.

When Gertrude Stein was quite young her brother once remarked to her, that she, having been born in February, was very like George Washington, she was impulsive and slow-minded. Undoubtedly a great many complications have been the result.

One day in this same spring we were going to visit a new spring salon. Jane Heap had been telling us of a young russian in whose work she was interested. As we were crossing a bridge in Godiva we saw Jane Heap and the young russian. We saw his pictures and Gertrude Stein too was interested. He of course came to see us.

In How To Write Gertrude Stein makes this sentence, Painting now after its great period has come back to be a minor art.

She was very interested to know who was to be the leader of this art.

This is the story.

The young russian was interesting. He was painting, so he said, colour that was no colour, he was painting blue pictures and he was painting three heads in one. Picasso had been drawing three heads in one. Soon the russian was painting three figures in one. Was he the only one. In a way he was although there was a group of them. This group, very shortly after

Gertrude Stein knew the russian, had a show at one of the art galleries, Druet's I think. The group then consisted of the russian, a frenchman, a very young dutchman, and two russian brothers. All of them except the dutchman about twenty-six years old.

At this show Gertrude Stein met George Antheil who asked to come to see her and when he came he brought with him Virgil Thomson. Gertrude Stein had not found George Antheil particularly interesting although she liked him, but Virgil Thomson she found very interesting although I did not like him.

However all this I will tell about later. To go back now to painting.

The russian Tchelitchev's work was the most vigorous of the group and the most mature and the most interesting. He had already then a passionate enmity against the frenchman whom they called Bébé Bérard and whose name was Christian Bérard and whom Tchelitchev said copied everything.

René Crevel had been the friend of all these painters. Some time later one of them was to have a one man show at the Galérie Pierre. We were going to it and on the way we met René. We all stopped, he was exhilarated with exasperation. He talked with his characteristic brilliant violence. These painters, he said, sell their pictures for several thousand francs apiece and they have the pretentiousness which comes from being valued in terms of money, and we writers who have twice their quality and infinitely greater vitality cannot earn a living and have to beg and intrigue to induce publishers to publish us; but the time will come, and René became prophetic, when these same painters will come to us to re-create them and then we will contemplate them with indifference.

René was then and has remained ever since a devout surréaliste. He needs and needed, being a frenchman, an intellectual as well as a basal justification for the passionate exaltation in him. This he could not find, being of the immediate postwar generation, in either religion or patriotism, the war having destroyed for his generation, both patriotism and religion as a passion. Surréalisme has been his justification. It has clarified for him the confused negation in which he lived and loved. This he alone of his generation has really succeeded in expressing, a little in his earlier books, and in his last book, The Clavecin of Diderot very adequately and with the brilliant violence that is his quality.

Gertrude Stein was at first not interested in this group of painters as a group but only in the russian. This interest gradually increased and then she was bothered. Granted, she used to say, that the influences which make a new movement in art and literature have continued and are making a new movement in art and literature; in order to seize these influences and create as well as re-create them there needs a very dominating creative power. This the russian manifestly did not have. Still there was a distinctly new creative idea. Where had it come from. Gertrude Stein always says to the young painters when they complain that she changes her mind about their work, it is not I that change my mind about the pictures, but the paintings disappear into the wall, I do not see them any more and then they go out of the door naturally.

In the meantime as I have said George Antheil had brought Virgil Thomson to the house and Virgil Thomson and Gertrude Stein became friends and saw each other a great deal. Virgil Thomson had put a number of Gertrude Stein's things to music, Susie Asado, Preciosilla and Capital Capitals. Gertrude Stein was very much interested in Virgil Thomson's music. He had understood Satie undoubtedly and he had a comprehension quite his own of prosody. He understood a great deal of Gertrude Stein's work, he used to dream at night that there was something there that he did not understand, but on the whole he was very well content with that which he did understand. She delighted in listening to her words framed by his music. They saw a great deal of each other.

Virgil had in his room a great many pictures by Christian Bérard and Gertrude Stein used to look at them a great deal. She could not find out at all what she thought about them.

She and Virgil Thomson used to talk about them endlessly. Virgil said he knew nothing about pictures but he thought these wonderful. Gertrude Stein told him about her perplexity about the new movement and that the creative power behind it was not the russian. Virgil said that there he quite agreed with her and he was convinced that it was Bébé Bérard, baptised Christian. She said that perhaps that was the answer but she was very doubtful. She used to say of Bérard's pictures, they are almost something and then they are just not. As she used to explain to Virgil, the Catholic Church makes a very sharp distinction between a hysteric and a saint. The same thing holds true in the art world. There is the sensitiveness of the hysteric which has all the appearance of creation, but actual creation has an individual force which is an entirely different thing. Gertrude Stein was inclined to believe that artistically Bérard was more hysteric than saint. At this time she had come back to portrait writing with renewed vigour and she, to clarify her mind, as she said, did portraits of the russian and of the frenchman. In the meantime, through Virgil Thomson, she had met a young frenchman named Georges Hugnet. He and Gertrude Stein became very devoted to one another. He liked the sound of her writing and then he liked the sense and he liked the sentences.

At his home were a great many portraits of himself painted by his friends. Among others one by one of the two russian brothers and one by a young englishman. Gertrude Stein was not particularly interested in any of these portraits. There was however a painting of a hand by this young englishman which she did not like but which she remembered.

Every one began at this time to be very occupied with their own affairs. Virgil Thomson had asked Gertrude Stein to write an opera for him. Among the saints there were two saints whom she had always liked better than any others, Saint Theresa of Avila and Ignatius Loyola, and she said she would write him an opera about these two saints. She began this and worked very hard at it all that spring and finally finished Four Saints and gave it to Virgil Thomson to put to music. He did. And it is a completely interesting opera both as to words and music.

All these summers we had continued to go to the hotel in Belley. We now had become so fond of this country, always the valley of the Rhône, and of the people of the country, and the trees of the country, and the oxen of the country, that we began looking for a house. One day we saw the house of our dreams across a valley. Go and ask the farmer there whose house that is, Gertrude Stein said to me. I said, nonsense it is an important

And it is a completely interesting opera

both as to words and music.

house and it is occupied. Go and ask him, she said. Very reluctantly I did. He said, well yes, perhaps it is for rent, it belongs to a little girl, all her people are dead and I think there is a lieutenant of the regiment stationed in Belley living there now, but I understand they were to leave. You might go and see the agent of the property. We did. He was a kindly old farmer who always told us allez doucement, go slowly. We did. We had the promise of the house, which we never saw any nearer than across the valley, as soon as the lieutenant should leave. Finally three years ago the lieutenant went to Morocco and we took the house still only having seen it from across the valley and we have liked it always more.

While we were still staying at the hotel, Natalie Barney came one day and lunched there bringing some friends, among them, the Duchess of Clermont-Tonnerre. Gertrude Stein and she were delighted with one another and the meeting led to many pleasant consequences, but of that later.

To return to the painters. Just after the opera was finished and before leaving Paris we happened to go to a show of pictures at the Galérie Bonjean. There we met one of the russian brothers, Genia Berman, and Gertrude Stein was not uninterested in his pictures. She went with him to his studio and looked at everything he had ever painted. He seemed to have a purer intelligence than the other two painters who certainly had not created the modern movement, perhaps the idea had been originally his. She asked him, telling her story as she was fond of telling it at that time to any one who would listen, had he originated the idea. He said with an intelligent inner smile that he thought he had. She was not at all sure that he was not right. He came down to Bilignin to see us and she slowly concluded that though he was a very good painter he was too bad a painter to have been the creator of an idea. So once more the search began.

Again just before leaving Paris at this same picture gallery she saw a picture of a poet sitting by a waterfall. Who did that, she said. A young englishman, Francis Rose, was the reply. Oh yes I am not interested in his work. How much is that picture, she said: It cost very little. Gertrude Stein says a picture is either worth three hundred francs or three hundred thousand francs. She bought this for three hundred and we went away for the summer.

Georges Hugnet had decided to become an editor and he began editing the Editions de la Montagne. Actually it was George Maratier, everybody's friend who began this edition, but he decided to go to America and become an american and Georges Hugnet inherited it. The first book to appear was sixty pages in french of The Making of Americans. Gertrude Stein and Georges Hugnet translated them together and she was very happy about it. This was later followed by a volume of Ten Portraits written by Gertrude Stein and illustrated by portraits of the artists of themselves, and of the others drawn by them, Virgil Thomson by Bérard and a drawing of Bérard by himself, a portrait of Tchelitchev by himself, a portrait of Picasso by himself and one of Guillaume Apollinaire and one of Erik Satie by Picasso, one of Kristians Tonny the young dutchman by himself and one of Bernard Faÿ by Tonny. These volumes were very well received and everybody was pleased.

Once more everybody went away.

Gertrude Stein in winter takes her white poodle Basket to be bathed at a vet's and she used to go to the picture gallery where she had bought the englishman's romantic picture and wait for Basket to dry. Every time she came home she brought more pictures by the englishman. She did not talk much about it but they accumulated. Several people began to tell her about this young man and offered to introduce him. Gertrude Stein declined. She said no she had had enough of knowing young painters, she now would content herself with knowing young painting.

In the meantime Georges Hugnet wrote a poem called Enfance. Gertrude Stein offered to translate it for him but instead she wrote a poem about it. This at first pleased Georges Hugnet too much and then did not please him at all. Gertrude Stein then called the poem Before The Flowers Of Friendship Faded Friendship Faded. Everybody mixed themselves up in all this. The group broke up. Gertrude Stein was very upset and then consoled herself by telling all about it in a delightful short story called From Left to Right and which was printed in the London Harper's Bazaar.

It was not long after this that one day Gertrude Stein called in the concierge and asked him to hang up all the Francis Rose pictures, by this time there were some thirty odd. Gertrude Stein was very much upset while she was having this done. I asked her why she was doing it if it upset her so much. She said she could not help it, that she felt that way about it but to change the whole aspect of the room by adding these thirty pictures was very upsetting. There the matter rested for some time.

To go back again to those days just after the publication of The Making of Americans. There was at that time a review of Gertrude Stein's book Geography and Plays in the Athenaeum signed Edith Sitwell. The review was long and a little condescending but I liked it. Gertrude Stein had not cared for it. A year later in the London Vogue was an article again by Edith Sitwell saying that since writing her article in the Athenaeum she had spent the year reading nothing but Geography and Plays and she wished to say how important and beautiful a book she had found it to be.

One afternoon at Elmer Harden's we met Miss Todd the editor of the London Vogue. She said that Edith Sitwell was to be shortly in Paris and wanted very much to meet Gertrude Stein. She said that Edith Sitwell was very shy and hesitant about coming. Elmer Harden said he would act as escort.

I remember so well my first impression of her, an impression which indeed has never changed. Very tall, bending slightly, withdrawing and hesitatingly advancing, and beautiful with the most distinguished nose I have ever seen on any human being. At that time and in conversation between Gertrude Stein and herself afterwards, I delighted in the delicacy and completeness of her understanding of poetry. She and Gertrude Stein became friends at once. This friendship like all friendships has had its difficulties but I am convinced that fundamentally Gertrude Stein and Edith Sitwell are friends and enjoy being friends.

We saw a great deal of Edith Sitwell at this time and then she went back to London. In the autumn of that year nineteen twenty-five Gertrude Stein had a letter from the president of the literary society of Cambridge asking her to speak before them in the early spring. Gertrude Stein quite completely upset at the very idea quite promptly answered no. Immediately came a letter from Edith Sitwell saying that the no must be changed to yes. That it was of the first importance that Gertrude Stein should deliver this address and that moreover Oxford was waiting for the yes to be given to Cambridge to ask her to do the same at Oxford.

There was very evidently nothing to do but to say yes and so Gertrude Stein said yes.

She was very upset at the prospect, peace, she said, had much greater terrors than war. Precipices even were nothing to this. She was very low in her mind. Luckily early in January the ford car began to have everything the matter with it. The better garages would not pay much attention to aged fords and Gertrude Stein used to take hers out to a shed in Montrouge where the mechanics worked at it while she sat. If she were to leave it there there would most likely have been nothing left of it to drive away.

One cold dark afternoon she went out to sit with her ford car and while she sat on the steps of another battered ford watching her own being taken to pieces and put together again, she began to write. She stayed there several hours and when she came back chilled, with the ford repaired, she had written the whole of Composition As Explanation.

Once the lecture written the next trouble was the reading of it. Everybody gave her advice. She read it to anybody who came to the house and some of them read it to her. Prichard happened to be in Paris just then and he and Emily Chadbourne between them gave advice and were an audience. Prichard showed her how to read it in the english manner but Emily Chadbourne was all for the american manner and Gertrude Stein was too worried to have any manner. We went one afternoon to Natalie Barney's. There there was a very aged and a very charming french professor of history. Natalie Barney asked him to tell Gertrude Stein how to lecture. Talk as quickly as you can and never look up, was his advice. Prichard had said talk as slowly as possible and never look down. At any rate I ordered a new dress and a new hat for Gertrude Stein and early in the spring we went to London.

This was the spring of twenty-six and England was still very strict about

Very tall, bending slightly, with dreaming and hesitatingly advancing, and beautiful

with the most distinguished nose I have ever seen on any human being

passports. We had ours alright but Gertrude Stein hates to answer questions from officials, it always worries her and she was already none too happy at the prospect of lecturing.

So taking both passports I went down stairs to see the officials. Ah, said one of them, and where is Miss Gertrude Stein. She is on deck, I replied, and she does not care to come down. She does not care to come down, he repeated, yes that is quite right, she does not care to come down, and he affixed the required signatures. So then we arrived in London. Edith Sitwell gave a party for us and so did her brother Osbert. Osbert was a great comfort to Gertrude Stein. He so thoroughly understood every possible way in which one could be nervous that as he sat beside her in the hotel telling her all the kinds of ways that he and she could suffer from stage fright she was quite soothed. She was always very fond of Osbert. She always said he was like an uncle of a king. He had that pleasant kindly irresponsible agitated calm that an uncle of an english king always must have.

Finally we arrived in Cambridge in the afternoon, were given tea and then dined with the president of the society and some of his friends. It was very pleasant and after dinner we went to the lecture room. It was a varied audience, men and women. Gertrude Stein was soon at her ease, the lecture went off very well, the men afterwards asked a great many questions and were very enthusiastic. The women said nothing. Gertrude Stein wondered whether they were supposed not to or just did not.

The day after we went to Oxford. There we lunched with young Acton and then went in to the lecture. Gertrude Stein was feeling more comfortable as a lecturer and this time she had a wonderful time. As she remarked afterwards, I felt just like a prima donna.

The lecture room was full, many standing in the back, and the discussion, after the lecture, lasted over an hour and no one left. It was very exciting. They asked all sorts of questions, they wanted to know most often why Gertrude Stein thought she was right in doing the kind of writing she did. She answered that it was not a question of what any one thought but after all she had been doing as she did for about twenty years and now they wanted to hear her lecture. This did not mean of course that they were coming to think that her way was a possible way, it proved nothing, but on the other hand it did possibly indicate something. They laughed. Then up jumped one man, it turned out afterwards that he was a dean, and he said that in the Saints in Seven he had been very interested in the sentence about the ring around the moon, about the ring following the moon. He admitted that the sentence was one of the most beautifully balanced sentences he had ever heard, but still did the ring follow the moon. Gertrude Stein said, when you look at the moon and there is a ring around the moon and the moon moves does not the ring follow the moon. Perhaps it seems to, he replied. Well, in that case how, she said, do you know that it does not; he sat down. Another man, a don, next to him jumped up and asked something else. They did this several times, the two of them, jumping up one after the other. Then the first man jumped up and said, you say that everything being the same everything is always different, how can that be so. Consider, she replied, the two of you, you jump up one after the other, that is the same thing and surely you admit that the two of you are always different. Touché, he said and the meeting was over. One of the men was so moved that he confided to me as we went out that the lecture had been his greatest experience since he had read Kant's Critique of Pure Reason.

Edith Sitwell, Osbert and Sacheverell were all present and were all delighted. They were delighted with the lecture and they were delighted with the good humoured way in which Gertrude Stein had gotten the best of the hecklers. Edith Sitwell said that Sache chuckled about it all the way home.

The next day we returned to Paris. The Sitwells wanted us to stay and be interviewed and generally go on with it but Gertrude Stein felt that she had had enough of glory and excitement. Not, as she always explains, that she could ever have enough of glory. After all, as she always contends, no artist needs criticism, he only needs appreciation. If he needs criticism he is no artist.

Leonard Woolf some months after this published Composition As Explanation in the Hogarth Essay Series. It was also printed in The Dial.

Mildred Aldrich was awfully pleased at Gertrude Stein's english success.

She was a good new englander and to her, recognition by Oxford and Cambridge, was even more important than recognition by the Atlantic Monthly. We went out to see her on our return and she had to have the lecture read to her again and to hear every detail of the whole experience.

Mildred Aldrich was falling upon bad days. Her annuity suddenly ceased and for a long time we did not know it. One day Dawson Johnston, the librarian of the American Library, told Gertrude Stein that Miss Aldrich had written to him to come out and get all her books as she would soon be leaving her home. We went out immediately and Mildred told us that her annuity had been stopped. It seems it was an annuity given by a woman who had fallen into her dotage and she one morning told her lawyer to cut off all the annuities that she had given for many years to a number of people. Gertrude Stein told Mildred not to worry. The Carnegie Fund, approached by Kate Buss, sent five hundred dollars, William Cook gave Gertrude Stein a blank cheque to supply all deficiencies, another friend of Mildred's from Providence Rhode Island came forward generously and the Atlantic Monthly started a fund. Very soon Mildred Aldrich was safe. She said ruefully to Gertrude Stein, you would not let me go elegantly to the poorhouse and I would have gone elegantly, but you have turned this into a poorhouse and I am the sole inmate. Gertrude Stein comforted her and said that she could be just as elegant in her solitary state. After all, Gertrude Stein used to say to her, Mildred nobody can say that you have not had a good run for your money. Mildred Aldrich's last years were safe.

William Cook after the war had been in Russia, in Tiflis, for three years in connection with Red Cross distribution there. One evening he and Gertrude Stein had been out to see Mildred, it was during her last illness and they were coming home one foggy evening. Cook had a small open car but a powerful searchlight, strong enough to pierce the fog. Just behind them was another small car which kept an even pace with them, when Cook drove faster, they drove faster, and when he slowed down, they slowed down. Gertrude Stein said to him, it is lucky for them that you have such a bright light, their lanterns are poor and they are having the benefit of yours. Yes, said Cook, rather curiously, I have been saying that to myself, but you know after three years of Soviet Russia and the Cheka, even I, an american, have gotten to feel a little queer, and I have to talk to myself about it, to be sure that the car behind us is not the car of the secret police.

I said that René Crevel came to the house. Of all the young men who came to the house I think I liked René the best. He had french charm, which when it is at its most charming is more charming even than american charm, charming as that can be. Marcel Duchamp and René Crevel are perhaps the most complete examples of this french charm. We were very fond of René. He was young and violent and ill and revolutionary and sweet and tender. Gertrude Stein and René are very fond of each other, he writes her most delightful english letters, and she scolds him a great deal. It was he who, in early days, first talked to us of Bernard Faÿ. He said he was a young professor in the University of Clermont-Ferrand and he wanted to take us to his house. One afternoon he did take us there. Bernard Faÿ was not at all what Gertrude Stein expected and he and she had nothing in particular to say to each other.

As I remember during that winter and the next we gave a great many parties. We gave a tea party for the Sitwells.

Carl Van Vechten sent us quantities of negroes beside there were the negroes of our neighbour Mrs. Regan who had brought Josephine Baker to Paris. Carl sent us Paul Robeson. Paul Robeson interested Gertrude Stein. He knew american values and american life as only one in it but not of it could know them. And yet as soon as any other person came into the room he became definitely a negro. Gertrude Stein did not like hearing him sing spirituals. They do not belong to you any more than anything else, so why claim them, she said. He did not answer.

Once a southern woman, a very charming southern woman, was there, and she said to him, where were you born, and he answered, in New Jersey and she said, not in the south, what a pity and he said, not for me.

Gertrude Stein concluded that negroes were not suffering from persecution, they were suffering from nothingness. She always contends that the african is not primitive, he has a very ancient but a very narrow culture and there it remains. Consequently nothing does or can happen.

Carl Van Vechten himself came over for the first time since those far away days of the pleated shirt. All those years he and Gertrude Stein had kept up a friendship and a correspondence. Now that he was actually coming Gertrude Stein was a little worried. When he came they were better friends than ever. Gertrude Stein told him that she had been worried. I wasn't, said Carl.

Among the other young men who came to the house at the time when they came in such numbers was Bravig Imbs. We liked Bravig, even though as Gertrude Stein said, his aim was to please. It was he who brought Elliot Paul to the house and Elliot Paul brought transition.

We had liked Bravig Imbs but we liked Elliot Paul more. He was very interesting. Elliot Paul was a new englander but he was a saracen, a saracen such as you sometimes see in the villages of France where the strain from some Crusading ancestor's dependents still survives. Elliot Paul was such a one. He had an element not of mystery but of evanescence, actually little by little he appeared and then as slowly he disappeared, and Eugene Jolas and Maria Jolas appeared. These once having appeared, stayed in their appearance.

Elliot Paul was at that time working on the Paris Chicago Tribune and he was there writing a series of articles on the work of Gertrude Stein, the first seriously popular estimation of her work. At the same time he was turning the young journalists and proof-readers into writers. He started Bravig Imbs on his first book, The Professor's Wife, by stopping him suddenly in his talk and saying, you begin there. He did the same thing for others. He played the accordion as nobody else not native to the accordion could play it and he learned and played for Gertrude Stein accompanied on the violin by Bravig Imbs, Gertrude Stein's favourite ditty, The Trail of the Lonesome Pine, My name is June and very very soon.

The Trail of the Lonesome Pine as a song made a lasting appeal to Gertrude Stein. Mildred Aldrich had it among her records and when we spent the afternoon with her at Huiry, Gertrude Stein inevitably would start The Trail of the Lonesome Pine on the phonograph and play it and play it. She liked it in itself and she had been fascinated during the war with the magic of the Trail of the Lonesome Pine as a book for the doughboy. How often when a doughboy in hospital had become particularly fond of her, he would say, I once read a great book, do you know it, it is called The Trail of the Lonesome Pine. They finally got a copy of it in the camp at Nîmes and it stayed by the bedside of every sick soldier. They did not read much of it, as far as she could make out sometimes only a paragraph, in the course of several days, but their voices were husky when they spoke of it, and when they were particularly devoted to her they would offer to lend her this very dirty and tattered copy.

She reads anything and naturally she read this and she was puzzled. It had practically no story to it and it was not exciting, or adventurous, and it was very well written and was mostly description of mountain scenery. Later on she came across some reminiscences of a southern woman who told how the mountaineers in the southern army during the civil war used to wait in turn to read Victor Hugo's Les Misérables, an equally astonishing thing for again there is not much of a story and a great deal of description. However Gertrude Stein admits that she loves the song of The Trail of the Lonesome Pine in the same way that the doughboy loved the book and Elliot Paul played it for her on the accordion.

One day Elliot Paul came in very excitedly, he usually seemed to be feeling a great deal of excitement but neither showed nor expressed it. This time however he did show it and express it. He said he wanted to ask Gertrude Stein's advice. A proposition had been made to him to edit a magazine in Paris and he was hesitating whether he should undertake it. Gertrude Stein was naturally all for it. After all, as she said, we do want to be printed. One writes for oneself and strangers but with no adventurous publishers how can one come in contact with those same strangers.

However she was very fond of Elliot Paul and did not want him to take too much risk. No risk, said Elliot Paul, the money for it is guaranteed for a number of years. Well then, said Gertrude Stein, one thing is certain no one could be a better editor than you would be. You are not egotistical and you know what you feel.

Transition began and of course it meant a great deal to everybody. Elliot

Paul chose with great care what he wanted to put into transition. He said he was afraid of its becoming too popular. If ever there are more than two thousand subscribers, I quit, he used to say.

He chose Elucidation Gertrude Stein's first effort to explain herself, written in Saint-Rémy to put into the first number of transition. Later As A Wife Has A Cow A Love Story. He was always very enthusiastic about this story. He liked Made A Mile Away, a description of the pictures that Gertrude Stein has liked and later a novelette of desertion If He Thinks, for transition. He had a perfectly definite idea of gradually opening the eyes of the public to the work of the writers that interested him and as I say he chose what he wanted with great care. He was very interested in Picasso and he became very deeply interested in Juan Gris and after his death printed a translation of Juan Gris' defence of painting which had already been printed in french in the Transatlantic Review, and he printed Gertrude Stein's lament, The Life and Death of Juan Gris and her One Spaniard.

Elliot Paul slowly disappeared and Eugene and Maria Jolas appeared.

Transition grew more bulky. At Gertrude Stein's request transition reprinted Tender Buttons, printed a bibliography of all her work up to date and later printed her opera, Four Saints. For these printings Gertrude Stein was very grateful. In the last numbers of transition nothing of hers appeared. Transition died.

Of all the little magazines which as Gertrude Stein loves to quote, have died to make verse free, perhaps the youngest and freshest was the Blues. Its editor Charles Henri Ford has come to Paris and he is young and fresh as his Blues and also honest which also is a pleasure. Gertrude Stein thinks that he and Robert Coates alone among the young men have an individual sense of words.

During this time Oxford and Cambridge men turned up from time to time at the rue de Fleurus. One of them brought with him Brewer, one of the firm of Payson and Clarke.

Brewer was interested in the work of Gertrude Stein and though he promised nothing he and she talked over the possibilities of his firm printing something of hers. She had just written a shortish novel called A

Novel, and was at the time working at another shortish novel which was called Lucy Church Amiably and which she describes as a novel of romantic beauty and nature and which looks like an engraving. She at Brewer's request wrote a summary of this book as an advertisement and he cabled his enthusiasm. However he wished first to commence with a collection of short things and she suggested in that case he should make it all the short things she had written about America and call it Useful Knowledge. This was done.

There are many Paris picture dealers who like adventure in their business, there are no publishers in America who like adventure in theirs. In Paris there are picture dealers like Durand-Ruel who went broke twice supporting the impressionists, Vollard for Cézanne, Sagot for Picasso and Kahnweiler for all the cubists. They make their money as they can and they keep on buying something for which there is no present sale and they do so persistently until they create its public. And these adventurers are adventurous because that is the way they feel about it. There are others who have not chosen as well and have gone entirely broke. It is the tradition among the more adventurous Paris picture dealers to adventure. I suppose there are a great many reasons why publishers do not. John Lane alone among publishers did. He perhaps did not die a very rich man but he lived well, and died a moderately rich one.

We had a hope that Brewer might be this kind of a publisher. He printed Useful Knowledge, his results were not all that he anticipated and instead of continuing and gradually creating a public for Gertrude Stein's work he procrastinated and then said no. I suppose this was inevitable. However that was the matter as it was and as it continued to be.

I now myself began to think about publishing the work of Gertrude Stein. I asked her to invent a name for my edition and she laughed and said, call it Plain Edition. And Plain Edition it is.

All that I knew about what I would have to do was that I would have to get the book printed and then to get it distributed, that is sold.

I talked to everybody about how these two things were to be accomplished.

At first I thought I would associate some one with me but that soon did not please me and I decided to do it all by myself.

Gertrude Stein wanted the first book Lucy Church Amiably to look like a school book and to be bound in blue. Once having ordered my book to be printed my next problem was the problem of distribution. On this subject I received a great deal of advice. Some of the advice turned out to be good and some of it turned out to be bad. William A. Bradley, the friend and comforter of Paris authors, told me to subscribe to The Publishers' Weekly. This was undoubtedly wise advice. This helped me to learn something of my new business, but the real difficulty was to get to the booksellers. Ralph Church, philosopher and friend, said stick to the booksellers, first and last. Excellent advice but how to get to the booksellers. At this moment a kind friend said that she could get me copied an old list of booksellers belonging to a publisher. This list was sent to me and I began sending out my circulars. The circular pleased me at first but I soon concluded that it was not quite right. However I did get orders from America and I was paid without much difficulty and I was encouraged.

The distribution in Paris was at once easier and more difficult. It was easy to get the book put in the window of all the booksellers in Paris that sold english books. This event gave Gertrude Stein a childish delight amounting almost to ecstasy. She had never seen a book of hers in a bookstore window before, except a french translation of The Ten Portraits, and she spent all her time in her wanderings about Paris looking at the copies of Lucy Church Amiably in the windows and coming back and telling me about it.

The books were sold too and then as I was away from Paris six months in the year I turned over the Paris work to a french agent. This worked very well at first but finally did not work well. However one must learn one's trade.

I decided upon my next book How To Write and not being entirely satisfied with the get up of Lucy Church Amiably, although it did look like a school book, I decided to have the next book printed at Dijon and in the form of an Elzevir. Again the question of binding was a difficulty.

I went to work in the same way to sell How To Write, but I began to realise that my list of booksellers was out of date. Also I was told that I should write following up letters. Ellen du Pois helped me with these. I was told that I should have reviews. Ellen du Pois came to the rescue here too. And that I should advertise. Advertising would of necessity be too expensive; I had to keep my money to print my books, as my plans were getting more and more ambitious. Getting reviews was a difficulty, there are always plenty of humorous references to Gertrude Stein's work, as Gertrude Stein always says to comfort herself, they do quote me, that means that my words and my sentences get under their skins although they do not know it. It was difficult to get serious reviews. There are many writers who write her letters of admiration but even when they are in a position to do so they do not write themselves down in book reviews. Gertrude Stein likes to quote Browning who at a dinner party met a famous literary man and this man came up to Browning and spoke to him at length and in a very laudatory way about his poems. Browning listened and then said, and are you going to print what you have just said. There was naturally no answer. In Gertrude Stein's case there have been some notable exceptions, Sherwood Anderson, Edith Sitwell, Bernard Faÿ and Louis Bromfield.

I also printed an edition of one hundred copies, very beautifully done at Chartres, of the poem of Gertrude Stein Before The Flowers Of Friendship Faded Friendship Faded. These one hundred copies sold very easily.

I was better satisfied with the bookmaking of How To Write but there was always the question of binding the book. It is practically impossible to get a decent commercial binding in France, french publishers only cover their books in paper. I was very troubled about this.

One evening we went to an evening party at Georges Poupet's, a gentle friend of authors. There I met Maurice Darantière. It was he who had printed The Making of Americans and he was always justly proud of it as a book and as bookmaking. He had left Dijon and had started printing books in the neighbourhood of Paris with a hand-press and he was printing very beautiful books. He is a kind man and I naturally began telling him my troubles. Listen, he said I have the solution. But I interrupted him, you must remember that I do not want to make these books expensive. After

This time they had a great deal to say to each other.

all Gertrude Stein's readers are writers, university students, librarians and young people who have very little money. Gertrude Stein wants readers not collectors. In spite of herself her books have too often become collector's books. They pay big prices for Tender Buttons and The Portrait of Mabel Dodge and that does not please her, she wants her books read not owned. Yes yes, he said, I understand. No this is what I propose. We will have your book set by monotype which is comparatively cheap, I will see to that, then I will handpull your books on good but not too expensive paper and they will be beautifully printed and instead of any covers I will have them bound in heavy paper like The Making of Americans, paper just like that, and I will have made little boxes in which they will fit perfectly, well made little boxes and there you are. And I will be able to sell them at a reasonable price. Yes you will see, he said.

I was getting more ambitious I wished now to begin a series of three, beginning with Operas and Plays, going on with Matisse, Picasso and Gertrude Stein and Two Shorter Stories, and then going on with Two Long Poems and Shorter Ones.

Maurice Darantière has been as good as his word. He has printed Operas and Plays and it is a beautiful book and reasonable in price and he is now printing the second book Matisse Picasso and Gertrude Stein and Two Shorter Stories. Now I have an up to date list of booksellers and I am once more on my way.

As I was saying after the return from England and lecturing we gave a great many parties, there were many occasions for parties, all the Sitwells came over, Carl Van Vechten came over, Sherwood Anderson came over again. And beside there were many other occasions for parties.

It was then that Gertrude Stein and Bernard Faÿ met again and this time they had a great deal to say to each other. Gertrude Stein found the contact with his mind stimulating and comforting. They were slowly coming to be friends.

I remember once coming into the room and hearing Bernard Faÿ say that the three people of first rate importance that he had met in his life were Picasso, Gertrude Stein and André Gide and Gertrude Stein inquired quite simply, that is quite right but why include Gide. A year or so later in referring to this conversation he said to her, and I am not sure you were not right.

Sherwood came to Paris that winter and he was a delight. He was enjoying himself and we enjoyed him. He was being lionised and I must say he was a very appearing and disappearing lion. I remember his being asked to the Pen Club. Natalie Barney and a long-bearded frenchman were to be his sponsors. He wanted Gertrude Stein to come too. She said she loved him very much but not the Pen Club. Natalie Barney came over to ask her. Gertrude Stein who was caught outside, walking her dog, pleaded illness. The next day Sherwood turned up. How was it, asked Gertrude Stein. Why, said he, it wasn't a party for me, it was a party for a big woman, and she was just a derailed freight car.

We had installed electric radiators in the studio, we were as our finnish servant would say getting modern. She finds it difficult to understand why we are not more modern. Gertrude Stein says that if you are way ahead with your head you naturally are old fashioned and regular in your daily life. And Picasso adds, do you suppose Michael Angelo would have been grateful for a gift of a piece of renaissance furniture, no he wanted a greek coin.

We did install electric radiators and Sherwood turned up and we gave him a Christmas party. The radiators smelled and it was terrifically hot but we were all pleased as it was a nice party. Sherwood looked as usual very handsome in one of his very latest scarf ties. Sherwood Anderson does dress well and his son John follows suit. John and his sister came over with their father. While Sherwood was still in Paris John the son was an awkward shy boy. The day after Sherwood left John turned up, sat easily on the arm of the sofa and was beautiful to look upon and he knew it. Nothing to the outward eye had changed but he had changed and he knew it.

It was during this visit that Gertrude Stein and Sherwood Anderson had all those amusing conversations about Hemingway. They enjoyed each other thoroughly. They found out that they both had had and continued to have Grant as their great american hero. They did not care so much about Lincoln either of them. They had always and still liked Grant. They even planned collaborating on a life of Grant. Gertrude Stein still likes to think about this possibility.

We did give a great many parties in those days and the Duchess of Clermont-Tonnerre came very often.

She and Gertrude Stein pleased one another. They were entirely different in life education and interests but they delighted in each other's understanding. They were also the only two women whom they met who still had long hair. Gertrude Stein had always worn hers well on top of her head, an ancient fashion that she had never changed.

Madame de Clermont-Tonnerre came in very late to one of the parties, almost every one had gone, and her hair was cut. Do you like it, said Madame de Clermont-Tonnerre. I do, said Gertrude Stein. Well, said Madame de Clermont-Tonnerre, if you like it and my daughter likes it and she does like it I am satisfied. That night Gertrude Stein said to me, I guess I will have to too. Cut it off she said and I did.

I was still cutting the next evening, I had been cutting a little more all day and by this time it was only a cap of hair when Sherwood Anderson came in. Well, how do you like it, said I rather fearfully. I like it, he said, it makes her look like a monk.

As I have said, Picasso seeing it, was for a moment angry and said, and my portrait, but very soon added, after all it is all there.

We now had our country house, the one we had only seen across the valley and just before leaving we found the white poodle, Basket. He was a little puppy in a little neighbourhood dog-show and he had blue eyes, a pink nose and white hair and he jumped up into Gertrude Stein's arms. A new puppy and a new ford we went off to our new house and we were thoroughly pleased with all three. Basket although now he is a large unwieldy poodle, still will get up on Gertrude Stein's lap and stay there. She says that listening to the rhythm of his water drinking made her recognise the difference between sentences and paragraphs, that paragraphs are emotional and that sentences are not.

Bernard Faÿ came and stayed with us that summer. Gertrude Stein and he talked out in the garden about everything, about life, and America, and

still will get up on gertrude stein's lap and stay there

themselves and friendship. They then cemented the friendship that is one of the four permanent friendships of Gertrude Stein's life. He even tolerated Basket for Gertrude Stein's sake. Lately Picabia has given us a tiny mexican dog, we call Byron. Bernard Faÿ likes Byron for Byron's own sake. Gertrude Stein teases him and says naturally he likes Byron best because Byron is an american while just as naturally she likes Basket best because Basket is a frenchman.

Bilignin brings me to a new old acquaintance. One day Gertrude Stein came home from a walk to the bank and bringing out a card from her pocket said, we are lunching to-morrow with the Bromfields. Way back in the Hemingway days Gertrude Stein had met Bromfield and his wife and then from time to time there had been a slight acquaintance, there had even been a slight acquaintance with Bromfield's sister, and now suddenly we were lunching with the Bromfields. Why, I asked, because answered Gertrude Stein quite radiant, he knows all about gardens.

We lunched with the Bromfields and he does know all about gardens and all about flowers and all about soils. Gertrude Stein and he first liked each other as gardeners, then they liked each other as americans and then they liked each other as writers. Gertrude Stein says of him that he is as american as Janet Scudder, as american as a doughboy, but not as solemn.

One day the Jolases brought Furman the publisher to the house. He as have been many publishers was enthusiastic and enthusiastic about The Making of Americans. But it is terribly long, it's a thousand pages, said Gertrude Stein. Well, can't it be cut down, he said to about four hundred. Yes, said Gertrude Stein, perhaps. Well cut it down and I will publish it, said Furman.

Gertrude Stein thought about it and then did it. She spent a part of the summer over it and Bradley as well as she and myself thought it alright.

In the meantime Gertrude Stein had told Elliot Paul about the proposition. It's alright when he is over here, said Elliot Paul, but when he gets back the boys won't let him. Who the boys are I do not know but they certainly did not let him. Elliot Paul was right. In spite of the efforts of Robert Coates and Bradley nothing happened.

In the meantime Gertrude Stein's reputation among the french writers and readers was steadily growing. The translation of the fragments of The Making of Americans, and of the Ten Portraits interested them. It was at this time that Bernard Faÿ wrote his article about her work printed in the Revue Européenne. They also printed the only thing she has ever written in french a little film about the dog Basket.

They were very interested in her later work as well as her earlier work. Marcel Brion wrote a serious criticism of her work in Echange, comparing her work to Bach. Since then, in Les Nouvelles Littéraires, he has written of each of her books as they come out. He was particularly impressed by How To Write.

About this time too Bernard Faÿ was translating a fragment of Melanctha from Three Lives for the volume of Ten American Novelists, this to be introduced by his article printed in the Revue Européenne. He came to the house one afternoon and read his translation of Melanctha aloud to us. Madame de Clermont-Tonnerre was there and she was very impressed by his translation.

One day not long after she asked to come to the house as she wished to talk to Gertrude Stein. She came and she said, the time has now come when you must be made known to a larger public. I myself believe in a larger public. Gertrude Stein too believes in a larger public but the way has always been barred. No, said Madame de Clermont-Tonnerre, the way can be opened. Let us think.

She said it must come from the translation of a big book, an important book. Gertrude Stein suggested The Making of Americans and told her how it had been prepared for an American publisher to make about four hundred pages. That will do exactly, she said. And went away.

Finally and not after much delay, Monsieur Bouteleau of Stock saw Gertrude Stein and he decided to publish the book. There was some difficulty about finding a translator, but finally that was arranged. Bernard Faÿ aided by the Baronne Seillière undertook the translation, and it is this translation which is to appear this spring, and that this summer made Gertrude Stein say, I knew it was a wonderful book in english, but it is even, well, I cannot say almost really more wonderful but just as wonderful in french.

Last autumn the day we came back to Paris from Bilignin I was as usual very busy with a number of things and Gertrude Stein went out to buy some nails at the bazaar of the rue de Rennes. There she met Guevara, a chilean painter and his wife. They are our neighbours, and they said, come to tea to-morrow. Gertrude Stein said, but we are just home, wait a bit. Do come, said Méraude Guevara. And then added, there will be some one there you will like to see. Who is it, said Gertrude Stein with a never failing curiosity. Sir Francis Rose, they said. Alright, we'll come, said Gertrude Stein. By this time she no longer objected to meeting Francis Rose. We met then and he of course immediately came back to the house with her. He was, as may be imagined, quite pink with emotion. And what, said he, did Picasso say when he saw my paintings. When he first saw them, Gertrude Stein answered, he said, at least they are less bêtes than the others. And since, he asked. And since he always goes into the corner and turns the canvas over to look at them but he says nothing.

Since then we have seen a great deal of Francis Rose but Gertrude Stein has not lost interest in the pictures. He has this summer painted the house from across the valley where we first saw it and the waterfall celebrated in Lucy Church Amiably. He has also painted her portrait. He likes it and I like it but she is not sure whether she does, but as she has just said, perhaps she does. We had a pleasant time this summer, Bernard Faÿ and Francis Rose both charming guests.

A young man who first made Gertrude Stein's acquaintance by writing engaging letters from America is Paul Frederick Bowles. Gertrude Stein says of him that he is delightful and sensible in summer but neither delightful nor sensible in the winter. Aaron Copland came to see us with Bowles in the summer and Gertrude Stein liked him immensely. Bowles told Gertrude Stein and it pleased her that Copland said threateningly to him when as usual in the winter he was neither delightful nor sensible, if you do not work now when you are twenty when you are thirty, nobody will love you.

For some time now many people, and publishers, have been asking Gertrude Stein to write her autobiography and she had always replied, not possibly.

She began to tease me and say that I should write my autobiography. Just think, she would say, what a lot of money you would make. She then began to invent titles for my autobiography. My Life With The Great, Wives of Geniuses I Have Sat With, My Twenty-five Years With Gertrude Stein.

Then she began to get serious and say, but really seriously you ought to write your autobiography. Finally I promised that if during the summer I could find time I would write my autobiography.

When Ford Madox Ford was editing the Transatlantic Review he once said to Gertrude Stein, I am a pretty good writer and a pretty good editor and a pretty good businessman but I find it very difficult to be all three at once.

I am a pretty good housekeeper and a pretty good gardener and a pretty good needlewoman and a pretty good secretary and a pretty good editor and a pretty good vet for dogs and I have to do them all at once and I found it difficult to add being a pretty good author.

About six weeks ago Gertrude Stein said, it does not look to me as if you were ever going to write that autobiography. You know what I am going to do. I am going to write it for you. I am going to write it as simply as Defoe did the autobiography of Robinson Crusoe. And she has and this is it.

Afterword

I am
LoAth
to leave
them .

This is a love story.

You know.

How two people, joined together,
become themselves.

They cannot breathe right
without each other.

Not breathe right without each other

Who did they know?
EVERYBODY.

This most singular time —

literature, art, music, dance, architecture
EXPLODING into a new era.

The world reinvented. Modernism.
PROBLEMS. FURIES. Betrayals. Alliances.

PREPOSTEROUS Notions. Malicious opinions.
Relentless drive. Enveloping beauty.

Many many many meals.

And within it all, Gertrude and Alice. Alice and Gertrude. Don't be deceived by Alice always in the background.

Nothing would have happened
without Alice. NO THING.

It could be that Alice did write
this book. It could be.

who holds the pen?
who has the ideas?

what is the atmosphere of the
living Room, Kitchen, bedRoom, salon?

what sharpness of vision. What Relishing
of things big and small.

great fame. A cozy home.

This is a singular story, embedded
in a singular time.

That is enough. And more.

MK
2019

with thanks to

Gertrude and Alice (of course)

Charlotte Sheedy who is indomitable and whose idea this was

Ann Godoff who sagely consults, or leaves you alone, as needed

Claire Vaccaro for her precise, elegant design

Casey Denis who organizes, channels, oversees with grace
Elisabeth Calamari for so thoughtfully and nicely publicizing the book
Darren Haggar for covering all covers so well

Ed Koren for gallantly making the introduction to

Elisabeth and Ron Beckman
who graciously brought me to Elisabeth Grunspan
who literally opened the door to the Stein apartment at
27 Rue De Fleurus and served me lemon pound cake and coffee no less.

Marie Helene Silvy-Leligois and Jean Silvy-Leligois
for opening the door to the family home in Bilignin where I sat in the garden
in the spot where Alice sat with her back to the view.

Julie Saul for being a great gallerist and great friend

Rick Meyerowitz for being the most willing and kind traveler to all destinations

And as always
to Lulu and Alex
for lighting the way
completely

leaf from Bilignin

from Rue de Fleurus

Carl Van Vechten · Claribel Cone · Georgiana King ·
Harry Gibb · Bernard Berenson · Mabel Dodge · Rousseau ·
Van Dongen · Rönnebeck · Kahnweiler · Poiret · H.G.
Wells · Frank Stella · Marsden Hartley · Roger Fry ·
Clive Bell · Vanessa Bell · Augustus John · Lamb ·
Wyndham Lewis · Prichard · Thomas Whittemore ·
Lady Cunard · Nancy Cunard · Jacques-Emile Blanche ·
Alphonse Kann · Lady Otoline Morrell · William Cook ·
Sabartes · Severini · Marinetti · Jacob Epstein · Emily
Chadbourne · Myra Edgerly · Genthe · John Lane ·
Constance Fletcher · Jo and Yvonne Davidson · Florence
Bradley · Mary Foote · André Gide · Muriel Draper ·
Paul Draper · Mina Loy · Haweis · Florence Bradley ·
Demuth · Picabia · Marcel Duchamp · Robert Jones ·
John Reed · Gordon Caine · La Argentina · Allan
and Louise Norton · Avery Hopwood · Alvin Langdon
Coburn · Hope Mirrlees · Alfred North Whitehead ·
Evelyn Whitehead · Lady Astley · Lytton Strachey ·
Bertrand Russell · Donald Evans · Princesse de
Polignac · Virgil Thomson · Sylvia Beach · Adrienne
Monnier · Tristan Tzara · Jean Cocteau · Ezra
Pound · Sherwood Anderson · Man Ray · Robert Coates ·
Djuna Barnes · Glenway Wescott · Robert McAlmon ·
T. S. Eliot · Jane Heap · Janet Scudder · George Lynes ·
F. Scott Fitzgerald · George Antheil · Tchelitchev · René
Crevel · Francis Rose · Natalie Barney · Edith Sitwell

nard Faÿ by Tonny. These volumes were very well received and everybody was pleased.

Once more everybody went away.

Gertrude Stein in winter takes her white poodle Basket to be bathed at a vet's and she used to go to the picture gallery where she had bought the englishman's romantic picture and wait for Basket to dry. Every time she came home she brought more pictures by the englishman. She did not talk much about it but they accumulated. Several people began to tell her about this young man and offered to introduce him. Gertrude Stein declined. She said no she had had enough of knowing young painters, she now would content herself with knowing young painting.

In the meantime Georges Hugnet wrote a poem called Enfance. Gertrude Stein offered to translate it for him but instead she wrote a poem about it. This at first pleased Georges Hugnet too much and then did not please him at all. Gertrude Stein then called the poem Before The Flowers Of Friendship Faded Friendship Faded. Everybody mixed themselves up in all this. The group broke up. Gertrude Stein was very upset and then consoled herself by telling all about it in a delightful short story called From Left to Right and which was printed in the London Harper's Bazaar.

It was not long after this that one day Gertrude Stein called in the concierge and asked him to hang up all the Francis Rose pictures, by this time there were some thirty odd. Gertrude Stein was very much upset while she was having this done. I asked her why she was doing it if it upset her so much. She said she could not help it, that she felt that way about it but to change the whole aspect of the room by adding these thirty pictures was very upsetting. There the matter rested for some time.

To go back again to those days just after the publication of The Making of Americans. There was at that time a review of Gertrude Stein's book Geography and Plays in the Athenaeum signed Edith Sitwell. The review was long and